ADOBE PHOTOSHOP MASTER CLASS

JOHN PAUL CAPONIGRO

AN ADOBE PRESS BOOK

Haboob, Allies, 1998

ADOBE PHOTOSHOP MASTER CLASS

JOHN PAUL CAPONIGRO

ADOBE PRESS

2000

Adobe Photoshop Master Class

John Paul Caponigro

Copyright ©2000 by John Paul Caponigro

This Adobe Press book is published by Peachpit Press.

For information on Adobe Press books, contact:

Peachpit Press

1249 Eighth Street

Berkeley, California 94710

800-283-9444

510-524-2178 (tel) 510-524-2221 (fax)

http://www.peachpit.com

Peachpit Press is a division of Addison Wesley Longman

For the latest on Adobe Press books, go to

http://www.adobe.com/adobepress

Cover and Interior Design by Alexandra Caponigro. Assistant Designers: Sarah Szwajkos and Zeb Ellis.

Cover Image: *Triple Goddess*, ©1996 by John Paul Caponigro

ISBN 0-201-35499-3

9 8 7 6 5 4 3 2 1

Printed and bound in the United States of America

DEDICATION

This book is dedicated to my students — past, present, and future.

ACKNOWLEDGMENTS

I would like to thank many people who have helped me along the way.

My wife Alexandra for her inspiration, initiative, encouragement, constructive criticism, unfailing support, and for helping make this book look so good in every way.

My mother and father for helping lay my foundations as an artist and person with guidance, support, mutual respect, inspiration, and love.

Zeb Ellis, my assistant, for respectfully challenging me to be thorough, getting what needed to be done done, taking the pressure off me when he could, and making the process more enjoyable, including exposing me to new music.

Sarah Szwajkos, my wife's assistant, for deftly helping her help me get things done with a great sense of humor and a keen eye.

Margaret Richardson for understanding and respecting the soul of this book, how to get that put into words, and so many other things.

Julieanne Kost for her kind sharing spirit and knowledgeable review.

Nancy Ruenzel at Peachpit for her graceful and energetic support, and Marjorie Baer and Kate Reber for their care in shepherding this book through the appropriate channels and seeing it through to production.

Those at Adobe who helped make it happen, in particular Tanya Wendling, Barabara Rice, and Karen Gauthier.

Canon USA and David Metz and for their continuous support.

Mike Newler at Canon USA for his generosity and for making it so much fun.

Mike Johnston at Photo Techniques for his early and continued support of the project.

Fabia Barsic Ochoa at Epson for her kind support.

Kanwal Sharma and John Santoro at Apple for their continued support and lively rapport.

The many people at The Center for Creative Imaging who helped me get my start digitally — in particular Robert Schwarzbach, John Macintosh, Kip Brundage, and Charles Altschul.

My colleagues for sharing their knowledge and providing feedback (in particular Jeff Schewe, Katrin Eismann, John Rueter, Timothy Morrissey, Huntington Witherill, Stephen Johnson, Brian Lawler, Joseph Holmes, Bruce Fraser, and Sean Kernan) and for their enthusiastic encouragement (in particular Joyce Tenneson, Chris Rainier, Tony Bannon, Barbara Bordnick, Douglas and Françoise Kirkland, Ryszard Horowitz, Arnold and Augusta Newman, Craig Stevens, and Chris James).

The workshops where I teach, which offered the many opportunities to meet with my students — The Maine Photographic Workshops (David Lyman), The Santa Fe Workshops (Reid Callanan and Jerry Courvoisier), Palm Beach Photographic Centre (Fatima and Art Nejame), The International Center of Photography (Adam Eidelberg), Toscana Photographic Workshops (Carlo Roberti and Alberto Cocchi).

My students for asking questions I couldn't answer at the time, pushing me to explore new areas of Photoshop I might not have on my own, and for challenging me to be as clear as I could be when offering explanations.

You for reading the book.

Finally, I would like to thank the book, which offered an interesting process of clarification both personally and technically, a journey anticipated for some time, which still yielded many surprises along the way.

TABLE OF CONTENTS

ABOUT THE AUTHOR

John Paul Caponigro's fine art work is exhibited and collected internationally. He has approximately twelve exhibitions each year at galleries, universities and museums around the world. His work resides in both private and public collections, including Princeton University, the Portland Museum of Art, and the Estée Lauder collection.

John Paul teaches and lectures internationally at workshops, universities and conferences. He teaches regularly at The Maine Photographic Workshops, The Santa Fe Photographic Workshops, Toscana Photographic Workshops, Palm Beach Photographic Centre, Rocky Mountain School of Photography and the International Center of Photography.

John Paul is a contributing editor for *View Camera* and *Camera Arts* magazines where his feature, *Dialogs*, conversations with other artists, appears regularly. His column, *The Fine Art of Photoshop*, appears in *Photo Techniques* magazine. His web feature, *Master Class*, appears monthly at www.apple.com/creative.

John Paul is one of Canon's Explorers of Light. Primarily a fine artist, he does select commercial work. Canon, Kodak, Adobe, and Apple are among his clients. His work is represented by Corbis stock agency.

For more information on John Paul see www.johnpaulcaponigro.com.

INTRODUCTION

"Know what the old masters did. Know how they composed their pictures, but do not fall into the conventions they established. These conventions were right for them, and they are wonderful. They made their language. You make yours. They can help you. All the past can help you." — Robert Henri

In the 1970s, while my mother was overseeing the production of Eliot Porter's book *Intimate Landscapes*, I was introduced to the world of digital imaging. After patiently sitting through endless press checks, I was rewarded with a tour of the Scitex computer room. My mother humorously referred to these machines as "million-dollar coloring books." I was thrilled by the potential of what I saw. In awe, I whispered under my breath a secret wish to be able to work that way. I thought it would be the better part of a lifetime before such an opportunity might present itself. Little did I know that little more than a decade later I would get my own "million-dollar coloring book." It cost a few thousand dollars. It was an Apple Macintosh with Adobe Photoshop. It was a dream come true. Both changed my life.

Photoshop has changed the way I make images irrevocably. As a result, I've begun painting and photographing differently. Considering and reconsidering the ways we make images is a large part of the spirit of this book. Given time, it is relatively easy to learn Photoshop. It works in definite ways, many of which have been defined. It's a fabulous tool. What I find more challenging, and ultimately more inspiring, is rethinking the ways images can be made, what they represent, and what they do. Photoshop is not a source of inspiration, but rather a gateway to it. People ask me for recommendations all the time. One of the questions I am most often asked is, "What book do you feel would be most helpful as I am learning to use Photoshop?" I answer, "There is not one book, but many." While there are many good books available, each approaches the problem differently, addressing specific needs, and so, necessarily, each has its strengths and weaknesses. Still, at the end of my recommendations, I found too often something was still missing. Many said, "You should write a book." And so I took that to heart. This then is the product of those queries.

This is not a monograph. This is not a book of theory. This is not a technical manual. This, like digital imaging, is a unique hybrid, something that is like what has gone before it and something that is completely new.

There are several fine encyclopedic surveys detailing all aspects of a very complicated program. They are good complements to the basic manual. There are also other fine books detailing specific recipes for specific problems. These are most useful when you repurpose the recipe for your individual needs. Few put the picture into a larger context. Placing information in a context is one of the primary goals of this book.

There was some debate over the title of this book. After reviewing hundreds of candidates, the editors decided on *Master Class*. Concerned that this might be interpreted as a volume filled only with advanced techniques to dazzle the most accomplished professional

Photoshop users with technical proficiency, I asked them to clarify what Master Class meant to them. The concensus was, "A Master Class is when an acknowledged practitioner works with aspiring professionals to have them reflect on their performances or art. Usually, it is a demonstration followed by the participants either also creating or asking profound questions in order to create. Essentially, the master works with aspirants because the master has resolved both art, form and technique and is so perceived." Some likened it to the spirit of a Maria Callas Master Class. While the concept/title was daunting, I appreciated the spirit of the suggestion as it placed technique in the service of vision, rather than technique before vision. I might have been more comfortable with Zen and the Art of Photoshop; then, my impulse to keep things simple would have been served. On the other hand, if a true Zen spirit were observed, nothing would be said save, "Look." So, I have tried to find a useful equilibrium in this book, a balancing point between many poles — East and West, personal and universal, aesthetic and technical, analog and digital, to name a few.

Some technique precedes most successful endeavors. In this book, essential (technical) chapters precede core (conceptual) chapters. The essential chapters sequentially outline the fundamentals of the digital process and guide you through it step by step. Though thorough, they are not exhaustive; they are efficient. They will be useful for anyone wishing an introduction, an overview, or a refresher. They outline many of the assumptions that future discussions of technique are based upon. Those who are more advanced may wish to skip ahead to the second, larger portion of this volume.

This book is as much about visual problem solving as it is about technical problem solving. You will note that the titles of the core chapters of this book are based on visual principles, not the words found in the program's interface, and not the technical language found in the process. In each of the core chapters, conceptual precedes technical. In truth, the one generates the need for the other. I have chosen to address the visual strategies that I find most useful, ones that may help you make images more successfully. You may even begin to make images in new ways. While not every technique will be suitable for the intentions and needs of every user, there is something for everyone here, purist and pioneer alike. Treat all as food for thought. Then make your own informed decision and take an action of your own making. You could do nothing better.

Above all, I recommend you look for strategy, not formula. Do not think of these demonstrations as recipes to be followed step by step without deviance. You will not be creating the same image and your working method will naturally vary from what is outlined here. Learning by rote provides only a superficial understanding of the process. Thoroughly understand the process conceptually and you can invent a formula yourself. Rigid adherence to a specific list of steps will fail you every time you encounter a unique situation. And every image can be a unique situation. However, you can benefit from another's previous experience. This is what I hope you do with what you find in this book. Once you grasp the underlying principle, you will find it much easier to apply these techniques to your own work. The strategies for solving certain problems may be carried forward and customized for solving others. It's much more important to learn to solve problems creatively than to apply specific formulas. It is my hope that this book will help you lay a solid foundation for future problem solving, both in Photoshop and in image making in general. First be mindful of what can be done, ask next what you want to do, seek out ways it has been done by others, and then do it your way. In short, improvise, but improvise knowledgeably. Try variations on a theme. Then every solution you find will be both informed and fresh.

There are ways of working in Photoshop that are more optimal than others. Certainly, I try to use these and I have attempted to alert you to these wherever possible. A caution must be issued here: the methods I use may not be the fastest. These images were all created to be displayed in fine art contexts. With that in mind, quality and future flexibility have taken precedence over expedience. Nonetheless, I value efficiency. If two paths offer equal quality, I favor traveling the shortest distance.

I have not filled the text with key commands. They make image editing more efficient, but they confuse the learning process. They clutter text. Everyone remembers a unique set of key commands — the ones used most often. Few remember them all. If you are relatively new to Photoshop, I recommend you let the words of the interface guide you; they are an excellent map to your needs. Should you decide to use key commands, they can easily be looked up in a nearby manual. In time, you will no doubt remember, from force of habit, the ones you find most useful. A good memory knows not only what to remember, but also what to forget.

There is little difference between Mac and PC versions of Photoshop. Consequently, while this volume is highly Mac-centric, only a few differences will be found for PC users. Most of them have to do with key commands. In this volume, PC users need simply substitute the Alt key for the Option key, the Control key for the Commmand key, and the Backspace for the Delete key.

It may seem there are some conspicuous omissions in the text: images have not been combined with text, none are heavily filtered or distressed, very few hand-drawn elements are included. While I have given, still give, and plan to give even more significant attention to these areas, after careful consideration it was determined that this volume would benefit from a more specific focus: photomontage — pursuit of a seamless or illusionistic aesthetic. Consequently, the concerns previously mentioned have been saved for a subsequent volume also with a specific focus: photocollage — an aesthetic that calls attention to the variety of sources, media, and visual languages that may be employed within a single image. I have more to say. There is much more to say about color. A separate volume will follow. Even some ideas that are appropriate for this volume have been omitted based on time and space. They may find their ways into subsequent editions. Some of these rogue chapters will be appearing periodically on my web page. For now, what is here is ample.

If there is one thing that I recommend you take to heart, it is this: Photoshop is many things to many people. Just because Photoshop can do so much for so many does not mean you should do it all. Whole bodies of work, even a lifetime of work, might employ only a single technique within these pages. It would serve you well to focus first on what you want to do, and second on how Photoshop can help you do it. Here is the secret to true Photoshop mastery: control it, don't be controlled by it.

As the images contained within this volume are personal and are clearly unified by a single vision, some attention has been given to the personal nature of the creation of each image. There is some attempt to answer the most difficult question, "Why?" The thoughts provided here are by no means definitive, but they may be illuminating. These words do not attempt to define the meaning of the work. Instead, they attempt to describe how the techniques were necessary for the creation of the images. While the images needed the techniques to find their fruition, the techniques did not bring forth the images. Seeing, feeling, and thinking did. The images contained herein are born of a vision, the product of a life lived. If you find inspiration in these images or words, if as a result you begin to look at image making or the world anew, or if you simply find pleasure in looking, I will consider that a blessing for us both. If you find some small measure of newfound clarity or feeling of empowerment for your personal vision here, my prayer for this book will have been answered.

If you take issue with what you find here, this will not disappoint me. It will only disappoint me if you do so without respect and consideration. Eliot Porter taught me that to disagree respectfully can be wonderfully stimulating for both parties. To do so asks us to be clear about our own positions while still recognizing that we will always have an enormous amount to learn, and that a newfound source of wisdom could be found anywhere or in anyone. Truly, there is a difference between being committed and being closed minded. I mean no disrespect. Consider the information in this book a set of thoughts based on my personal experience. The words you find here are no more than suggestions of possibilities rendered in the spirit of sharing.

This book contains both answers and questions. Eugene Ionesco remarked, "It's not the answer that enlightens, but the question." It is my hope that after reading this book you will be left with as many, or more, questions than answers, and that you will find this is a positive thing, and continue searching for your answers.

ESSENTIAL CHAPTERS

Understanding the architecture of Adobe Photoshop and its way of operating will greatly facilitate your progress in creating and modifying an image. This, then, is an attempt to strip it down to its essentials.

The words found in the interface of Adobe Photoshop are wonderful. Let them be your guide. The menu words (File, Edit, Image, Layer, Select, Filter, View, Window, Help) are straightforward and explanatory, categorizing the features within the menus. Layer offers options to

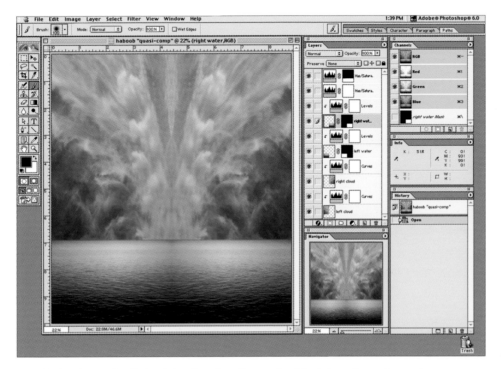

1. The Photoshop interface. Black and white channels combine to make a full-color image. Separate images exist on separate layers, each with their own channels. Adjustment layers contain no image information. An adjustment layer makes a correction to all the layers below it or to the one layer it is grouped with. A layer mask makes an image layer less visible or an adjustment layer's correction less visible.

affect layers. Select offers options to affect selections. Window allows you to make visible tool and function windows. In addition to the words in the menus there are graphic displays of keyboard shortcuts; by depressing the appropriate modifier and shortcut key you can activate a function. For example, Command H toggles between Hide Extras and Show Extras, which include active Selection Edges, Target Path, Grid, Guide,

Slices, Notes, and Color Sampler Points. We all memorize a unique set of key commands based on our image editing habits. If you are just starting, let the words and icons guide you. In time you will learn to use these shortcuts.

From top to bottom, the Tool Bar presents several divisions. First, there are the selection tools used for making or affecting selections (an exception is the Move tool, which affects image placement); second, the basic painting tools; third, vector based tools for making paths and working with text; fourth, viewing and information tools; fifth, foreground and background color specifiers; sixth, the Quick Mask icons; and seventh, monitor display mode options. If a tool has variable functions, you can make the window containing its controls visible by double-clicking on any tool. Note the small black arrows on some. These areas indicate hidden functions (submenus) throughout the program, in this case other tools. Many more words could be used to describe all of these tools (this is ably done in other volumes), but there is no substitute for direct experience. My advice is to play first. Play fearlessly. Don't be intimidated or self-conscious. Play. It won't hurt a thing. It will help you.

The menu Window allows access to a set of palettes to control various features of Photoshop, which can be shown or hidden at will. Each palette comes in a folder which you can file with (combine) or take away (separate) from others to save screen space. (Click and drag into each other to combine; click and drag out of each other to separate.) Palettes can also be filed in the Tool Options bar palette dock for easy access.

Once opened (File: Open or double-click on its icon on the desktop), finding your way through an image is facilitated by a series of tools. You can view an image at various magnifications up to 1600%. (Past a certain point, your screen will not be able to display the entire image.) The Navigator palette, whose size can

2. A pixel is the building block of digital images.

3. Many pixels combine to form a single image.

4. When the pixels are so small and numerous that they can no longer be seen by the naked eye, the image looks like a continuous tone image.

be changed by dragging its lower right corner, displays the full image no matter what magnification you are at. (Note that 100% is the only magnification that truly represents sharpness the way your image will look when printed.) A red rectangle indicates the portion of the image you are currently viewing. You can reposition it and you can adjust its size with the slider below it. Hold the Command key and you can redraw it to change your current view.

You can easily move through the current display window without using the Navigator. The side and bottom arrows move the image vertically or horizontally, or click on the gray track above or below the box indicating the current position to move a screen at a time. In addition there are two tools in the tool bar that can be used to move through an image, the Hand tool and the Zoom tool. You use the Hand tool to move the image inside the current display window, just click and drag. You use the Zoom tool to increase or to decrease magnification. Click to zoom in, and where you click becomes the center of the window. Hold the Option key and click to zoom out. Double-click the Zoom tool to see the image at 100% magnification. Double-click the hand icon to see the largest size full image which can be displayed by your monitor. Checking the option Resize Windows to Fit will resize the window when zooming. Unchecking it will maintain the current size of the window. Command - (minus) will decrease the image window along with magnification; Command + (plus) will increase it. In addition, no matter what tool you activate, if you depress the spacebar with the Option key, you temporarily activate the Zoom Out tool. If you depress the spacebar with the Command key, you temporarily activate the Zoom In tool. (This shortcut is well worth learning as you will be zooming in and out constantly.)

You can create more than one window to be visible simultaneously for a single file (View: New View). Each separate window can have a different magnification. You may find it useful to have one window at a magnification that displays the whole image (double-click on the hand icon) and one that displays the image at 100% which is, of course, the only magnification that accurately displays the level of detail the image will have when printed (double-click on the magnifying glass).

It is important to remember that bitmapped (photographic) digital image files are composed of pixels (squares). Every pixel is stored numerically. It takes so many bits to store it. A kilobyte (K) is a thousand bits. A megabyte (MB) is a million bits. At one bit per pixel you can display black or white, on or off. This is binary code at its most basic. As the number of bits per pixel rises, you can display more shades of gray. By increasing the number of bits per pixel to 8, you are able to display 256 values of gray (2 to the power of 8). (Note the maximum numerical range for RGB, or Red, Green, and Blue channels is 0–255, or 256 numbers, as seen in Levels.)

While 8-bit is the standard image editing color depth (8 bits per channel with 3 channels

5. The red channel.

6. The green channel.

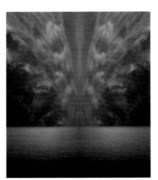

7. The blue channel.

in RGB thus 24-bit color, so 2 to the 24th equals 16,777,216 colors), there has been a gradual move forward to 16 bits per channel or 48-bit color. The advantages of working in a higher bit depth color space include greater dynamic color range, improved shadow detail, less gapping in Histograms after correction, smoother gradations, and improved conversions to CMYK (cyan, magenta, yellow, black). The disadvantage is increased file size. You also need to know that while some scanners are capable of producing 16-bit information, few software programs are able to utilize this richer information and monitors cannot display it. Adobe Photoshop does offer limited support for 16-bit color.

Located in the Channels palette, channels contain the information of an image. Each channel is a grayscale (black-and-white) image. Where it is white (256), it lets 100% of the color of that channel show through, and where it is black (0), 0%. A gray, in between black and white, is perceived as a percentage of that color based on its density: lighter equals more; darker equals less. (100% of three channels in RGB equals pure white; 0% equals pure black.) The composite of channels comprises the full image information. Grayscale has only one channel (black-and-white), RGB has three, CMYK has four. Note that you use the letters of the color space to identify the order of separate channels that comprise the full image.

For example, when you look at the Channels palette for an RGB file, you will see four divisions. The top line is the composite (Master channel or RGB) of the three below it (Red, Green, Blue). You can view each channel separately. Simply click on the channel you wish to see. In the well to the left, the icon of an eye indicates which channel(s) is visible. The highlighted area indicates which channel you are working on. If you highlight a channel, but don't have the eye turned on, you will not be able to affect it. You can, however, look at more than one channel and affect only one. (Be careful here. Make sure you are targeting the right channel (highlighted) when making corrections.) You can also access individual channels by pressing Command 1 for the first channel, Command 2 for the second channel, Command 3 for the third channel, and so on. Command ~ highlights all channels.

In Photoshop you have the ability to see channels in the color they specify rather than in grayscale (Edit: Preferences: Displays & Cursors). This makes evaluating a channel's information harder and so I do not recommend it. Seeing channels in grayscale is more useful.

Also located in the Channels palette, alpha channels are both similar and different from channels. Both are grayscale images. Both contribute similar amounts to your file size. But one is active and the other is passive. Channels are active; they build the image. Alpha channels are passive; they store selections. Once created, they can be used to load selections. Create a selection and save it (Selection: Save Selection). Instantly, an alpha channel appears. Or, create a new alpha channel (Click on the Create new

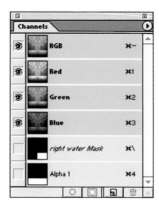

8. Grayscale channels (separate) combine to form full-color images (Master). Alpha channels store selections. A highlighted layer mask will also appear in the Channels palette and can be used to load a selection.

9. Separate images exist on separate layers. Adjustment layers make flexible corrections — linked are layer specific; unlinked are not. Layer masks hide either images or corrections.

channel icon) and paint a grayscale image. Either way, the alpha channel created is used to create a selection at a later date (Selection: Load Selection). That's all alpha channels do. They're storage devices, nothing more. When highlighted layer masks also appear in the Channels palette, they too can be used to load a selection. Just like channels and alpha channels, layer masks are grayscale images. You can do anything to a channel, alpha channel, or layer mask that you can do to a grayscale image — lighten it, darken it, increase or decrease its contrast, blur it, sharpen it, paint on it, etc.

Layers are individual images placed on top of each other like a deck of cards. Each layer has its own set of channels. A single source image, such as a "straight" photograph, typically has only one image layer. A multiple source image, a composite, typically has multiple layers stacked on top of one another. The top layer obscures the ones below it. Transparent areas of a layer are specified by a gray-and-white checkerboard pattern. The layers can be shuffled to change their order. Click, hold, and drag the layer to move it to any position. Watch the line separating these layers turn bold. When it does, you have found the position that will allow you to make the change. Release to drop the layer in place. The background is anchored to the bottom of the layer stack; it cannot be moved unless you change its name, making it like any other layer. (To change the name of a layer, an adjustment layer, or a channel, double-click on its icon and type in a new name.)

You can drag a layer from one document to another simply by clicking on, holding, and dragging the layer on top of the image area of another document. As the layer is dragged on top, the image will be highlighted with a bold outline around the image area. Release, and the new layer will be placed on top of the targeted layer in the destination document. Hold the shift key before releasing to center the position of the introduced layer.

Every layer has an opacity (degree of transparency) and a mode (manner of blending).

Actions typically performed to layers can be found in the Layer menu, the submenu in the Layers palette (click on the black arrow), and the icons at the bottom of the Layers palette.

With adjustment layers, you can make corrections to an image. Adjustment layers provide great flexibility when applying corrections to the image. After the correction is made with an adjustment layer, you can modify it in a variety of ways indefinitely. You can reduce its opacity, diminishing the intensity of the corrections to the percentage you specify. You can change its blending mode. Or you can change its values; just double-click on the name. Uncheck the eye to the left to hide an adjustment layer. Or you can eliminate the adjustment layer by clicking on it, holding, and dragging it into the trash icon at the bottom of the Layers palette.

You can reduce the opacity of a layer selectively with a layer mask. To create a layer mask, first create a selection (with a selection tool or load an alpha channel to activate a previously created selection). Then go to Layers: Add A Layer Mask: Reveal All. You will see a second thumbnail appear to the right of the layer highlighted, the mask. Fill the selection with black.

Click on the layer mask thumbnail to work on it (a dotted circle surrounded by gray will appear between the eye and the layer icon). Click on the layer thumbnail to work on it (a paint brush will appear between the eye and the layer icon). Check

this carefully before performing any function. It is easy to mistake which you are working on. To view a layer mask, hold the Option key and click on its thumbnail. (As a rule, if you are ever looking for a hidden function, try the Option key first.) To see a mask and the layer's image simultaneously, hold the Option and Shift keys and click on its thumbnail. The black areas of the mask will be represented by red at 50% opacity. To change the color of the mask, first make it visible (hold Option and Click on its thumbnail) and then double-click on its thumbnail. Specify a new percentage of opacity or click on Color to pick another color. To turn a mask off or on, hold the Shift key and click on its thumbnail.

To selectively reduce the intensity of the correction made, use adjustment layer layer masks. As adjustment layers contain no image information, their thumbnails all look like histograms. Unlike image layers whose masks are not created automatically, blank masks for adjustment layers are created automatically. To change an adjustment layer layer mask, simply activate a selection and fill the adjustment layer or use a paint tool to create the mask.

The architecture of Photoshop can be complex. It is a bit like a Chinese puzzle box. It is easy to get lost or to trip up if you move too fast. If things aren't working as you expected, check these three things first. Are you working on the right layer? Are you working on the right channel? Do you have a selection hidden?

You will make mistakes. Everyone does. There are several safety nets you need to know about. First is Command Z. Set to the default preference (Edit: Preferences: General), Command Z will toggle between undoing or redoing (Edit: Undo and Edit: Redo) the last action taken. Change the Redo preference and Command Z will step back in History states while Command Shift Z will step forward and Command Option Z will take you to the most recent History state. If you're just starting, keep it simple. Use the default preferences, and develop the Command Z twitch almost every Photoshop user has. It's great for quickly undoing a mistake. It's also great for toggling a view of an image between before and after states of a correction.

The History palette is extremely useful. It's a great safety net. Photoshop automatically keeps a record of each command that is performed to an image as you work and adds each state to the History palette. The default number of states History records is 20, but this number can be increased or decreased. To step back to a previous state, simply click on it. Performing a new action will delete states ahead of the state highlighted. You can turn the History feature to Allow Non-Linear History editing. This causes the working file to increase necessitating greater amounts of free hard drive space. You can use the History Brush to restore previous states of an image selectively rather than globally. Activate the History Brush icon to the left of the appropriate History state in the History palette, select the History Brush from the Tool Palette, and begin painting on the area to be restored. If you need to go back to a stage prior to an available state, you can click on a Snapshot. Every image has an initial Snapshot and other Snapshots can be taken along the way.

As a last resort, you can revert the file (File: Revert) to its last saved version. Save (Command: S) often since that's your best safety net. Set an egg timer to remind you if it helps. You can save a file that has been changed as another document leaving the original untouched (File: Save As and rename the file). Successive stages can be saved this way. A copy of a corrected image can also be saved midstream during corrections (File: Save a Copy). This does not preserve your original document, but instead it allows you to continue editing the original rather than a duplicate at a later stage of transformation. Or you can duplicate an image (Image: Duplicate) to create another

simultaneously active version of a document. Regardless of which method(s) you use, creating safety nets is a good habit to develop. After all, you never know when your computer will crash.

The following are recommended steps for making a digital image listed in order of execution. Each of these is explained further in the following chapters:

1   Calibrate: Once a week.

2   Scan: Set resolution to your output device's resolution and scan to the maximum size desired.

3   Tone & Color: Set dynamic range (Levels).

4· Make global corrections to tone, color, and saturation (Curves and Hue/Saturation).

5   Make local corrections (with Selections) to tone, color, saturation (Curves and Hue/Saturation).

6   Comparison: Compare multiple versions side by side to check color balance (Variations).

7   Retouch: (Rubber Stamp tool).

8   Save: Save an unsharpened version.

9   Sharpen: (Unsharp Mask).

10 Check Retouching.

11 Save: Save a sharpened version.

12 Convert: If necessary, convert to the output device's specific color space (generally CMYK).

13 Check color: out-of-gamut colors may have changed slightly.

14 Proof: On a device capable of simulating the color gamut of the final output device.

15 Print.

16 Save: Save a device-specific version.

Before you begin to work on your images, it is wise to establish that what you see is finally what you get. Calibration and characterization are the keys to controlling results.

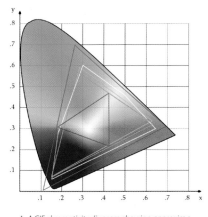

1. A CIE chromaticity diagram showing approximations of various color spaces decreasing in size throughout the imaging process. LAB (visible) (black), Joseph Holmes' Ekta Space (film) (green), a generic scanner (white), Apple Multiscan 17 monitor (orange), Adobe RGB (editing) (cyan), CMYK SWOP (print) (red).

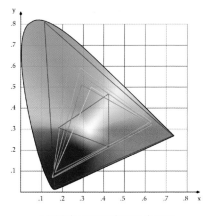

2. A CIE chromaticity diagram showing approximations of various Working Spaces — LAB (black), Wide Gamut (purple), Adobe RGB (cyan), Apple RGB (orange), Colormatch RGB (gray), sRGB (yellow), and CMYK SWOP (red).

THE PROBLEM

Here's the problem. It won't go away. We see two different types of light when looking at prints and monitors. When we look at prints, we see reflected light. When we look at monitors, we see transmissive light. When we see transmissive light, the light strikes our eyes directly from its source. When we see reflected light, the light strikes the object first, part of it is absorbed, and the rest is reflected — we see what's left. When looking at monitors and prints, there are other incidental factors involved, such as their surfaces, which can reflect glare from additional light sources. This may not be crucial, but it is not insignificant, and it can and should be minimized. The basic problem remains. Reflected light is never as strong, pure, or brilliant as transmissive light. Getting a perfect match between a transmissive display (RGB phosphors — additive) and a reflective print (CMYK inks — subtractive) is impossible; they're two different beasts. We can only simulate one with the other. Nevertheless, we can get close, and closer and closer by degrees. So we calibrate our monitors and characterize the ways the devices we use represent color to match input and output as closely as possible. This allows us to make educated guesses about the final outcome. The closer the match, the more refined our expectations can become. Close is, in the end, a relative term. Some will have much wider ranges of acceptability; others will have tighter tolerances. Even if you're a perfectionist, you can get very close.

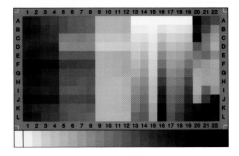

3. An IT8 target is used to generate an ICC profile.

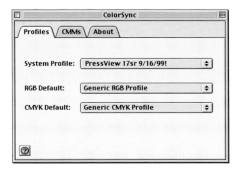

4. ICC profiles are stored in the ColorSync folder and can be accessed in the ColorSync window.

COLOR SPACE

You need to focus on the nuances of color in order to calibrate and characterize all your devices effectively. There are various ranges of colors — wavelengths of light — some that we see and some that we don't. In very general terms, a transparency can represent 75% of what the human eye can see, a monitor 50%, and a print 25%. Each has a different color space. If you compare the CIE Yxy chromaticity diagrams of the LAB, various RGB, and CMYK color spaces, you will see that each one grows progressively smaller (not in file size but in color gamut). As the color space grows smaller, certain colors, typically very saturated ones, become unattainable or "out-of-gamut."

Which color space should you work in? It depends on your needs. The CMYK color space is a favored working space for many, even though it is the smallest color space and it is device-specific. Those who favor it typically expect a one-time use on a particular printing device for their images. One advantage to working directly in CMYK is that you will be editing directly in the color space of your final output device and will not be editing colors that are impossible to reproduce. With a closed loop of one scanner, one monitor, and one printer, it's possible to control color very accurately. However, those who wish to see their images reproduced in many media over time will

favor a richer color space. For most uses, LAB color space (the device-independent international standard from the Commission Internationale d'Eclairage, or CIE) is overly rich, making it difficult to work subtly. This leaves RGB. There are many RGB color spaces. Larger than CMYK, RGB files generally must be converted into the smaller color space of CMYK before printing (see Output). It's better to go from RGB to CMYK, from larger to smaller, than to go the other way. Throwing information away that is no longer useful is not as difficult a problem as trying to reclaim useful information once it has been lost. For the greatest amount of flexibility, it's better to build a rich RGB file and convert a copy to CMYK for a specific device when you need to print, retaining the rich RGB file for other uses.

From smallest to largest, Apple RGB, Colormatch, and Adobe RGB are the most commonly used RGB color spaces. All are suitable for professional-quality output. It is likely that Adobe RGB will become the most used color space. Just because a monitor is an RGB device does not necessarily mean it will display the entire RGB spectrum. There may be information within a file that cannot be displayed, but this is rarely a problem as the monitor typically displays more information than can be printed. The best RGB color space to operate in is one that is slightly wider than the monitor's color space and encompasses the full CMYK space.

COLOR MANAGEMENT SYSTEM

Before today's color management systems existed we still managed color; that is, we implemented methods for controlling it. Color management today generally means using sophisticated sets of software to do so. A color management system (CMS) is a set of software tools that attempts to maintain consistency in the appearance of colors between different devices (monitor, printers, etc.). There are many different CMSs. Here we discuss Adobe Photoshop's color management system. Use one system. Do not use multiple systems. One stacked on top of another will likely spell disaster. In any color management system there are three basic components: the reference color space, the color matching engine, and profiles. The color space is essentially a language used for describing color. The reference color space defines a device-independent perceptually-based color space as a go-between for two different device-dependent color spaces. The color matching engine (or color matching method) is the software that actually converts information from one device-specific color space (monitor) into another device-specific color space (printer) based on profiles of the two devices. Profiles describe the color behaviors of different devices (cameras, scanners, monitors, printers) with a device-independent color language. Using a common language, profiles tell the color management system what a color on a particular device looks like and how the same color differs on another device. Profiles are interpreters. You specify a source profile (scanner or monitor), where the color came from, and a target profile (printer), where the color is going to. The color engine makes the conversion or color space transformation (translation). With the exception of the translation from the editing color space to the monitor color space (which is done on the fly and does not change the file), every conversion involves some change (and likely, loss) of data, even between equal color spaces. This is nothing to be overly concerned about; you simply want to minimize the number of conversions as much as possible. You should be careful converting from a larger color space to a smaller color space. Once converted, the rich information contained in the larger color space will be lost, even if the color is subsequently converted back into the richer color space. Converting from a smaller color space to a larger one does not automatically increase the color depth of the information a file contains. Typically, the only way information can be expanded beyond the originating color space is for you to edit the file.

PROFILING

The single biggest problem with color management prior to Photoshop 5 was the lack of standards. Now we have standards, namely ICC profiles and defined device-independent color spaces. ICC (International Color Consortium) profiles characterize a device-specific color space in terms of a device-independent color language. To generate ICC profiles, we first measure the colors a particular film can record, a particular scanner can scan, a particular monitor can display, or a particular printer can print. A profile is generated for each separate component involved. We measure wavelengths of light using spectrophotometers (such as X-Rite's Colortron) on IT8 color targets, which display a large range of colors. To measure the color gamut of film, you photograph a standard IT8 target illuminated by a known light temperature, process the film (carefully, to known standards), and measure each swatch using a known light source. To measure the color gamut of a scanner, you scan an IT8 target (film for transmissive, printed for reflected). To measure the color gamut of a monitor, you measure the display of a standard IT8 target file. To generate the profile, the resulting measurements are entered into an ICC profile-generating software (such as Kodak's Colorflow). You need not generate these profiles yourself. Preexisting (generic) profiles are readily available from manufacturers and there are many service providers who will generate new (device-specific) profiles for you.

In calibrating a monitor, you set its dynamic range and neutralize any color casts. You bring it to a known state. You will want to allow half an hour for the monitor to "warm up" before calibrating. A recently activated monitor will gradually brighten over this time. If you calibrate in the first five minutes of its operation, your results may no longer be accurate after it has been operating for a longer period of time.

Before you start, make sure your monitor background color is a neutral gray (Apple: Control Panels: Appearance). Other colors, particularly very bright, dark, or saturated colors, will alter your perception of color and prejudice your decisions.

All monitors are not created equally. Some monitors are self-calibrating, such as the AppleVision monitors. Some monitors ship with calibrating software and hardware, such as Barco. You can buy third party hardware/software solutions for any monitor from manufacturers such as X-Rite. Or, you can use a visual comparator method, such as the Adobe Gamma utility. Use either the manufacturer's calibration scheme or the Adobe Gamma utility, but not both. In general, hardware solutions are more accurate and more expensive.

The monitor's settings are extremely important. I recommend monitors that have buttons with onscreen programming or numerical readouts that indicate brightness and contrast settings. Dials do not provide the same level of accuracy. I marvel at monitor manufacturers who give us dials without numerical values to refer to; no stereo manufacturer would think of doing such a thing. If you have dials, you may want to tape them down once you have calibrated to ensure that they are not accidentally changed. You are locking down the variables into a known state so that you can reasonably predict your re-

sults. You have to be thorough, methodical, and scientific about this to get consistent results.

Once calibrated, and only once calibrated, a profile may be generated to describe a monitor's specific behavior. Typically, both calibration and characterization are accomplished with the Adobe Gamma utility, but other software and hardware configurations can be used to do this.

One critical aspect of calibration has nothing to do with either hardware or software. It's the environment you work in. Consider the following to establish an optimal working environment. Avoid light sources, natural or artificial, that shine directly on your monitor. Aside from causing eye strain, reflections can alter your perception of color. Similarly, it is very difficult to work comfortably and effectively if your monitor is strongly backlit. Some monitors ship with neutrally colored hoods that keep glare off the viewing surface. You can make one for any monitor with cardboard, paint, and duct tape. Windows with blinds are preferred. You can do all but the finest correction with windows open. (It's good to look out them periodically, as staring at a single fixed distance for long periods of time can cause eye strain and has the potential for causing problems in the future — the equivalent of carpal tunnel syndrome for the eyes.) But when it comes to critical calibration and color correction, you don't need any outside influences, so draw the blinds. Use caution in the presence of bright colors. A brightly colored wall behind a monitor can change your perception of color. Likewise, color from an adjacent brightly colored wall, even the clothing you wear, can be reflected onto your monitor, a highly reflective surface, and this can influence your color perception. I know of one manufacturer who included a black jacket with its monitor to be used when correcting color. Wear a black shirt and you'll achieve the same thing. Remember to specify a neutral gray background without a pattern for your monitor. Another color (particularly a bright color) can alter or bias your eye. In order to achieve critical accuracy, you need an unbiased eye, or as few biases as possible.

The light you view your prints under is also very important. You can see a monitor without another light source, but you can't see a print without one. Different lights have very different temperatures: tungsten is very warm, halogen is a little cooler, fluorescent is much cooler. The standard viewing temperature in the prepress industry is 5000 K (Kelvin), a light temperature that approximates early afternoon light. It is a very cool light source. Very few people actually look at images under such light. Most homes have tungsten, and galleries favor halogen. Both are much warmer than 5000 K. So what use is the standard? It's useful because it is a standard. Users can view their prints at the same light temperature and communicate meaningfully with one another over long distances. Manufacturers, like Softview, make viewing boxes that are balanced to the 5000 K standard. You don't have to buy an expensive viewing box to achieve 5000 K lighting. You can buy a 5000 K bulb and an inexpensive lighting fixture at your hardware store. 5000 K lighting helps you communicate with service providers or clients, but it won't help you determine how a print will look on display. Determine the light temperature your images are most likely to be viewed under, and make final prints for that setting (gallery, office, home, outdoors, etc.).

THE OLD VERSUS THE NEW

The old way of working and the new way of working differ in fundamental ways. In the old way, the RGB editing color space was defined by the color space of a particular monitor matched to a particular output device; it was device-specific. The LAB color space, a device-independent color space, was (and still is) used to translate color from RGB to CMYK, both device-dependent color spaces. (The CIE, Commission Internationale de L'Eclairge, created LAB color space in the 1930s. Other versions of LAB have been created since in an attempt to describe the range of light the human eye can see. It has since become a device-independent standard.) CMYK colors were displayed onscreen through this translation in tandem with the settings in Printing Inks and CMYK Separation Setup, along with the Monitor Setup. With this system, the consistency of images from monitor to monitor and platform to platform was far less than ideal. Change the destination of an image and you need to recalibrate. Recalibrate and you need to change the file. Thus, the file necessarily undergoes a number of successive transformations, sometimes compromising its quality.

In the new way, device-independent RGB color spaces have been defined. A monitor profile is generated to interpret how a specific monitor displays RGB data while the actual RGB values conform to a universally recognized standard. Provided other users have followed the correct calibration procedures, they will see the same RGB color on their monitors and systems that you do, even if they use equipment made by another manufacturer or an entirely different platform (Mac, PC, etc.). Color consistency is maintained through ICC profiles which translate the image data, making compensations for varying conditions. When you work with an image that has an ICC profile embedded in it, the profile is recognized when the file is opened. If the profile does not match your current working color space, the image data is transformed appropriately. The ICC profiles create standards for color spaces and standard ways of translating from one color space to another. (Think of the use of profiles as a handshake made by a skilled diplomat with a translator.) If you intend multiple destinations for a single image, at one time or over a long period of time, operating in a device-neutral color space makes sense. It will minimize the number of transformations and corrections necessary to achieve optimal results. And it works with a known, readily identifiable standard, creating a common language. Change the destination and you only need to specify a new profile.

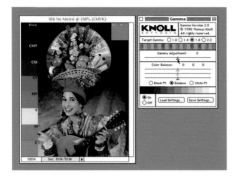

5. The Knoll Gamma utility and Ole No Moire file.

6. Upon opening Adobe Gamma, you may select Step By Step (Assistant) or Control Panel. Both do the same task. Use the assistant until you become familiar with the process.

The ultimate goal is a color management system in which the user calibrates his/her monitor and everything else falls into place. In theory, it should no longer be necessary to recalibrate to match a device's output. It's a nice, neat, simple dream; the reality is somewhat more complex. On the whole, the use of profiles has increased color consistency between differing software, devices, and platforms. It has not achieved perfection, but it is doing so by degrees. A significant problem with the new system is that it is only as good as the profiles used. If the profiles aren't perfect, the translation won't be either. By making semi-automatic what was once deliberate and conscious, the danger of making incorrect conversions by specifying incorrect or less-than-perfect profiles has risen. The profiles change your files. And it's difficult to change the way profiles change your files. To perfect profiles, you need expensive hardware and software. (Some manufacturer's are addressing this issue, making profiling easier and more affordable for the average consumer. As well, many new service providers have begun to fill this need, creating custom profiles for others.) It's guaranteed that as conditions change, you will need to change your profiles. If profiles are essential to controlling changing conditions, it is certain that the ability to change profiles is similarly essential. To some, this will be prohibitively costly and Byzantine in complexity. If you're confused, you're not alone. No topic is more likely to raise a heated debate. The jury's still out on whether color management has arrived (it will certainly continue to improve, hopefully becoming easier to use) or whether, like Esperanto, it remains a good idea in theory, one that never caught on when confronted with practical realities. I'm betting on the first, provided it becomes less costly and easier to implement for the average user. After all, it is likely that every new user will implement it. Already, since the writing of the first draft of this chapter to its revisions twelve months later, I have sensed increased momentum towards the use of color management, and I have personally experienced its many positive benefits.

HOW IT "USED" TO BE DONE
— PHOTOSHOP 4 AND BEFORE

You need to know how it used to be done before Photoshop 5, and how it is still being done by many. For a variety of reasons, not everyone has adopted the new color management options introduced in Photoshop 5. Depending on who you talk to, either the industry still hasn't caught up, or color management hasn't caught on. If you are working with someone

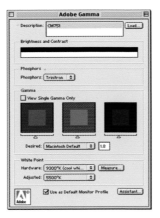

7. The Adobe Gamma Control Panel.

who is not implementing Photoshop's new color management system, you will need to know how they are working in order to better work with them.

The first step is to open and print the file on the device you intend to use. Next, under controlled lighting (the standard is 5000 K, but you may want to calibrate to the light temperature your image will be viewed under in its final use), compare the print to the monitor.

The file Ole No Moire (Adobe's Carmen Miranda) is useful for this procedure (when converted to RGB using the default CMYK settings). It has several merits. First, it represents a wide range of colors, including pure cyan, magenta, yellow, red, green, blue, black, white, and middle gray, generated with numeric targets. A file that represents the full color spectrum is very helpful. In the absence of one range of colors, a bias might not be detected. Second, it has neutral colors in the the background that quickly display color imbalances. Third, it has flesh tones, which we are particularly sensitive to; we can detect color casts that much more readily in these areas. If a sacrifice must be made between the pure color swatches and the neutral background and flesh tones, favor the latter two. Fourth, an exact duplicate ships and is installed with every copy of Photo-

shop, making it an ideal reference for many users. Fifth, few will be heavily invested in making the image look good, encouraging users to aim for an accurate match — not a work of art. Any similar file will do. Regardless of which file is used, you must be absolutely certain not to change the file or the process will be rendered inaccurate. The file matched must be identical to the one that created the output.

Looking at output from a given device under controlled lighting and the RGB file that was used to generate it on the monitor to be calibrated, use the Gamma control panel (Previously Thomas Knoll, now Adobe, it is located in Photoshop: Goodies: Calibration. Upon installation, it should subsequently be placed in the system folder for Mac computers.) to change the way the monitor displays the file to match the output. The key here is that the file itself is not changed; only the way the monitor displays it. When you use any of the correction tools in Photoshop, you change the numerical values of the digital file. When you use the gamma utility, you don't; you only change the way the monitor displays them. In both cases the image on the screen looks different. Again, when using the gamma utility you are running a subprogram operating within Photoshop, but you are no longer in Photoshop. Think of these as two separate programs that run at the same time. The name of the game is to match the monitor's display with the output, constraining its color space to the output's color space, without changing the file. If you changed the file in Photoshop, the reference print would no longer be an accurate reference print. The aim is not to make the image look good with the gamma utility; it is simply to match the monitor with the output. If the output is dark and magenta, make the monitor look dark and magenta. With the older Knoll utility, you can alter the color of highlights separately from shadows for a much closer match. Do this only if necessary and after going as far with midtones as possible. Think of gamma target (number) as contrast: a higher number will increase contrast and vice versa. Think of gamma adjustment (slider) as brightness. Generally, you will need to turn your monitor's controls to maximum contrast levels. Brightness will vary. Once set, make a note of their settings or tape the controls down so that they can only be changed deliberately. If a perfect match is achieved, you can expect your images to print out exactly as you see them on the monitor. Thus, when you make them look good on your monitor using Photoshop, they should look good when printed. Once you achieve optimal settings, save them. Give them a meaningful name: include the output device, the monitor's name, its brightness and contrast settings, and the date. The date is useful as conditions may change. For instance, your inks may change or your monitor may age. You create different settings for different output devices. You can save and load multiple settings. Save a backup copy in a safe place, as these settings represent a significant amount of work. If you change output devices, to compensate for the difference you change your file in Photoshop based on the display at the settings generated for that device. Don't think this process will happen instantly. It takes time. Expect to make continual refinements.

The CMYK Setup (now called Working Space) does affect calibration. It affects the way CMYK files are displayed (you may be looking at a CMYK file or you may have the CMYK preview turned on) and how files are converted (transformed) from another color space into CMYK or from CMYK into another color space. Achieve a match between your monitor displaying an RGB file and your output and it is likely that Photoshop's default conversion settings will work well. When necessary, these settings can be fine-tuned for greater accuracy.

HOW IT'S DONE AFTER PHOTOSHOP 5

Implementing Photoshop's new color management scheme bears many similarities to the old scheme. Here again you calibrate your monitor, but unlike the Knoll Gamma utility, with the Adobe Gamma utility you also generate a profile for the monitor. Using the Adobe Gamma utility to generate a profile for your monitor is very straightforward. You can use the Adobe Gamma Assistant to guide you through the process. Open the Adobe Gamma control panel (Apple: Control Panels: Adobe Gamma). Choose either Step by Step (Assistant) or Control Panel. Start with the Assistant. Then compare it to the Control Panel. Both do the same thing, but one, the Assistant, offers more help. Next, press the Load button and select an ICC profile that describes your monitor. If your monitor is not represented in the list of ICC profiles, choose the Generic RGB profile. Next, using the monitor controls, set the brightness and contrast of your monitor. Contrast is almost always set to maximum. For brightness, find a setting that displays both bright whites and barely discernable separation between the inside and outside black boxes seen on your monitor. Next, set your monitor phosphor type. (Check the documentation that came with your monitor. If you can find the custom numerical values for your monitor, use them. If you have to guess, Trinitron is your best bet.) Next, set your monitor gamma. Use the recommended standard for the platform you are working on (1.8 for Macintosh,

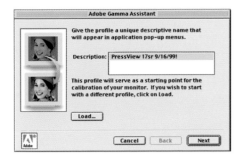

8. You may specify an ICC profile as the basis for subsequent calibration and characterization by loading a previously existing one.

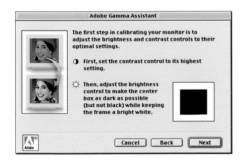

9. When proper settings of contrast and brightness are achieved, you will see faint separation between the inside and outside black squares.

10. Set you monitor phosphor type based on the manufacturer's specifications. These often come with accompanying literature or may be obtained from the manufacturer. If you are unable to locate this information, specify Trinitron as it is the most common model.

2.2 for Windows). Then squint and use the color sliders to make the inside square match the tone of the outside square for each color box, namely R, G, and B. Additionally, you can use the Single Gamma slider. Check it, and the three color boxes become one gray box. Compare both methods. You will note that if you use the Single Gamma slider after the separate sliders, this will reset the color sliders. If you want to use the two in conjunction, first set the Single Gamma slider, and then set the separate color sliders. For best results, try to get the middle square to blend with its surrounding square in both the single and the separate color sliders. Next, choose the Hardware White Point of your monitor. If your monitor allows you to choose a white point, set it before running Adobe Gamma and then choose that setting here. As with the phosphor specification, if

the monitor manufacturer recommends a custom setting you can set the white point more accurately using those numbers. To measure your monitor's white point, press the Measure button for instructions. Press Next. Then, select a gray for the middle square that is absolutely neutral (the one on the left will look cooler and the one on the right will look warmer). To make the middle square cooler, click on the square to the left; to make the middle square warmer, click on the square to the right. Next, set the Adjusted White Point. You can choose to work at a different white point than your monitor's hardware setting, for instance to simulate output on different substrates whose whites may vary considerably. Many favor the 6500 K setting. It's fine to choose an Adjusted White Point that looks pleasing to the eye, but you must specify the Hardware White

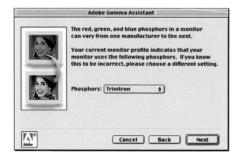

11. Custom coordinates may be specified for increased accuracy in describing phosphor characteristics.

14. Specify the hardware white point based on the manufacturer's recommendations. Custom will allow you to enter specific coordinates.

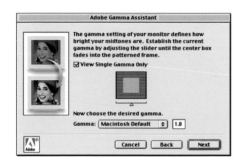

12. Specify either Macintosh or Windows default and move the slider until the inner square blends with the outer square. It often helps to squint.

15. If you cannot find manufacturer specifications, you can determine the white point visually by clicking Measure.

13. Uncheck the View Single Gamma Only box and repeat this process with the three separate color boxes. Be careful since returning to the Single Gamma window and making additional corrections to it often resets these settings.

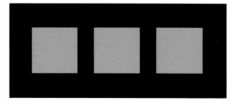

16. Select a gray that is neutral, one that is neither warm nor cool. Clicking the gray square to the right makes the gray increasingly warm (yellow), while clicking the gray square to the left makes the gray increasingly cool (blue). Place the most neutral gray in the middle and click on it.

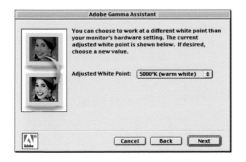

17. You can choose to work at a different white point than your hardware's white point.

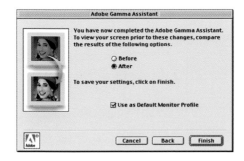

18. The final window will allow you to compare previous settings to new settings. Make sure to provide important information in the newly generated profile's title and to save it in the Color Sync folder.

19. The Color Settings window.

Point exactly. Next, you can use the Before and After buttons to toggle the display between the way it was previously and the way it is now. Give the file a meaningful name. (I recommend the name of your monitor, with numerical settings for its brightness and contrast settings, and the date. A monitor's display can change over time and may need updating in the future.) You can save many monitor profiles if you wish. This is especially helpful if you work with multiple monitors on a single system. To load a previous profile, just open the Adobe Gamma utility and load it. Back these settings up. Save the profiles you create on a separate disk, and if anything goes wrong with your hard drive, you will not have to recreate these settings. Whether you use the Assistant or the Control Panel, you have just calibrated and generated a profile for your monitor. If

you use other software to create a monitor profile, you will need to load it in the ColorSync control panel. The Adobe Gamma utility does this automatically.

COLOR SETTINGS

Once the monitor has been calibrated and the profiles generated, you need to specify how you would like the color management engine to handle transformations.

Photoshop 6 has consolidated the four components of Color Settings (RGB Setup, CMYK Setup, Grayscale Setup, and Profile Setup) found in 5 and 5.5 (under File) into a single window Color Settings (found under Edit).

First, Settings allows you to choose from several standard color management set ups, among them U.S. Prepress Defaults,

Emulate Photoshop 4, and Web Graphics Defaults. Each will specify Working Spaces and Color Management Policies for you. Or, you can specify them yourself to customize the setup to your needs by choosing Custom.

Second, Working Spaces (combining the former RGB Setup, CMYK Setup, and Grayscale Setup) allows you to specify which RGB color space you edit in. This information is used to make transformations to and from the RGB color space. It is also used to translate data to your monitor's color space for display. (Usually the monitor's RGB space is different than your editing RGB space. I state this emphatically, as it is critical that you not confuse the two.) Select your desired RGB editing space under RGB. (One of the following is recommended: Adobe RGB, Apple RGB, or ColorMatch.) You can define your own color space. (How to do this is a subject beyond the scope of this book and is recommended only for expert users with very specific needs.) If you use one of the predefined color spaces, Gamma, White Point, and Primaries will all be set for you. Change them and you will be specifying a custom color space. (Again, don't change them unless you have a definite need to.) Don't confuse the gamma and white point of your working space with the gamma and white point of your monitor.

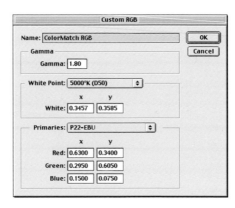

20. The Custom RGB window.

21. The Custom CMYK window.

22. The Custom Gamma window.

23. The Custom Dot Gain window.

They're different. (In 5 and 5.5 under RGB Setup, enable Display Using Monitor Compensation. This option is eliminated in 6.) You can display the embedded profile of a given file by going to the submenu at the bottom of the image window and checking Document Profile.

Working Spaces next allows you to specify what the inks you are using look like and how you want to use those inks to reproduce your images in the CMYK menu (formerly CMYK Setup). Photoshop also uses the settings to display CMYK data or to "softproof" (simulate) it. Photoshop's CMYK preview (View: Proof Colors or Proof Setup: Working CMYK) and Gamut Warning capabilities use the information in the CMYK setup to determine how colors are displayed and to determine which colors are out-of-gamut. The default settings offer very good standards for standard web offset printing (SWOP). Nevertheless, the behavior of offset presses varies so much that it is wise to obtain the recommendations of your service provider to fine-tune these settings or provide you with an accurate ICC profile. The gamut of other media (most inkjet printers, including Epson, Iris, and Encad, film recorders, and even hexachrome printing on offset presses) may be much larger; thus, the gamut warning will give an overly conservative report. To get the most accurate

24. The Profile Mismatch window.

25. The Missing Profile window.

report, you will need to change the settings appropriately. The capabilities of 5 and 5.5's Built-In, ICC, and Tables have been combined into a single menu — CMYK. There you can choose between several defaults including U.S. Web Coated (SWOP), or a specific ICC profile, or create a Custom CMYK setup (formerly Built-In). Each is a different method for specifying how to make CMYK conversions and how to display CMYK files. Unless you are familiar with creating settings manually (Custom CMYK) or your service provider can specify accurate settings, specify the appropriate ICC profile for the printer you intend to use. Remember, device-specific profiles will be more accurate than generic profiles provided by the printer's manufacturer, though these can work surprisingly well. You might try the generic profile before deciding to create a new profile yourself or have one created by a knowledgeable service provider.

Working Spaces also allows you to specify how Photoshop makes translations to and from Grayscale under Gray (formerly Grayscale Setup). You can specify this in two ways, standard Dot Gain settings and Gray Gamma settings, and both can be customized. Use Gamma (default 1.8) settings for destinations that are true RGB devices (monitors, film recorders). Use Dot Gain (default 20%) for images whose destinations are ink and paper (or an equivalent substrate), typically CMYK devices. The default settings are generally quite good.

Third, Color Management Policies (formerly Profile Setup) allows you to specify whether or not to embed profiles (saving)

and how profile mismatches (opening) or files with missing profiles will be handled (opening) to make accurate translations. In the case of each type of file (RGB, CMYK, and Grayscale), you can convert files to the working color space, or Preserve Embedded Profiles, or turn the function Off.

If you are routinely opening files from a known source, you can automate the procedure by specifying the appropriate settings and convert files to the working spaces on the fly. Uncheck Ask When Opening, and no Missing Profile or Profile Mismatch dialog box will appear. Files will simply be converted. Otherwise, it is wise to specify Preserve Embedded Profiles and Ask When Opening. Then, upon opening a file, if either the Embedded Profile Mismatch or the Missing Profile dialog box appears, you can knowledgeably specify how or whether to convert a specific image with its unique situation in mind.

When you encounter a Missing Profile or Profile Mismatch dialog box upon opening files, you are presented with three choices: Use the embedded profile (instead of the working space), Convert document's colors to the working space, or Discard the embedded profile (don't color manage). If you specify "Use the embedded profile (instead of the working space)", the subsequent editing you perform to that file will occur in the color space of the embedded profile. No conversion will be made and the original embedded profile will be preserved. (This is best when your current editing space is smaller than the space the image was created in.) If you specify "Convert document's colors to the working space," the image will be converted to the current working space specified in Color Settings, subsequent editing will take place in that color space, and a profile for that color space will replace the profile of its previous color space. (This is usually the safest course for RGB and grayscale files.) If you specify "Discard the embedded profile (don't color manage)," the profile will be discarded, no new profile will be embedded, and subsequent editing will occur in the working space. (This may redefine color values, possibly changing the file to something quite different.)

Color management in Photoshop 6 has been updated, streamlined, and significantly improved. Aside from the many other new features in 6, this alone is a compelling reason to upgrade. Before 6, you could use only one editing space at a time — the one specified in RGB Setup. In 6, you can edit several files, each in separate spaces, without having to reconfigure the RGB Setup. When open, the name of the editing space of a particular file is displayed in the lower left corner of the image's window. For this reason, when working with documents in different color spaces, you may encounter a Paste Profile Mismatch. When you encounter a Paste Profile Mismatch, you can choose between Convert (preserve color appearance) or Don't convert (preserve color numbers). As a result, many unnecessary conversions are eliminated and conversions are made more consciously, resulting in greater color accuracy and better color management practices. While 5 and 5.5 offered application-specific color management, 6 offers document-specific color management.

All "legacy" files (without profiles, typically created before Photoshop 5), generated before the use of profiling, will not have profiles. If you choose to use profiling, you should bring these files up to date, converting them to your choice of color space, and embedding profiles for them.

When you encounter a Missing Profile dialog box, you will be presented with three choices: Leave as is (don't color manage), Assign working RGB, or Assign Profile. "Leave as is (don't color manage)" which makes no change to your document. Use this if you don't wish to use color management. "Assign working RGB" assigns the profile of the current working space. Use this if you're uncertain of the file's previous working space and wish to convert it to the current working color space. "Assign profile" allows you to embed the profile of an alternate working space. Use this if you know the alternate working space the file was created in. This feature also enables you to convert the document to the working RGB space if you desire. If you do not convert the file, you will edit in the space of the assigned profile.

If you check Advanced in the Color Settings window, you will find two additions: Conversion Options and Advanced Controls. Conversion Options specifies which separation engine (most favor Adobe (ACE), some prefer Apple ColorSync) you want to use to convert images and its rendering Intent (most favor Perceptual). The defaults favoring Adobe and Perceptual are excellent. Advanced Controls enables you to make various compensations for the display of your monitor. Desaturate Monitor Colors By helps users visualize the full range of colors in spaces larger than the monitor is capable of displaying. Blend RGB Colors Using Gamma reduces edge artifacts. Both are recommended only for expert users working in unusual situations.

Finally, the Color Settings window also provides a useful Description for each setting.

Color management is evolving rapidly, and good sources of information aren't easy to find. I will be posting updated informration on my web site (www.johnpaulcaponigro.com) periodically. You can find a great deal of useful information on the web. See www.color.org, www.color.com, and www.colorsync.com.

MAKING NEW VERSIONS
WORK LIKE OLD VERSIONS

If you do not wish to implement the new color management capabilities of Photoshop 5 and higher, you should not fear upgrading. You don't have to use it. The many additional features, such as the History feature, will make upgrading worthwhile to users of previous versions.

You can make new versions of Photoshop manage color like old versions of Photoshop. You can use the new Adobe Gamma control panel just like the old Knoll Gamma control panel to control the appearance of your monitor's display. Rather than using Step by Step, use the Control Panel and change the monitor's appearance as you desire. Then, go to RGB Setup, specify the RGB working space as Monitor RGB, and uncheck Display Using Monitor Compensation. Next, go to CMYK Setup and use the Built-in default settings. Finally, turn off color management. Under Profile Setup, uncheck Embed Profiles, specify None for Assumed Profiles, and Ignore for all Profile Mismatch Handling. Also, be aware that dot gain settings have been changed between 4 and 5. 20% does not mean the same thing in 5 that it does in 4. If you are accustomed to using previous dot gain settings, you can change the settings to compensate. Many prefer the new settings, and if you are new to Photoshop, or new to this aspect of Photoshop, there is no need to change the settings. Some think the new settings are in fact an improvement.

In Photoshop 6, managing color exactly as it did before 5 is harder (Display Using Monitor Compensation has been eliminated); however, 6 offers a very easy and convenient way to simulate 4. Go to Edit: Color Settings and under Settings, specify Emulate Photoshop 4. The Working Spaces will be set automatically to Apple RGB, Photoshop 4 Default CMYK, Gray Gamma 1.8, and Dot Gain of 20%; Color Management Policies will also be turned Off.

TWEAKS

If you are working with service providers, they can supply you with accurate profiles and color space setup information. If you are not, fortunately, there other ways to compensate for imperfections in calibrating and profiling. If you are using a printer you control, you can create a set of custom settings with the printer's software that tweaks the output to compensate for any variances that occur. Once determined through testing, use those settings each time you print. Or, you can establish a custom CMYK conversion for a particular device to transform the file precisely before printing, doing the conversion manually. Or, you can create a custom adjustment layer in Photoshop that tweaks the file before conversion, and apply it to every file before printing. Whichever route you pursue, consistency is the key. You must know the status of each variable to control the entire process.

A PROBLEM YOU NEED TO KNOW ABOUT

Photoshop 5.0 shipped with a problem. There may still be some users using 5.0 who don't know the problem exists. You need to know about it to avoid possible problems when working with those people. 5.0 set the default working color space to sRGB — excellent for the Web but inferior for printing. If an unwary user opens a file in Photoshop 5.0 without changing the Profile Setup settings, the file will be converted to sRGB automatically, often degrading it. Users will not be asked if they wish to convert; they will simply see a progress bar with the words "converting colors." Some will not know that the file has just been changed, and that it is now numerically different from the original file. Two people in two places may be looking at very different files, assuming that they are the same, when in fact they are not. You can avoid this in 5.0 by specifying another RGB working space and changing the Profile Mismatch Handling to Ask When Opening. 5.02 quickly fixed this problem. It does not exist in subsequent versions.

Image size, how large the file size is and how large it will be output, is determined by the number of pixels it contains.

A pixel is a square that has no height and no width. Its height and width are "x" or variable. That's the hardest concept to grasp here. It still throws me a little. It throws me because I'm more comfortable dealing with concrete things, not abstractions. A pixel is an abstraction. It's the visual representation of mathematical code. The code specifies a tone and a color within a square boundary of indeterminate size.

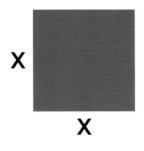

1. A pixel's height/width is variable.

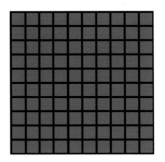

2. A file's size is measured in numbers of pixels. This comprises file size in megabytes. As a pixel has no set physical size, neither does the image file. A single file will print at various sizes on printers with varying resolutions.

The pixel can be printed at any height, large or small, but it's still just a colored square. It's a fluid square of color.

Digital images, photographic or bitmapped ones, are comprised of a grid of colored squares. Like the grain of film, when pixels are small enough our eyes cannot see them individually, but when many are placed together we see the whole image they create.

Your image size, your file size (measured in megabytes) and how large your image will be printed (measured in inches or centimeters) are determined by the number of pixels the image contains. Therefore, it is important for you to be able to calculate the size of your image and see the relationships between the various numbers used to represent it.

Before I start tossing numbers around let me assure you that it might look complex, but it's not. There's nothing more involved here than multiplication and division. For those of you who like math, the equation to calculate file size follows. Height (in pixels) x width (in pixels) x bytes per pixel (the number of channels) = total number of bytes. To convert bytes into megabytes, divide by 1,048,576. There are 1024 bytes in a kilobyte and 1024 kilobytes in a megabyte. While kilo- means a thousand and mega- means a million, the terms are approximate here. The precise number is a factor of 2, in this case, 2 to the 8th power because we are dealing with 8 bits per channel.

Let's take a hypothetical file, 1000 pixels high x 1000 pixels wide or 1,000,000 pixels.

Output	Resolution	Pixel	MB (RGB)
35mm transparency	2032 PPI	2800 x 2240	18
6x6 cm transparency	1524 PPI	3600 x 3600	37.1
4" x 5" transparency	1219 PPI	4876 x 6095	85.1
8" x 10" transparency	1016 PPI	8128 x 10160	236.3
8" x 10" print	300 PPI	2400 x 3000	20.6
11" x 14" print	300 PPI	3300 x 4200	39.7
16" x 20" print	300 PPI	4800 x 6000	82.4
20" x 24" print	300 PPI	6000 x 7200	123.6
30" x 40" print	300 PPI	9000 x 12000	309

3. Total pixel counts and flattened file sizes in megabytes for various forms and sizes of output.

File Size (Pixels)	MB (RGB)	Resolution	Output Size
2400 x 3000	20.6	72 PPI	33.33" x 41.66"
2400 x 3000	20.6	100 PPI	24" x 30"
2400 x 3000	20.6	300 PPI	8" x 10"
2400 x 3000	20.6	600 PPI	4" x 5"
2400 x 3000	20.6	1500 PPI	1.6" x 2"

4. Even if file size remains constant, output size may vary based on the resolution of the output device. Here resolutions for monitor, electrostatic printer, inkjet printer, a high line screen offset film, and film recorder are listed respectively.

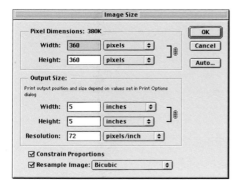

5. Use the Image Size dialog box to change the size of your image. If Resample Image is checked, this will change the total pixel count to make the image larger or smaller.

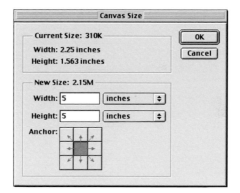

6. Use the Canvas Size dialog box to add new imaging area. The gray square indicates the position of the current image information in relationship to the new imaging areas seen in white. The total number of pixels comprising the original image remains the same.

1000 x 1000 x 1 = 1,000,000 for Grayscale

1,000,000 ÷ 1,048,576 = .95 MB or 977 K

1000 x 1000 x 3 = 3,000,000 for RGB

3,000,000 ÷ 1,048,576 = 2.87 MB

1000 x 1000 x 4 = 4,000,000 for CMYK

4,000,000 ÷ 1,048,576 = 3.82 MB

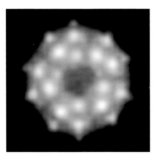

7. Image scanned at 10 PPI and up-sampled to 300.

The previous equation works for 8-bit color spaces. If you are working in 16-bit color spaces your files size will double.

For those of you who don't like math, to calculate a file size, simply begin to create a new document in Photoshop. Once the dialog box appears, specify height, width, and resolution. Photoshop will do the math for you, giving you readouts of numbers of pixels and megabytes. (There's no need to create this file, so just cancel out of the dialog box which we were only using as a calculator.)

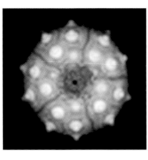

8. Image scanned at 25 PPI and up-sampled to 300.

Once you have determined the size of your image file, the total number of pixels and the number of megabytes will remain the same unless you use software to modify or resample (add or subtract through averaging calculations) it. However, that same file (with a fixed number of pixels) may print out at different sizes on different printers. Why? Because the resolution of the output device in combination with the resolution of the file determines the physical size of a print. Each output device will need so many pixels to create an inch. That's its resolution. A monitor needs 72 PPI, a printer typically needs

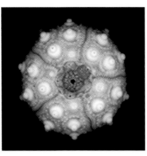

9. Image scanned at 50 PPI and up-sampled to 300.

300 PPI, a film recorder typically needs 1500 PPI. In the case of printers, these figures represent resolutions that are optimal as typically they can take less or more but output quality may suffer. An image file has a fixed number of pixels (height x width). Divide the number of pixels by the output device's resolution to get the final print size. Again it's simple math. Output our hypothetical file on a 100-DPI printer and the resulting print will be 10" wide and 10" tall — the height/width (1000 pixels) divided by the output resolution (100) or 1000 ÷ 100 = 10. Take that same file and output it on a 1000-DPI printer and the resulting print will be 1" — 1000 ÷ 1000 = 1. The file itself remains unchanged, as it still has 1,000,000 pixels. The print size varies according to the resolution of the printer. Output devices have inches (or centimeters) and resolutions. Digital files do not. A digital file has a grid of pixels. We talk about a digital file having so many inches at a given resolution because these are our real-world equivalents for dealing with the abstraction of pixels. But it's best to keep in mind that the true file size is measured in total numbers of pixels and that resolution and print size is variable. They are linked since increasing one decreases the other.

Often the terms PPI, pixels per inch, and DPI, dots per inch, are used interchangeably. They are not the same thing. Pixels are square. You find pixels in digital files. Dots are any number of shapes, typically round or elliptical. You find dots in reproductions (prints, books, magazines). Scanners create pixels. (Even if their interfaces say "dots," it's a misnomer.) Digital files do not have dots, hence, no DPI; rather they have PPI. Printers turn pixels into dots, namely DPI (a process called Raster Image Processing or ripping). Now knowing the distinction between PPI and DPI, you must realize that many in the industry often use the terms interchangeably. With the above in mind, you'll know what they're talking about and when to translate when they use the incorrect term.

Be careful with printer manufacturer specifications of resolution. The Epson Stylus Photo printers will quote a resolution of 1720 DPI. This does not mean you need to create image files at 1720 PPI. This means the printer is capable of reproducing type with sharp edges that will yield the equivalent of 1720 DPI. It is also capable of producing multiple dots from single pixels. It's rare that you get one dot for one pixel. Photographic images will need dramatically less resolution, roughly 300 DPI. You get diminishing or no returns in quality from higher resolution image files. You get reduced image quality with lower resolutions. If you really want to find out what the optimal resolution for your printer is, test it yourself. Scan an image at varying resolutions (250, 275, 300, 325, 350, 400), print the different files, and compare them side by side. You will be able to see the difference in quality and determine the optimal image resolution for your printer optically rather than relying on manufacturer specifications.

Because of varying printer resolutions, the physical dimensions of output (prints, film, video) of a digital file may vary without chang-

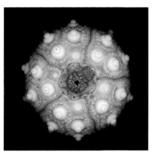

10. Image scanned at 75 PPI and upsampled to 300.

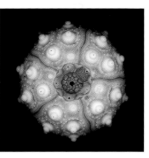

11. Image scanned at 300 PPI.

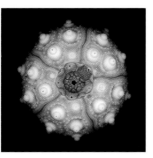

12. Image scanned at 1500 PPI and downsampled to 300.

ing the total pixel count. While adding layers, adjustment layers, layer masks, and alpha channels can increase your working file size (right number in the lower left hand corner of the image window), the flattened file size (left number in the lower left hand corner of the image window) can only vary if you change the file by adding or subtracting pixels (resampling). Three tools within Photoshop can be used to change the size of your file in this way: the Crop tool, Canvas Size, and Image Size. (Additionally you can use the Rectangular Marquee tool and go to Image: Crop.)

You use the Crop tool to eliminate part of an image. Crop an image and you remove the pixels outside the cropping boundary. The pixels within the cropping boundary remain. You can also use the Crop tool to enlarge or reduce a file, changing the pixel count within the cropping boundary. Enter a Fixed Size in the Crop tool dialog box that is larger or smaller than the size of the area to be cropped and crop it. This is essentially no different than resampling the image with Image Size and cropping.

Similarly, while you can crop an image with Canvas Size (Image: Canvas Size) by entering values smaller than the image affected, Canvas Size is most often used to increase the area of the working image. Canvas Size adds more imaging area without altering the image seen. It adds more "canvas" to work with, a uniform set of pixels. If you suddenly realize you need "a bigger piece of paper" to place new material on, you can create it, at any time, with Canvas Size. The color of the new area is specified by your background color. Though it's generally white, it can be any color.

Then there's the Image Size feature. If the Resample Image box is not checked, this tool will simply change your resolution, and it changes physical size readings along with it. What does not change is the total pixel count. All that has changed is the way Photoshop displays the numbers, and nothing about the file has actually changed. If on the other hand the Resample Image box is checked, this feature actually changes the image; it adds or subtracts pixels. This is one area that can get you into trouble. Resampling, or interpolation, uses software to perform sophisticated averaging calculations to add or subtract pixels, making your total pixel count (megabytes) smaller or larger. Both operations soften the structure of your image; that is, the transitions the pixels describe become less defined. Reduced images suffer very little from this softening process, since the sampling algorithms are very sophisticated and smaller images look sharper to the eye. You can take advantage of this softening when scanning prescreened originals. When half-toned originals are scanned larger than necessary and then sized down, the image information describing the edges of the dots is softened and the likelihood of moiré patterns is reduced. You can even scan a prescreened original at an angle (30 degrees is favored) and then rotate it to make it square, as rotation at any angle not a factor of 90 (90,180, 270, 360) will also soften an image. If you do size down an image and you want to be able to return to a larger size, remember to save the Resampled Image as a new document. That way you will have both large and small versions to choose from. Reduction is generally not a problem, but enlargement is. (The only time I can think of reduction being a problem is if the small image created will later be enlarged, say in the case of 35mm film that is destined for enlargement in the traditional darkroom.) When an image is "upsampled," information is added, information calculated by software. No matter how good the algorithms, to date, nothing beats the real thing, optically captured (scanned) information. It is much better to capture the maximum amount of information you will need optically as the quality of the information will be superior. Telltale signs of upsampling are softness and brittle artifacts that look like "stair steps" in the image.

Try it for yourself. Scan an image at 300 PPI. Scan the same image at 75 PPI and upsample it to 300 PPI. Compare the information at a magnification of 100%. The one with optically captured information will be superior.

If you must upsample an image rather than upsampling to your final size in one step, do it in many steps — go a quarter of the way, then to half, then to three quarters, and finally all the way. Artifacting will be reduced. Fractal algorithms have been employed to upsample images with even greater success. Look to a program called Genuine Fractals for your most critical upsampling needs.

4. INPUT SCAN

A scanner converts analog information into digital information. A scanner reads the information from an original (print, film, object) and creates a digital file capable of reproducing that original as a two-dimensional image. Scanners break images into pixels (squares), creating a grid of information. Each pixel specifies a color and a tone, nothing more. The principle applies to Impressionist paintings, Pointillist paintings, and halftone reproductions equally. Put enough small pieces of information together in a given space, and the

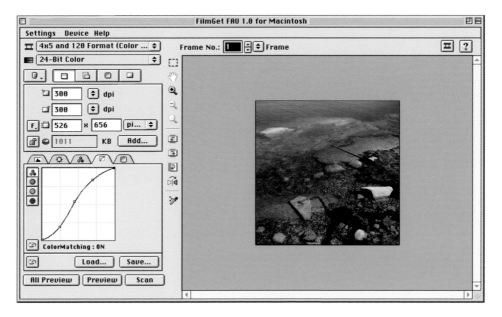

1. A scanner interface. One essential feature of any software package is the ability to apply a curve at the scan level.

human eye will read them as one continuous whole rather than as separate pieces. The quality of the image information is largely determined by the quality of the scan.

You can evaluate the quality of any scanner and compare it to another by being mindful of five significant factors: resolution, dynamic range, bit depth, software, profiles. These are the areas you need to be aware of when choosing and using a scanner.

RESOLUTION

Measured in pixels per inch, this factor simply determines how much information is packed into an inch. (It's like grain in film.) The more information, the bigger the file, the higher the quality, the larger the image can be printed without loss of quality. Be careful when reading specifications provided by manufacturers. Often these specifications quote resolutions that are achievable through scanner software interpolation, the quality of which will not be as good as information that is captured purely by optics. You do not need scanner software to interpolate (enlarge or reduce, essentially add or subtract pixels, with software averaging schemes). You can interpolate easily in Photoshop. Photoshop can even do it better than most scanners can. The "true," "native," or "optical" resolution of the scanner is what counts.

2. A scan with low contrast.

4. A scan with normal contrast.

6. A scan with high contrast.

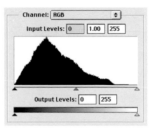

3. The corresponding histogram. No
information is lost. Minor gapping in
the histogram will occur as
corrections will not be major.

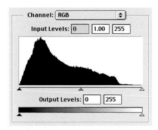

5. The corresponding histogram. No
information has been lost. Little or no
gapping will occur as corrections will
be minor.

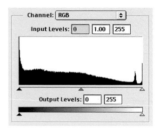

7. The corresponding histogram.
Some information has been lost, both
in the highlights and the shadows. No
amount of correction will reclaim it.

DYNAMIC RANGE

Dynamic range is a measure of the scanner's ability to see the information in your original. It's essentially the length of the tonal scale the scanner is capable of reproducing. Typical dynamic ranges of a scanner run from 3.0 to 4.2. The higher the number, the more sensitive the scanner will be. A more sensitive scanner will be able to get more information out of difficult areas in originals. This is true for originals that are too bright and, more often than not, those that are too dark. As the scale is measured logarithmically (like the scale used to measure earthquakes), each increase of .1 is more significant than you might imagine. A respectable dynamic range is 3.0–3.2 and will handle most average originals adequately. A more respectable dynamic range is 3.3–3.4 and will handle most average originals well.

A good dynamic range is 3.5–3.6 and will handle most originals very well. A very good dynamic range is 3.7–3.8 and will handle all but the most difficult originals exceptionally well. The 3.9–4.2 range is state-of-the-art quality, and it will handle even the most difficult originals exceptionally well.

BIT DEPTH

Bit depth is a measure of a scanner's ability to make subtle distinctions between tone and color. Bit depth is measured in factors of three. It's a measure of so many bits per channel and the RGB color space (the one used by scanners, even for scanning grayscale images) has three channels. Typical bit-depth ratings are 24 (respectable), 36 (good), and 48 (exceptional). A scanner with a lower bit depth is not capable of making distinctions between two subtly different colors and will create a file in which they are reproduced as the same color, whereas a scanner with a higher bit depth will be capable of recognizing them as being different and representing them differently.

SOFTWARE

Software should be easy to use, and it should have the ability for you to see a large enough preview of the image you are scanning so that you can comfortably evaluate and make corrections at the scan level. It should also enable you to make sophisticated corrections at the scan level. In a nutshell, the most important factor in choosing software is the ability to apply a curve at the scan level. Applying the curve while scanning, rather than after the scan, creates files with undistorted histograms. Ideal software provides higher quality optically captured information rather than average quality information that is later digitally enhanced. Don't think that all corrections must be made at the scan level or that all histograms must be completely undistorted. Just think: a little is better than a lot. Use the scanner for gross adjustment, and use Photoshop for fine-tuning. Agfa's software has a simple but very powerful scanning ability I have not seen in other software packages, something I think would improve all software packages if it were included. With it you can make a quick first low-resolution scan at the scanner's default settings. Open the file in Photoshop. Correct your file with a curve. Save that

8. This histogram indicates that the scan was too dark and shadow detail was lost. Rescan.

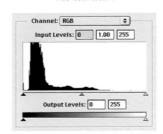

9. This image is very dark. No tones exist above the midpoint and shadow detail has not been lost. The scan is fine.

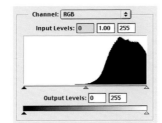

10. This histogram indicates that the scan was too dark and highlight detail was lost. Rescan.

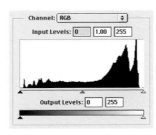

11. This image is very light yet highlight detail has not been lost. The scan is fine.

curve. Import that curve at the scan level for a second scan, this time at high resolution, yielding a pristine, undistorted histogram in a file that needs little or no further adjustment. Simple. Wonderful.

As well as being a map of the relative distribution of tones throughout an image, a file's histogram will tell you a great deal about the quality of information it contains. Gapping occurs from excessive corrections made to a file and may cause unwanted artifacts such as posterization and noise. While there is no ideal shape for a histogram (every image's histogram will be unique in shape), there is another thing to look for. The altitude of a line is not a concern, it simply represents a great quantity. However, a high solid line of information at the black point or white point indicates information has been lost, and in all likelihood exists in the original below or above those points. The histogram should slope down to these points; then information will not be lost. (Remember to crop black film borders before evaluating a histogram, as that information will alter the shape of the histogram.)

PROFILES

All profiles are not created equally. Some are more accurate than others. It's difficult to evaluate the quality of profiles. An expert, in-depth, and objective comparison between multiple manufacturers of multiple input and output devices would be necessary. What would make such a comparison more complicated is the speed at which things are changing, which would require continual reevaluation of the results. This is not something you are likely to be able to evaluate. You can correct Profiles with other software packages, but this is prohibitively complicated and expensive to the average user. Word on the street has it that the following manufacturers have profiles that are a cut above the rest — Agfa, Epson, Imacon, Linotype Hell. Keep your ear to the ground as, again, this information is continually changing. I see a trend toward monitors that are self-profiling. They take stock of their current operating conditions and generate an ICC profile that reflects that state, resulting in a more accurate profile. I expect a similar trend to follow with scanners.

To make a purchasing decision, compare these factors and weigh them against their relative costs. All factors being equal, you may want to make your decision on ease of use or reputation of manufacturer, perhaps even the responsiveness of a manufacturer's technical support (which, hopefully, you won't require).

TO MAKE A SCAN

Place the original in the scanner. Whenever possible place it on the scanner in a way that will avoid later rotation of the image. (Rotating the image in Photoshop can degrade your image. It's not something to worry about a great deal. A little rotation is fine. Rotating an image many times is not recommended.) Preview the image. Select the area to be scanned. For in-

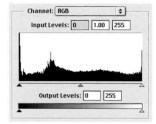

12. Both highlight and shadow detail have been lost. Rescan.

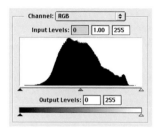

13. An excellent histogram without gapping.

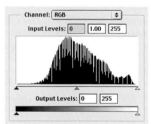

14. A fine histogram with minimal gapping.

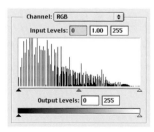

15. A severely distorted histogram … expect trouble.

creased precision, crop generally with the scanner software, selecting a little more than you are likely to need. Crop tightly in Photoshop after the scan has been made. Make obvious corrections in tone or color with the scanner software. Favor using Curves over Brightness and Contrast sliders. Set the resolution to create a file of your maximum desired size at the resolution of your final output device. Finally, scan the image. If you are going to create a digital file that will be used for multiple purposes, create the largest file you are likely to need. It's better to scan too large than scan too small as sizing up degrades quality much more than sizing down. Often, I simply scan at the maximum optical resolution of the scanner at 100%. This avoids interpolation or up-sampling (the addition of pixels through software averaging) which can be done better in Photoshop or with Genuine Fractals than with scanner software. When the file is finished, I size copies of that large file down when necessary.

Making a good scan is like making a good exposure. If you're using a digital camera, it is the exposure. A digital camera simply puts a scanner behind a lens, scanning the world, instead of reproductions of it. If you are scanning film or a photographic print, that scan is essentially a second exposure. All the rules that apply to making a good traditional exposure apply to making a good scan. In general, capture a maximum amount of information, favoring full detail in shadows and highlights and accurate color.

16. An evenly distributed
histogram favoring the
three-quartertones.

18. The histogram for a dark image
with little information
above the midpoint.

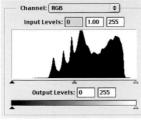

17. The histogram for a light image
with little information in the three-
quartertones and below.

19. An evenly distributed
histogram.The spike at the black
point is created by the black sky
where loss of detail is not an issue.

5. TONE LIGHT AND THE ZONE SYSTEM

While your methods may or may not change when working digitally, the language of the Zone System will always be useful. The Zone System, codified by Ansel Adams in the 1940's, presents us with a way to describe and measure light, and to capture it. "Previsualization" is the term used to explain the process of imagining what we want a photograph to look like in its final incarnation before we make the exposure. We translate what we see originally into what we see finally using the Zone System, a language of light.

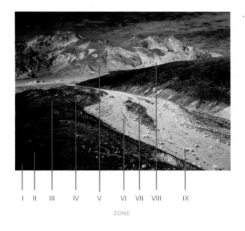

1. The zones identified in She iii.

The Zone System divides an image into 11 zones or tones. The Roman numerals from 0 to X identify successive zones. 0 represents pure black. I represents black with no detail but not maximum black. X represents pure white. IX represents white with tone but no detail. II through VIII represent the tones with detail ranging from very dark to very light. V represents middle gray, halfway between pure black and pure white. The relative relationships between the tones from black to white are graphed on a characteristic curve, 0 at the bottom or the black point and X at the top or the white point. Each material (or device) has its own characteristic curve or way of recording relationships of light; some are contrasty, some are not. The curve of each will have a different shape. To control the relative relationships of tone you modify the curve, traditionally through exposure (light and time) or development (chemistry and time).

Zone V, middle gray, is used as a key measurement. If it is optimally set, it will be reproduced as a normal color/tone as if you were looking at it under normal lighting conditions and your eyes had adjusted to that lighting situation. After measuring the dynamic range (the total range of tones from dark to light) of a scene, you usually set the exposure to its middle value. Information that is too bright or too dark to fit within the dynamic range of the capture device will be lost, at one end of the scale, or the other, or both. Set the exposure to a value brighter than the middle of the range and more highlight detail will be captured, but shadow detail will be lost. Set the exposure to a value darker than the middle of the range and more shadow detail will be captured, but highlight detail will be lost. "Expose for the shadows and develop for the highlights." This simple phrase distills the essence of the Zone System in

	ZONE									
0	I	II	III	IV	V	VI	VII	VIII	IX	X

RGB VALUE

0	26	51	77	102	128	153	179	204	230	255

GRAYSCALE PERCENTAGE

100	90	80	70	60	50	40	30	20	10	0

2. A grayscale strip with corresponding numerical values.

3. The Brightness/Contrast window offers two points of control.

practice. It's a way of setting the dynamic range, capturing a maximum amount of information, and sacrificing detail in less important areas to preserve it in more important areas.

After exposure, in the traditional darkroom you then modify tonal relationships (the curve) using chemical reactions. In the digital darkroom you modify tonal relationships (the curve) using mathematical codes. While electricity replaces chemistry in digital imaging, the principles of the Zone System are just as valid and useful before, during, and after capture. The materials may change, the methods may differ, but the essence of the practice does not.

In Photoshop you look to three tools for tonal correction — Brightness/Contrast, Levels, and Curves. The tools ascend in sophistication in that order.

Brightness/Contrast offers two points of control: a slider between dark and light for brightness and a slider between more and less for contrast. Both tools uniformly modify the ends of an image's curve, or the black and white points. With Brightness you move a straight curve vertically up (brighter) or down (darker). With Contrast you bring the end points closer together in equal proportions. You change all the other tones in between in relationship to, not independently of, these two points. It's perfectly fine to use the Contrast in Brightness/Contrast, though you can affect contrast with a great deal more sophistication with Levels or Curves. Watch Brightness carefully, as

it will reduce your dynamic range, making your whites darker (gray) when decreased or your blacks lighter (gray) when increased. Brightness/Contrast has the right name, but it can lead to problems so easily that I recommend that you don't use it.

Levels offers three points of control: a white point, a black point and a midpoint. You can modify each point independently from the others. When you are moving the sliders in Levels you are specifying a value below which no information will appear (black point), a value above which no information will appear (white point), and a value that is midway between those two points (midpoint). To increase contrast, simply move the black and white points in towards the midpoint. Unlike the Contrast slider in Brightness/Contrast, you can move these points separately and to different degrees. To increase or decrease brightness, move the midpoint slider — left for lighter, right for darker. Unlike the Brightness slider in Brightness/Contrast, this will not change your dynamic range, as the end points of your dynamic range remain fixed; blacks remain black and whites remain white. If you wish, you can darken or lighten an image and still change its black point or white point or both in Levels. Simply move them. You'll note that sliding the black point or white point will move the midpoint as well; the proportional distance between the black point and white point remains the same. To decrease contrast, move the output sliders. Moving the black output slider will lighten your blacks; it will make them

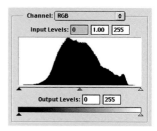

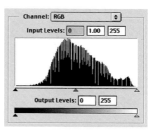

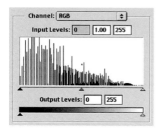

4. An excellent histogram without gapping.

5. A fine histogram with minimal gapping.

6. A severely distorted histogram … expect trouble.

gray (as Brightness does). Moving the white output slider will darken your whites; it will make them gray (as Brightness does). For this reason, you might not use the output levels often. On occasion you might use them to screen images back (making them darker or lighter), for example when an image is lightened or darkened, to increase the visibility of text placed on top of it.

The histogram, above these points of control, is a graphical representation of the tonal values throughout an image. On the far left is the black point; on the far right is the white point, in between are all the shades of gray from dark to light that form the continuum between them. The height of the black line above the value on the baseline indicates how much of the image is comprised of that tone: the higher the line the more that tone will be found in the image, the lower the line the less that tone will be found in the image. A histogram with a peak at the left will be weighted towards the darker end of the tonal scale. A histogram with a peak at the right will be weighted towards the lighter end of the tonal scale. A histogram that is equally high from left to right will have an even distribution of all tones. The histogram of every image will be unique; there is no perfect shape for a histogram. (One exception: if the original histogram has very high peaks at either end, black point or white point, it is likely that the scan was too dark or too light and information was lost. You may want to rescan.) However, there is a perfect state: without gaps. As you alter an image, the information in the image is redistributed with software; that is, bits are stretched and squeezed. The histogram records the effects of these subsequent changes. If you make substantial changes, "gapping" in the histogram will occur. A gap is where a white line breaks the black mass of the histogram at its baseline. Gapping and the likelihood of artifacting occurring (posterization or noise, for example) increases in proportion to the amount you manipulate an image. A little bit of gapping presents no problem. Dramatic gapping may. (Editing in 16-bit color dramatically reduces or eliminates such gapping.)

You can use the histogram as a guide for your image correction. The first move is to set your dynamic range by specifying a black point and a white point. Drag the white point slider to the point on the histogram at which information begins to appear. Next, drag the black point to the point on the histogram at which information begins to appear. Some recommend clipping off what they consider to be insignificant amounts of information and moving the sliders to points where a substantial amount of information begins. I don't because I prefer to maintain the longest tonal scale possible, maintaining all the information I possibly can in the highlights and shadows and so, as a rule, I generally consider all information significant. Once you set the dynamic range, slide the midpoint slider to a point that achieves an overall desired tone: dark, medium, light. The histogram graph is a great way to

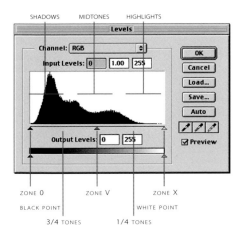

7. The Levels window with histogram
for the preceding image.

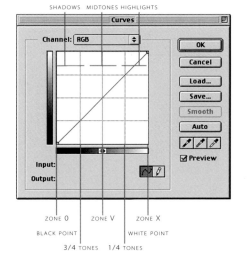

8. The Curves window. The straight curve equals no
change where values for input (the horizontal axis) and
output (the vertical axis) are equal.

evaluate the quality of an image's information. If it weren't for the histogram in Levels, I'd recommend you only use Curves, but the histogram is such a useful reference for evaluating an image and making corrections based on those evaluations that I can't recommend that.

Levels and Curves have several things in common. Both have an auto button and black point, white point, and gray balance eyedroppers. The Auto button will tell Photoshop to search all the values of an image and make the darkest value black and the lightest value white. You can use the eyedropper tools to do this by hand and be more selective. Click on the black point eyedropper; now go into the image and click on the area you would like to specify as black. Use the white point eyedropper the same way. You can get Photoshop to indicate where the lightest and darkest values in the image are before deciding where to specify white points and black points. With the Levels dialog box activated, uncheck the preview box and hold down the Option key. Slide the white point slider. The first areas of the image to

appear out of blackness will be the lightest values. Do the same with the black point slider to find the darkest values that will appear out of white. (This is called video LUT animation.) You would think the gray balance eyedropper would specify a midpoint value, but it does not. It is actually a color correction tool. Whatever you click the gray balance eyedropper on will become a neutral gray, without a color cast of any kind, and all other colors will be shifted accordingly.

You can change the values that the black point and white point eyedroppers specify. With the Levels or Curves dialog box activated, double-click on the white point eyedropper. Default values are 0/0/100 in HSB (hue, saturation, brightness). Values of 0/0/96 are recommended. Do the same for the black point eyedropper. Default values are 0/0/0 in HSB; values of 0/0/4 are recommended. The default values are a little extreme. Generally you will want to hold a hint more detail in those areas.

Be careful of rules and default settings. They're great for a majority of circumstances, but every one of them will have its

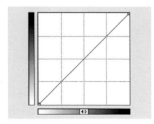

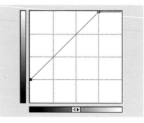

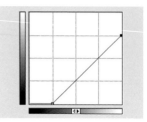

9. Click the arrows to reverse the placement of shadows and highlights.

10. Option click on the grid to change the curves grid of four to ten.

11. The curve for increased lightness with Brightness/Contrast.

12. The curve for decreased lightness with Brightness/Contrast.

exceptions. You need to know when to make those exceptions and override the defaults. A case in point is that some images will not have a black point (white stallion in a snowstorm), and some will not have a white point (black stallion at midnight). If you specify one, your image will become too dark or too light and in the process you will lose a great deal of useful, even necessary, information.

More often than not, I determine the dynamic range of the image by first looking at the histogram. Then I move to Curves. Curves offers the greatest number of points of control — 16. You can do everything with Curves that you can do with Brightness/Contrast and Levels. You can't do everything with Brightness/Contrast and Levels that you can do with Curves. I highly recommend you learn to use the power of Curves.

If I were forced to throw away everything in Photoshop but one tool, I'd keep Curves. The curve is the heart of tonal and color correction. Of all the digital tools at your disposal it is the most useful. With Curves you can do in the "digital darkroom" most of what is done in the traditional darkroom.

Like the histogram, the curve is a graphical representation of the tones that exist within an image. Unlike the histogram, which is unique for every image, the curve looks the same for every image before correction. The curve is a grid and a line. It

represents the black point (lower left corner), quartertones (move up and over one grid), midtones (dead center), three-quartertones (three grids up, three grids over), and highlights (top right corner). (This order is reversed and reversible in Grayscale mode. Click the arrows at the bottom of the curve.) The bottom line or x-axis represents input level; the y-axis represents the output level. The line that connects the black point and white point represents the change from input to output.

A straight diagonal line represents no change. (This is what you see every time before you make a correction.) By placing a point along the line and raising or lowering it, you raise (brighten) or lower (darken) the values in the picture represented along the line. A curve that bulges up in the middle represents a lightening of values. A curve that bulges down in the middle represents a darkening of values. Moving the white point to the left sets the white point to a lower value clipping off information at the very top of the scale, and then gray becomes white (the same as moving the white point slider with Levels). Moving the black point to the right sets the black point at a higher value clipping off information at the very bottom of the scale, and gray becomes black (the same as moving the black point slider with Levels). If you increase the angle of ascent (from left to right), you increase contrast. If you

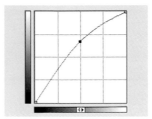 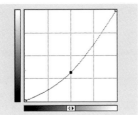 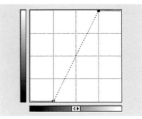 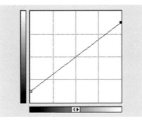

13. The curve for increased lightness with levels. White point and black point remain fixed, maintaining dynamic range and minimizing loss of detail.

14. The curve for decreased lightness with Levels.

15. The curve for increased contrast with Brightness/Contrast. White point and black point can only be changed equally

16. The curve for decreased contrast with Brightness/Contrast. White point is lowered (gray whites) and black point is raised (gray blacks) reducing dynamic range. The same can be done with the Levels output sliders.

move the black point to the right, you increase contrast; if you move the white point to the left, you increase contrast. If you move both the black point to the right and the white point to the left, you increase contrast even more.

All of these moves increase contrast while changing the ends of the dynamic range. You can increase contrast without changing the ends of your dynamic range. An "S curve" increases contrast without changing the white and black points — something you can only do with Curves. This kind of curve is achieved by placing a point for highlights (typically at the three quarter tones) and raising it and then placing a point for the shadows (typically at the quarter tones) and lowering it. A "reverse S curve" reduces contrast without changing the white and black points. Lowering contrast with Brightness or using the Output controls in Levels will both affect your white and black points. You can do the same thing with Curves by raising the black point and lowering the white point. This is a move that is not frequently made as it reduces an image's dynamic range, resulting in an image where there is no true white or black.

You may notice that while it is relatively easy to increase an image's dynamic range, it is more difficult to reduce it effectively. If a light gray value with information is to become a pure white with no information, that is a choice you make intentionally. If, on the other hand, a white point with no information is to become a lower tone with information, you have a conundrum. The information it is to represent must be created out of nothing. Out of pure white, Curves will only create a flat gray area for those lower tones, without photorealistic texture. It is better to capture a maximum amount of information initially. If in doubt when making exposures or scans, err towards lower contrast. It is much easier to add contrast than to remove it. (Don't overdo this; just favor it.) Similarly, it is easier to fine-tune a superior exposure than it is to resurrect an inferior exposure. Past a certain point, no amount of digital wizardry will make a bad exposure look good. Digital technology is clearly no substitute for traditional skills; it is rather a marvelous extension of them.

There are even more sophisticated curves that are impossible to build with any other tool. A "lock down" curve places either one or two points on either side of the range of tones to be affected, so that change will not occur above or below them, and then raises or lowers the middle, so that only those tones are affected. A curve that raises the black point to the top (the white point) and lowers the white point to the bottom (the black point) inverts the tones creating a negative image. Invert (Image: Adjust: Invert) does just this, and you can do it manually if you prefer.

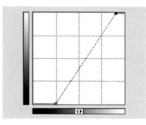

17. The curve for increased contrast with Levels. White point and black point can be changed equally or unequally.

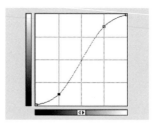

18. An "S" curve increases contrast, lightening highlights and darkening shadows.

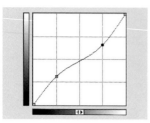

19. A reverse "S" curve decreases contrast darkening highlights and lightening shadows.

Unlike Levels, Curves does not tell you how much of a given tone exists in an image or where along the dynamic range image information begins and ends. Like Levels, Curves provides a method for analyzing an image not found in other tools. With the Curves dialog active, position your cursor on the image (the arrow will change to an eyedropper) and click and hold on an area of an image. A circle will appear on the curve, marking the point at which that tone occurs. You can use this to pinpoint corrections to a specific range of tones very precisely. Ask first what areas of an image seem most important to the image. Locate the top and bottom of the range of tones for those areas on the curve with the eyedropper and place a point at each end. Then steepen the curve between those two points. The added contrast to these areas will direct the eye's attention to them. You'll notice that increasing the slope in one part of the curve will decrease it in another. Essentially, you make sacrifices in less important areas of an image to highlight more important areas; you prioritize the information.

When building custom curves for naturalistic effects, create smooth curves and always maintain an angle of ascent. Failure to do this creates unnatural transitions. Flattening a part of a curve will eliminate contrast in that area of the curve, making it look gray. For a dramatic example of what happens when you flatten a part of the curve, flatten the entire curve by lowering the white point and raising the blackpoint to the midpoint. The entire image will become a flat even gray. That will happen within a smaller range of tones if you flatten only a portion of a curve. Raising a point to the left above another to its right will create solarization: tones will reverse and colors will change. If you want to solarize an image, you'll have more control doing it this way than using the filter Solarize.

A few tips in navigating will help you more easily master Curves. When the Curves dialog box is active, clicking in the image will produce a circle identifying where that tone is along the curve. Clicking anywhere on the curve will insert a point. Clicking, holding, and dragging a point will change its position. If you drag it outside the Curves grid, it will disappear. When a point is selected it will be dark, and unselected points will be light. To skip to the point above a selected point, you can click on another point to activate it. If you're not careful, you may move it slightly. For delicate work, you can skip to another point with key controls and not run that risk: press Command: Control+Tab to skip to the point above the active point. To skip to the point below, press Command: Control+Tab+Shift. You can change the standard grid from four divisions to ten by holding the Option key and clicking on the grid. You can make the

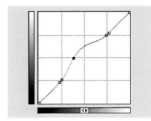

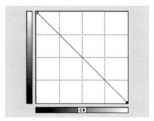

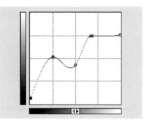

20. A lockdown curve where only a select portion of the curve is modified. Here the ends are locked down.

21. An inverted curve. Black becomes white and vice versa, producing a negative.

22. A very bad curve. Lowering a point to the right of another to the left causes solarization while flattening a portion of a curve so that there is no angle of ascent reduces all the tones in that range to a single flat gray tone.

Curves window bigger or smaller by clicking on the box at the top right. You can also change the grid of the curve from four to ten by holding the Option key and clicking on it.

Just as with making adjustments to an image with Levels, applying successive Curves corrections one after another will successively degrade your file and distort the image's histogram. Favor efficiency; try to achieve your desired result in the fewest steps possible. Favor flexibility; use adjustment layers.

Curves does everything the other tools do and more. Learn to build beautiful curves. Few areas of Photoshop will offer such rewards.

Remember, curves are not new to digital imaging. The terminology is repurposed from traditional photography and prepress techniques. Many aspects of this program have their origins here. To a large degree Photoshop represents the marriage of the two disciplines. If you have a background in one or both of these traditions you will find it much easier to make the transition to working digitally if you simply look for the ways in which you can repurpose your previous experience. Those of you who don't have this experience would do well to learn about the history and methods of these disciplines as they will

prove to be an invaluable foundation to build upon.

While it might be possible to achieve many of the results of tonal manipulation achieved with Curves by employing traditional methods, it would not be half so easy, flexible, or fast. Using digital tools, you can make test strips in seconds. You can try many variations of an image in minutes and see them all side by side for comparison. An enormous advantage of working digitally is the ability to work in the light and to see the changes you are making as they are being made. As you can see the changes you are making instantly, you will be encouraged to try more variations and work an image to a fuller completion. With Curves you can simply and effectively achieve tonal control that traditionally in a darkroom would require much greater effort, for example using contrast filters, polycontrast papers, differing paper chemical combinations, developing agent additives, or complex masking (many of which are not available for color images). Some of these effects may be so difficult to achieve in the traditional darkroom that they will not be attempted there. Digital technology removes these impediments. That leads to greater freedom and ultimately greater control.

Photoshop provides a variety of tools for working with color. Each has strengths and weaknesses.

Variations (Image: Adjust: Variations) is marvelous for this kind of visual evaluation. It's quick and extremely intuitive. It's great for figuring out how to get started. There are, however, more powerful and sophisticated ways to make color corrections, including Color Balance. (See Comparison for more on Variations.)

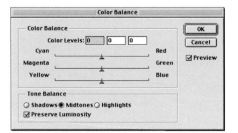

1. The Color Balance window is clear and intuitive.

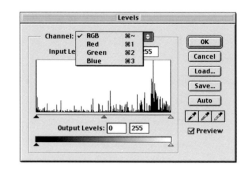

2. Levels offers greater sophistication.

Perhaps the most intuitive of all color correction tools found in Photoshop is Color Balance. It's powerful, simple, and graphic. For anyone who is shy on color theory, Color Balance graphically demonstrates the interelatedness of colors. Three color sliders present themselves: you'll see cyan, magenta, and yellow (CMY) on the left and red, green, and blue (RGB) on the right. Notice the two most used color spaces are represented and each slider affects a single channel. You can visibly see the relatedness between the opposing colors: cyan and red, magenta and green, yellow and blue. Add more of one of these pairs to an image and you take its opposing color out. Add cyan and you remove red. Add magenta and you remove green. Add yellow and you remove blue. You can't add one without removing the other; they're forever linked. The Color Balance tool graphically shows you this. Move the sliders left and right and you will see this visibly demonstrated in any color image. When you are first introduced to this it is harder to

make the distinction between cyan and blue or magenta and red; green and yellow tend to be easier. Think of cyan as a cool blue (more green/ice blue) and blue as a warm blue (more red/blueberry blue). Think of magenta as a cool red (more purple/fuschia) and red as a warm red (more yellow/cherry red). Think of green as a cool yellow (bluer) and yellow as a warm yellow (redder). Harder still is the process of developing an eye for making such distinctions when approaching color correcting an image. Sliding the Color Balance sliders back and forth will help you quickly evaluate an image's color bias and train your eye in the process. With time and experience you will develop a critical eye for color.

Color Balance also offers you the ability to correct shadows, midtones, and highlights separately. Think of these three ranges of tones as portions of a spectrum and you will realize that it's difficult to affect one without affecting the others. In affecting the shadows you will affect the midtones to a degree and the highlights very slightly. The majority of the correction will fall into the range you select. If you use this option you may find that you will need to make a slightly stronger correction in one end of the scale (shadows or highlights) and make another correction in the midtones to compensate for the first correction creeping into those areas. You can flick back and forth between all three zones to find the proper balance in each separate slider (cyan/red, magenta/green, yellow/blue). However, before you start making elaborate changes, ask yourself if you need to. An overly complex solution to a simple problem often produces further problems. Savor efficiency.

When you move the color sliders, these affect the separate channels of the file, making them darker or lighter. The position of the slider arrows is relative. The same correction can be produced with many different settings. The values 10/0/0, 20/10/10, 30/20/20, 40/30/30, and 50/40/40 all produce the same color correction, a 10 point increase in red (otherwise known as a 10 point decrease in cyan). You might as well keep it simple by shifting only one slider. (Stay with 10/0/0.) What matters is the relative relationships of the sliders.

One notable feature of the Color Balance dialog is the Preserve Luminosity option. The default setting has it activated. This feature attempts to keep the tonal values of the file constant while altering the color. When one channel is lightened the other two are darkened. It does well for mild color corrections but the tone still shifts for very large color corrections, yet less than would occur if this feature were deactivated. Compare a correction with and without Preserve Luminosity by checking it on and off before applying a very strong color correction.

With all this talk about channels, you might guess you could produce a color correction with Levels or Curves. And you would be right. With Color Balance you have three points of control (shadows, midtones, highlights). With Levels you have three points of control (black point, midtones, white point). To make a color correction with Levels go to the pull-down menu and choose the appropriate channel (R,G,B or C,M,Y,K); this allows you to affect onè channel only. Brightening or darkening a single channel with Levels does the same thing that Color Balance does, with one exception: Levels does not offer a Preserve Luminosity option. To alter the color and keep the tonal relationships the same with Levels, you must first correct the color on a single channel and then go back to the composite channel (RGB or CMYK) to correct for the resulting shift in tone.

Just as it does with tone, for color, Curves offers the ultimate in sophistication. Curves also produces changes in the channels, i.e. it lightens or darkens them. It also does not offer a Preserve Luminosity option. What it does offer, that no other tool offers, is a nearly unlimited number of points of control. You can make certain kinds of subtle and sophisticated corrections with it that you cannot make with any other tool. Master Curves and it is highly likely that you won't need the other tools.

The standard procedure for image correction in Curves is to set the highlights (white point), set the shadows (black point), set the midtones to produce a desired tone (midpoint slider or midpoint on the curve), then find a neutral area in your image on which to base corrections. Neutral colors (whites, blacks, but more particularly grays) display shifts in color more readily than other colors. Because of the absence of competing color, any introduction of unwanted color in neutral areas becomes that much more apparent.

In the RGB color space neutral colors are represented by equal values in all three channels: 10/10/10 or 128/128/128; both represent pure neutral colors without a bias of any kind, albeit a lighter and a darker one. (The numbers are different in CMYK. They are not equal. Generally cyan has higher values. The Info palette will display both RGB and CMYK values simultaneously.) Now look to the gray balance eyedropper since it drives the values of the area you click on to equal values in all three

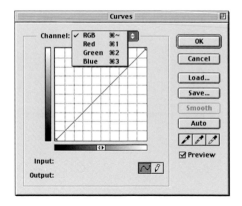

3. Curves offers the ultimate in sophistication.

channels. It does not drive them to a middle gray (128R, 128G, 128B or 44C, 33M, 33Y, 11K), but simply goes to the average of the three values found at any given point. Similarly, you can manually drive the values of any area to known values, in this case equal, with Levels or Curves. First, use the eyedropper and place a point in the image, hold the shift key while clicking. Next, make a Levels or Curves correction and alter the individual channels so that the numerical readouts of all three channels are equal in the Info palette (Window: Show Info). To do this you will probably need to make varying corrections in the separate channels. Don't make this complicated unless you absolutely need to. Start by raising or lowering the midtones in Levels or the area of the curve where you placed the point. Make the minimum correction necessary to neutralize the area (equal values). If the area you specify is truly a neutral gray (a gray card or pavement) and you do this properly, it is likely that all the other colors will fall into place along with the neutral color. Most images tend to have a consistent overall color cast, crosses are the exception.

If you don't have a neutral tone to guide you, you can find the numerical representation for another known color within the image and drive that area to the appropriate set of num-

bers. We are particularly sensitive to flesh tones. This is natural. Subtle shifts in a person's complexion often indicate emotion or a state of health. Consequently, flesh tones are the colors looked to most often after neutral colors. Often in an image they are even more important, for when people are in an image, they often become the focus of attention. It may be more desirable to have pleasing fleshtones and a slight cast in neutral tones than pure neutral tones and the wrong cast in flesh tones. Some recommend values for Caucasian flesh tones (186–278R, 133–173G, 108–136B or 0–20C, 35–45M, 35–45Y, 0=2K). These are fine baselines, but the bottom line is that there is enormous variety in flesh tones and every printer will likely need a slightly different set of numbers to produce the same color. If you haven't had previous experience with an individual's skin color, it is very difficult to make accurate assessments of any color bias there. You can only make generalizations. Nevertheless, many do, and this is not all bad. Critical accuracy is not generally the point; a pleasing effect is. Quite often if you simply make the flesh tones look pleasing, rather than merely accurate, you create a more pleasing image.

Lacking both, or wanting another point of reference, it is possible to test your printer by printing a set of colors and

4. Selective Color is highly sophisticated. Its control of the black plate, even in RGB, is exceptional.

noting the numerical values that produced them. Then you will have generated a useful set of reference numbers for comparison. Some say this is the ultimate calibration scheme, provided you train your eyes to make very precise distinctions in color and are able to translate that sensitivity into numerical values. Prepress professionals have been correcting color by the numbers for years. Many still distrust the monitor, sometimes for good reason, and prefer to rely on their years of experience to guide them. You may not have years of experience with a single printer and may not want to wait years to produce pleasing results. A well-calibrated monitor should give you enough confidence to approach any color problem. Make cultivating an understanding of the numbers your continuing education. It will come in handy, especially when setting highlight, shadow, and neutral values.

For more delicate color correction work, Selective Color (Image:Adjust: Selective Color) offers the ability to adjust single ranges of color without affecting others: cyans, blues, magentas, reds, yellows, greens, whites, neutrals, and blacks. You can select each range of colors in the dialog box's pull-down menu. The interface gives color readouts in CMYK, but the tool will also work well in RGB. You use percentages to increase or decrease each component in the range of colors specified. At the bot-

tom of the dialog box you can specify one of two methods for adding or subtracting that percentage: relative or absolute. Absolute adds the percentage you specify to those areas. With relative you use the percentage of color that exists in the selected area and increase it proportionally. Make a correction of +10% cyan to an area containing 50% cyan. If you use absolute, then 50% becomes 60% (50% + 10%=60%). If you use relative, then 50% becomes 55% (10% of 50%=5% so 5%+50%=55%). Selective Color does just what it promises, namely, it corrects color selectively. You don't need to make a selection by color range to make a Selective Color correction, since Selective Color will constrain a correction for you. Perhaps the most often used color ranges are whites and neutrals. Before correcting neutrals with Selective Color, or any color for that matter, make sure the color cast you see doesn't also exist in other areas of the picture. Work globally before working locally. While neutral colors display artificially introduced color casts most readily, neutral colors also display naturally reflected color more readily than other colors. Sometimes there's an enormous amount of unexpected but nonetheless real color in neutrals. These colors are not the artifacts of a film type's bias, imprecise processing, or a scanner's lack of precision; they exist in the original scene.

5. Hue/Saturation makes very strong color corrections. It is the only color correction tool that allows independent control of color's saturation component.

Whether you decide to correct an artificial cast or change a natural reflection depends on both the situation and your intention.

Hue/Saturation is a very powerful color correction tool, often too powerful. It's an essential tool, but one that should be used with some caution. It's the only tool that allows control of saturation independent of lightness or hue. Beware of the lightness control in Hue/Saturation. Like the brightness control in Brightness/Contrast, it will play havoc with your dynamic range, quickly diminishing whites and blacks. Use caution with the Hue slider, since it produces dramatic shifts in color very quickly. In a heartbeat, you may find you've changed one color into another. Hue is not so much for color correction as it is color transformation. Its values from -180 to +180 clearly refer to a color wheel, the Apple Color Picker, so hues that are 180 degrees apart are opposites or complements. The rainbow at the bottom of the dialog presents the color wheel as a straight line where the beginning and end points of the line represent the same color. Slide the Hue slider, for example, and you'll notice that the top color bar becomes offset from the bottom one. This is a visual demonstration of the transformation you are making, before (bottom) and after (top). Enter a positive or negative number and the hue of the color is shifted around the color wheel accordingly. Slide Hue to +/-180 and cyan becomes red, magenta becomes green, and yellow becomes blue; the colors are inverted.

In addition to Master, which affects all the colors, the pulldown menu offers a choice of reds, yellow, green, cyan, blue, and magenta. You can use each of the controls — Hue, Saturation, and Lightness — to affect specific ranges of colors singly or to different degrees. You can control the breadth of this range as well. Slip into a single range and you'll notice a set of sliders appear between the two color bars lines that allows you to define a very narrow range of related colors or a very broad one. Degrees define the range. Hue/Saturation uses the Apple Color Picker to define values for the ranges of color. Colors are specified by degrees in a circle — red 0, yellow 60, green 120, cyan 180, blue 240, magenta 300; each is 60 degrees apart. The areas in between represent the transition in spectrum from one to the other. You can see this graphically demonstrated in Hue/Saturation along the rainbow of color found there. Two straight bars define the range of the color selected, while two triangles defined the degree of fall-off into other colors. You can widen or narrow a range of colors or the degree to which they fall-off by shifting the sliders. You can even define a new

6. The Channel Mixer is used for the extremely sophisticated
color correction technique of channel blending.

range of colors to affect by using the eyedropper in the dialog box to sample a new range of colors within an image.

As a rule I don't use Lightness (only on flat colors as it reduces dynamic range), I occasionally use Hue (particularly for color transformations rather than corrections), and I frequently use Saturation. Saturation is the key component with this tool doing what no other tool does. It is essential. Nonetheless, along with Filters, there is perhaps no other feature of Photoshop that is more misused than Saturation. With Saturation you can turn the intensity of color up. But intensity for intensity's sake can become visual noise. I do not mean to suggest that the world of saturated color is not magnificent; it is. Let me simply remark that the more intense the colors you use, the more carefully you must orchestrate them to use them effectively. As you raise the saturation of colors, you raise the stakes and the challenge of using color in a meaningful way increases. Certainly it can be done. Think Pierre Bonnard. Think Willem DeKooning. Think Mark Rothko.

There's another reason for being cautious with shifting Hue and increasing Saturation. Both produce such radical transformations of color that the subtle underpinnings of color, the overtones and undertones if you will, tend to get lost. They yield simple solutions. Complex harmonies existing within a subject often tend to be distilled; their uniqueness is wiped out in the process. The Renaissance painters often used a green undercoloring for flesh tones to make the pinks more vibrant in contrast. The Expressionist painter Edvard Munch used an intense red, introducing a violent psychological undercurrent to his work. Accompanying colors have a profound effect on the final result. Accept simple solutions and you may sacrifice the potential contribution of these colors to an image.

Far too often, the realm of less saturated colors is overlooked. Turn Saturation all the way down and you end up with a black-and-white image. Don't go quite so far and you've got a very interesting hybrid, neither full-color nor black-and-white. These resulting hybrid images have qualities similar to hand-colored photographs or tinted drawings, but they also an even greater complexity of color. Sometimes a whisper's more effective than a scream. The subdued color palette can be exquisite.

Compare the color sensibilities prevalent in the 1950's (Cadillac yellow, avocado, Mary Kay pink) with those prevalent in the 1980's (neon yellow, neon green, neon pink, electric blue). There's nothing wrong with any of these colors in and of themselves, but which complement each other better? One's a chorus

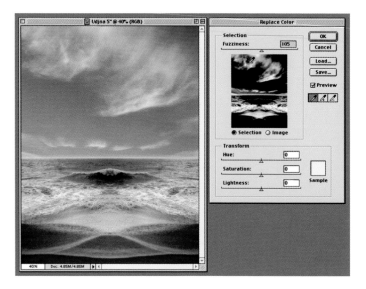

7. *Replace color functions as the Hue/Saturation with the selectivity of Select by Color Range.*

subtly interacting while the other is the equivalent of a color shouting match. Choose your color carefully and you are likely to move, rather than overwhelm, your viewers by your color choices.

We are still trying to get photographic capture as rich as the images we see with the naked eye. We lose a lot of information along the way. Sometimes we need increased saturation to overcome the limits of our capture devices. On the other hand, today's films like Ektachrome VS (very saturated) and Velvia favor high saturation, delivering images that you may want to calm down rather than perk up. (Adding saturation is easier than removing it, so for this reason I favor shooting a fairly neutral film, Ektachrome.) Accuracy aside, to serve an expressive end you might intensify or subdue color. Whatever your destination, you can get there from here.

If I were forced to keep only two controls in Photoshop and throw the rest away, I'd pick Saturation after Curves. The two are producing a quiet revolution in color photography. Digital control of color is simply astonishing. It offers the possibilities of bringing a painter's control of color to photographic

information. At the heart of this miracle is the ability to independently control color's three critical components — hue (color), saturation (intensity), and brightness (value).

Last and least, the Replace Color feature marries the Select by Color Range and Hue/Saturation tools. In actuality, it does not offer the full functionality of the Hue/Saturation tool as it lacks the ability to customize specific ranges of colors. Unlike all the other color correction tools, it cannot be used as an adjustment layer. Consequently it's more difficult to modify once changes have been applied to the image. For this reason I don't use it. You can do the same thing another way and retain flexibility. First create a selection using Select by Color Range and then create a Hue/Saturation adjustment layer. The active selection that was created by Select by Color Range will automatically be turned into an adjustment layer layer mask. With this arrangement, the values you set with Hue/Saturation and the mask itself (its contrast and density among other characteristics), you can make changes at any time, now or in the future. While I prize efficiency, I will go out of my way to retain flexibility.

7. COMPARISON SEEING THINGS SIDE BY SIDE

Whether you work in black and white or color, when correcting your images it is helpful to compare multiple versions side by side. Photoshop provides sophisticated tools to aid this process.

One Photoshop tool, Variations, offers a wonderful visual reference for color correction. Its interface simultaneously provides views of seven variations in color: the current pick surrounded by images that contain more cyan, red, magenta, green, yellow, and blue. The corrections of-

fered are the kind that can be found in Color Balance, including the ability to correct midtones, highlights, and shadows separately. The strength of the corrections can be increased and decreased. Click on any variation and that variation becomes the center image, or Current Pick. You can then make further corrections based on it. You can also switch the type of correction to saturation; you view a less saturated version and a more saturated version which straddle your Current Pick. On the right, you make the image lighter or darker with a brightness option. In the top left-hand corner, you view before and after images that show the original image before corrections and the Current Pick after corrections.

Variations has its limitations. The increments between corrections are not as fine as those found in Color Balance. You cannot make as complex a correction as you can with Curves. You cannot modify only one range of colors as you can in Selective Color (unless of course you make a selection first). Nor can you affect the saturation of only one range of colors as you can with Hue/Saturation. And while Variations offers the possibility of tonal correction, it offers the most limited kind, the kind found with Brightness/Contrast. Variations is great for getting started if you're not sure which way to go, but you're better off actually making specific corrections separately with other tools.

Unfortunately, the other tools don't offer the marvelous visual reference available in Variations. The ability to see multiple versions of an image side by side is of paramount importance to me. There is not a single image I work on that I don't com-

pare multiple variations of the image side by side. Why? Our eyes adapt. They adapt, for example, to a lighting situation which might include neutralizing its predominant color temperature. In short, as our eyes get used to a lighting situation they lose the ability to recognize its biases. A side-by-side comparison will shock the eyes into objectivity. When you look at a single image, it is far more difficult to recognize a color bias than it is to recognize it when comparing multiple versions.

So how do I compare variations of an image without using Variations? I create my own. You can too. I create at least four duplicates of an image and open them simultaneously so that I can compare them side by side. You may be working on a large file and be concerned that your system will not be able to handle four very large files simultaneously. I routinely work on very large files, so at this stage I create low-resolution versions for comparison. I simply size my main document down to a relatively small file size, save the smaller version as a separate document, and create multiples of it for comparison. Here's a quick way to get started. Open a file. Go to Image: Image Size and check the Resample box, as you will be removing pixels to reduce your file size. Specify a lower resolution or a smaller size since both are equally good paths towards reduction. Either way, it's the total number of pixels which are left that's important. I generally favor a 5" file simply because I regularly have a use for images that size for my promotional materials. You may have a different need. The final size is unimportant, but what is important is that you can work on four to six identical files

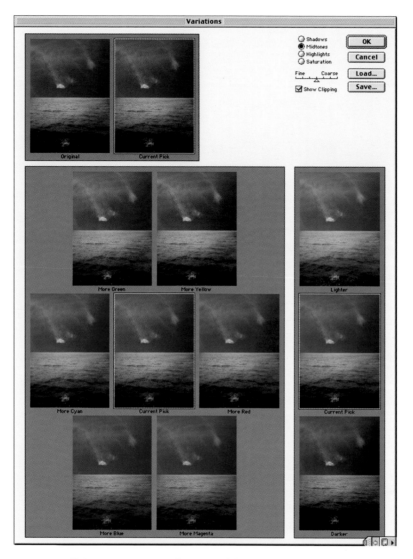

1. The Variations preview is visually intuitive and allows simultaneous comparison.

2. In variation 1, no color
correction is made.

3. In variation 2, the sky is
more green.

4. In variation 5, the sky is
more magenta.

quickly and easily. Determine your file size accordingly. Then save the picture as a new document (File: Save As: new name). I often include the letters "lr" in the title to signify that the file is a low-resolution copy. Then you duplicate the file at least three times. Save a copy (File: Save a Copy) with a new title (I usually just number copies 1, 2, 3 etc. to distinguish each individual version). Now open all the files simultaneously. Leave the first version alone since that's your original. In your second version, create an adjustment layer to make a variation in color (pick an appropriate color correction method). In your third version, repeat this sequence but make a different correction. Do the same again in the fourth. You can create any kind or number of adjustment layers. Now you have many sophisticated variations and you can make side-by-side comparisons. Modify the corrections as you see fit at any time simply by double-clicking on the adjustment layers and changing the corrections.

When you decide which variation is the best, the set of adjustment layers you created for the low-resolution version can be imported into the high-resolution version. It's a simple matter of opening the high-resolution version with the best low-resolution version and dragging the adjustment layers from one to the other. Click on, hold, and drag the first adjustment layer in the low-resolution version into the high-resolution version. Repeat for all subsequent adjustment layers created for the low-resolution version. Make sure you maintain the same order in the layer stack or you will find the final version may differ. To ensure you do this, you may want to number the adjustment layers to indicate their order before dragging them into the high-resolution version. Numbering the order of your adjustment layers is a good general practice.

Several software packages work with Photoshop to create test strips that show multiple variations of a single image. They can be useful for making visual determinations just as Variations is, but I rarely find that the kinds of corrections offered are as powerful as a set of adjustment layers. You can build your own test strips by creating adjustment layers with adjustment layer layer masks. Create an adjustment layer with the strongest correction you might want to make; in fact, overcorrect a little. Show your ruler and use the Rectangular Marquee tool to select a portion of a picture (the first inch perhaps). Fill your selection with 100% black. Select the next portion of your image (the second inch) and fill it with a lower percentage of black. Repeat this

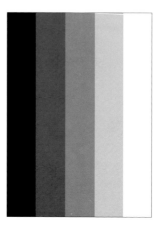

5. In variation 4, the sky is more saturated.

6. Tests strips are easily made with adjustment layers with layer masks.

7. The adjustment layer layer mask used for the test strip.

process across the entire image until you have created a series of step wedges with lowering opacities. The first should be 100% black (unaffected), and the last should be 0% black (totally affected). You can then see what lesser corrections will look like across an image and use the variations to determine a final correction. To choose a final correction intensity, fill the adjustment layer with the percentage of black found in the strip with the best result. Or fill the adjustment layer with white, eliminating the mask, and turn down the opacity of the layer to the same percentage yielded by that portion of the mask (if 50% black then 50% opacity, if 75% black then 25% opacity, if 30% black then 70% opacity). This can be done for any kind of adjustment layer. You can import the adjustment layer with its mask into any other image and change the settings, eliminating the need to remake the layer mask. Even if the resolution of the files differs, you can repurpose the layer mask since resizing the layer mask will not degrade quality. You can enlarge some

masks (Image: Adjust: Scale), those that are soft, without hard transitions, gradient masks for instance. Some masks you cannot enlarge, those with hard edges (though filtering the mask, specifically Unsharp Mask, Maximize, and Minimize, can go a long way towards fixing softening created by upsampling), luminance masks for instance, so you must recreate them. If you need to make a complicated hard-edged mask for a correction, do it roughly in the low-resolution variation and spend time finessing it in the high-resolution file.

Generally, comparing variations is one of the last things I do to an image. It's a final critical review that I find absolutely necessary. No matter how well I think a session has gone, I make these comparisons. It's a discipline I find extremely rewarding. Occasionally, I'm surprised by what I see and find I need to make further refinements. Often these are refinements that I would not have seen without making the comparison.

Think globally, then act locally. It's a very sound practice to attempt correcting the entire image before moving on to the details. In a majority of cases, you will find the same deficiencies in a single area of an image throughout the entire image. The trouble is, these flaws may not seem as apparent in other areas at first glance. The odds indicate it's likely they are there too. If you start correcting the deficiencies in one area only to find out they occur throughout the entire image, you then have to make corrections to all the other areas. What's

1. The image.

more, you may be tempted to make corrections of varying intensity or even to make different corrections throughout the image and end up producing an unsettling imbalance. This is equivalent to removing a loop in fishing line; small problems can quickly become big ones, resulting in a hopeless tangle. The chances of your success increase dramatically if you take a consistent and well-planned approach to correcting your images. Efficiency favors looking at the big picture before moving on to the details. The time and energy you save in doing so can be better spent on further refinements to an image or even to another image.

That said, local or selective correction is part of the art of image making. Its judicious application can make or break an image. Not every image will need it, but many do. The principle is simple: you apply a correction to a specific area but not to

2. A rough selection made with the Magic Wand of a simple area.

3. The selection refined with multiple clicks at varying points with varying tolerances.

4. The selection saved as an alpha channel.

the other surrounding areas of an image. To do this you make a selection to constrain the correction. With a selection active, any action you perform to the image takes place inside the outline. A correction in this case could be any action from changing hue, value, or saturation to retouching, replacing, or painting on the image; to sharpening and blurring — almost anything can be done to an image selectively.

The Lasso, the Marquee tool, and the Magic Wand are the standard tools for making a selection. Each can be used to create a selection outline delineated by a moving dashed line. Click on the desired tool, click inside the image, and hold and drag to create a selection. Let go and the selection will be complete. Think of drawing selections with the Lasso in closed outlines or complete loops. If you do not, a straight line between your starting point and finishing point will be made to complete the loop. Every selection is a closed loop or a set of closed loops. In the Tool Options bar, click on the Add icon (or hold the Shift key) to add to a selection, click on the Subtract icon (or hold the Option key) to subtract from it, or click on the Restrict

icon (or hold the Option and Shift keys) to create a selection from the intersection of two selections. You can use all of the selection tools in combination with each other to refine a single selection. Once created, the selection outline itself can be distracting. Luckily, you can hide it or reveal it by pressing command H (H for hide). If you hide a selection outline you will have to remember it is "active" as it will be invisible.

There's only one Magic Wand. It defines a selection outline for you. It has a variable sensitivity that detects differences in tone and color. Click on an area and all adjacent areas with values/hues similar to it will be encompassed. The degree of similarity sensed is determined by the tolerance of the tool, which you can change. (All tools have a corresponding options palette to control their functions; simply double-click on the appropriate tool to make it appear.) A high tolerance will be less discriminating and select more information, and a low tolerance will be more discriminating and select less information. Areas that are not contiguous or do not touch each other but have the same values/hues will not be selected, unless you

5. There is no need to save this channel and the previous channel. It can be achieved by inverting the previous channel before loading or by checking inverse upon loading or by inversing the selection after it is loaded.

6. The previous alphachannel refined by filling the area of the floating figure with black paint. This alpha channel selects everything but the sky, while its inverse selects the sky and the floating figure.

7. A rough selection made with the Lasso tool.

uncheck the contiguous box in the options palette. (You can also choose between using all layers or single layers.) You must select them additionally. There is a way to get Photoshop to do this for you; find Similar under the Selection menu. This allows you to select all similar values/hues throughout an entire image. When making selections always try to get the image to do the work for you. The Magic Wand is one tool that will do this. When it fails, consider making a luminance mask to create the selection. Getting the image to do the lion's share of the work is a great strategy; however, it won't work for all situations. You have to make some selections by hand.

Not in the tool bar, but under the Select menu, and related to the Magic Wand, is Color Range. This feature allows you to quickly select all the values/hues of a single color or set of colors throughout an image in one move. The related values or colors do not have to be adjacent to each other as they will all be selected. The accompanying dialog allows you to select a color by pull-down menu or by using the eyedropper tool. You may add or subtract additional colors by using the + and - eye-

droppers. The tolerance of the tool's selectivity is controlled by a "fuzziness" factor, which expands or contracts the selection. It's very fluid and powerful. And remember, what you create with it can be continually modified with any or all other selection techniques, including using it within an existing selection.

Most tools in the tool bar have their variants, which can you reveal by clicking and holding the submenu arrow below each one. The Lasso offers three options. The standard Lasso allows you to draw freeform outlines. When using the Lasso tool, think of drawing closed shapes: circles, triangles, squares, polygons, etc. The Polygonal Lasso tool allows you to draw selections with straight lines. Click to define the beginning of a line, let go and move the cursor to the end of the line, and click again; continue until a complete outline has been defined. You can do this with the standard Lasso tool by holding the Option key after the first click, let go to return to freeform, and hold it down to get back to straight lines; the Straight Line Lasso works in reverse. The Magnetic Lasso tool is sensitive to areas of contrast, making it easier to draw around areas, particularly complex

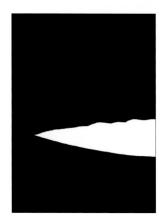

8. The rough selection moved into Quick Mask mode and refined by painting with a black brush on the resulting temporary alpha channel while simultaneously viewing the RGB channels as a guide.

9. The selection saved as a permanent alpha channel. Moving out of Quick Mask mode, the mask becomes a selection which can then be saved.

10. Alpha channels 6 and 9 may be combined to create a selection of the middle ground only. First load one. Second load the other one, while the first is active, and check the Add to Selection button. Combining alpha channels avoids unnecessary work. You rarely have to create the same outline twice.

areas, because you can draw more generally. It will refine the outline. It's like a lasso with a Magic Wand's sensitivity.

With the Marquee tool you make geometric selections, namely rectangles or squares, ellipses or circles. Click and drag and you will create a selection from start to finish. To create a selection from the center of the figure, hold the Option key before clicking and dragging. To make a square or circle, hold the option and shift keys before clicking and dragging. To reposition a marquee while drawing, hold down the spacebar.

Once you create a selection you can modify it in many ways: add to (hold the Shift key), subtract from (hold the Option key), expand (Selection: Modify: Expand), contract (Selection: Modify: Subtract), grow (Selection: Grow for contiguous information or Selection: Similar for noncontiguous information), transform (Selection: Transform), reverse (Selection: Inverse), or you can soften its edge (Selection: Feather). You can use any

selection tool in combination with the others.

You can store selections as alpha channels, layer masks, or paths. You store a selection so that you can use it at a later date without having to recreate it. These storage methods have distinct advantages. Most typically you will store a selection as an alpha channel, an additional channel that does not affect the way an image looks. In its most basic form it is nothing more than a record of a selection. Alpha channels are fundamentally different from channels in that they do not comprise the image, but they are like channels in two respects: they are grayscale images and they add an equal amount to file size. Depending on how complex it is, an alpha channel can add as much size to a file as a single channel — one half in grayscale, one third in RGB, or one quarter in CMYK. If they are comprised of large areas of single tones they will be compressed more than complex alpha channels when saved. Once you create a selection,

11. A hard-edged mask.

12. Blurring a mask achieves the same thing as feathering a selection

13. Save simple selections, without gray tones and uniform edges, as paths. While it would not have been as easy to make these selections with Paths, all of these selections could be saved as paths to reduce file size. Similarly, there is no need to save an alpha channel and a layer mask that define the same selection. Either can be turned into a selection, so one will do.

go to Selection: Save Selection and create a new alpha channel. You'll find it in the Channels palette. I recommend giving each new alpha channel a meaningful name when you create it or you'll soon be lost in a stack of numbered alpha channels. You can rename any alpha channel after creation simply by double-clicking on it and typing in a new name.

To turn an alpha channel into a selection, load it (Selection: Load Selection) or click on its icon in the Channels palette and drag it to the first icon on the bottom left of that window, a dotted circular line.

Selections are the active side of alpha channels; alpha channels are the passive side of selections. One creates the other. A selection creates an alpha channel when it is saved. An alpha channel creates a selection when it is loaded.

Alpha channels are black-and-white or grayscale images. The white areas of an alpha channel represent the areas of an image that will be affected or selected once the selection is loaded. The black areas represent the areas of an image that will not be affected or selected. Gray values in an alpha channel allow only partial correction based on their density, i.e., a darker gray will allow less correction, a lighter gray will allow more correction. You can modify alpha channels with any filter, paint, or correction tool to darken, lighten, or change its character, globally or locally. The changes you make to an alpha channel modify the selection it will create.

You can save alpha channels in a separate document. When you save alpha channels in another document you cut down on file size. Simply specify a new document when you save the selection. A multichannel document of the appropriate size will be created to store the alpha channel. Just as you can save an alpha channel in another document, you can load a selection from one document into another.

14. A selection can be used to affect an alpha channel or layer mask, not just to create one.

15. Similarly, a selection can be used to affect a Quick Mask, not just to create one.

You can also save selections as layer masks. Create an adjustment layer with an active selection and an adjustment layer layer mask is created that is in every respect similar to an alpha channel. You can even load the layer mask as a selection at a later date. It will not appear in the Channels palette unless that layer is activated (click on it). Once activated, load it as a selection. I've found that, for some odd reason, selections saved as layer masks take up slightly less space than selections stored as alpha channels. An adjustment layer that made no correction with a layer mask could actually reduce file size, thus increasing efficiency, but the clumsiness of having to activate the layer to turn it into a selection is generally not worth the small savings and can lead to confusion. However, do bear in mind that there is no reason to have an alpha channel that is identical to an existing layer mask. You can save significant file size by having just one, the layer mask. Likewise, there is no reason to save both a selection and its inverse as two alpha channels. Upon loading, or after loading, the selection can be inversed. One alpha channel will do for both figure and ground or positive and negative space.

Selections can also be saved as paths. You create paths with the Pen tool. The Bézier curves created are challenging. Without a great deal of practice, they are tedious and difficult to work with. I recommend starting elsewhere. However, they are superior for drawing rigidly geometric forms most often found in images of man-made objects or environments. If this is your challenge, then it is well worth your while to learn to work with Bézier curves.

Yet, you do not need to know how to draw with Bézier curves to use Paths. A path can be used both as a drawing tool (stroke a path with a brush and that brush is run along the path from beginning to end) and as a selection tool (turn a path into a selection by using the pull-down menu in the Paths palette and going to Make Selection). Selections and paths (like selections and alpha channels) can be linked; that is, one can create the other. A selection outline can be saved as a path. With a selection active, go to the Paths palette and use the submenu to find Make Work Path. A low tolerance will make the path very tight with many points. A high tolerance will make the path outline looser with fewer points. I generally favor a low tolerance (1.0). Oddly, this does not save the path, as

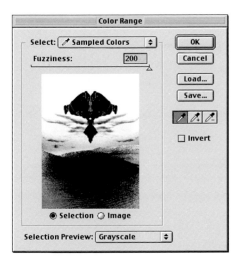

16. Color Range creates selections based on sampled colors.
Not all images have enough variety for it to be useful.

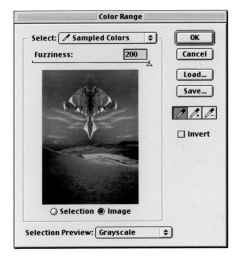

17. Temporarily increasing saturation or shifting hue with
an adjustment layer may aid the selection process.

it is only temporary. To make the path permanent, return to the submenu and go to Save Path. Give it a meaningful name for easy access. A path has the advantage of taking up very little file space. Adding an alpha channel can increase file size significantly (up to the space it takes to save a single channel — 33 MB more on a 100MB RGB file), while a path, regardless of file size, takes up far less space (less than a megabyte, often just a few kilobytes). A path, unlike an alpha channel, cannot store gray values. It can only define an outline. Simple masks that are black-and-white and hard-edged are best saved as paths. Complex masks with varying shades of gray must be saved as alpha channels. The selections made by paths can be feathered before or after they are created so the gray transitions of feathered edges in a selection can be recreated if they are uniformly soft. Paths stay visible until turned off, so when you have finished using them, turn them off (submenu Turn Off Path).

Quick Masks are an invaluable selection tool. Quick Masks are temporary alpha channels. They allow you to create a selection using the paint brush. To enter Quick Mask mode, find the icons near the bottom of your tool bar, a dotted circular line surrounded by white next to a dotted circular line surrounded by gray, and click on the dark one to the right. Then use a black brush to mask out areas that are not to be affected. Use a white brush to reveal areas that are. Use a combination of both to refine a selection. A gray brush will create a partial resist based on its value. As you paint you will see a red overlay appear; that's the mask. It's transparent so that you can see the image underneath it while you create it. If you double-click on the Quick Mask icon, you can change the default color and opacity. (I rarely do unless I'm masking something red, then it's hard to see the mask. Otherwise, the default is excellent. The Quick Mask is transparent red in part because it looks like a rubylith, the material used traditionally in prepress to mask things out.) You can create a feathered edge with a soft brush. The larger the brush, the longer the smooth transition. I often paint with the edge, rather than the center, of varying sizes of soft brushes to selectively control the degree of feathering I wish to create. When the mask is finished, click on the left icon (the dotted line surrounded by white) to turn the Quick Mask into a selection. Make sure to save the selection instantly because the Quick

Mask is only temporary and has to be saved if you wish to use the selection that was created again. You will notice the Quick Mask icon in the Channels palette disappears when it is turned into a selection. It is easy to forget to save it. If you do forget and the selection is deactivated, you may lose it and have to recreate it. (The History palette may help you recover it.) More often than not, I favor making a rough selection with the Lasso tool and then entering Quick Mask mode to refine the selection with a brush. You can go back and forth between mask and selection modes using any combination of selection or brush tools to refine a mask.

What you can accomplish in Quick Mask mode you can also do by painting on an alpha channel while simultaneously viewing the other channels. To do this, click on an existing alpha channel or create a new one. Activate the eye icons of the other channels to see them but do not affect them. Paint on the new alpha channel. This will look exactly like the Quick Mask mode. Make sure you do not activate the image channels and paint on them; this will damage your image. It's not quite as easy to change the alpha channel into a selection as it is to dip out of Quick Mask mode, but you will be less likely to forget to save your work this way. This way, you do not need to save your work, because changes to alpha channels are automatically saved.

One essential quality of any selection or mask created is its edge quality. Many selection outlines are typically too hard-edged when first created, resulting in unnaturally abrupt transitions. You can soften any selection by feathering it (Select: Feather). This creates a smoother transition. Feather a selection too much and you may run the risk of creating halos. The right degree of softness is critical to achieving a convincing effect. You will quickly develop an eye for it. Bear in mind that larger files have more pixels in them and so can withstand greater amounts of feathering. A selection can be feathered when it is created, before it is saved, or after it is loaded. In a majority of cases I favor the latter as it is easier to feather a selection than it is to convincingly make it more hard-edged. Blurring an alpha channel (or layer mask) achieves the same thing as feathering. If file size allows, you might want to save both a blurred and an unblurred alpha channel until you are certain you will no longer need one or the other.

Remember to zoom into the image to check the precision of your selection. At greater magnification you may find inaccuracies you'll wish to correct. You may want to create many selections starting at high magnification. More often than not, you will need to zoom in and out frequently throughout the process of creating a selection.

A key perceptual skill in creating selections is to always keep figure (object)/ground (environment) relationships in mind. Take an image of a butterfly on a white background. The quickest way to select the butterfly? Select the white background, which is everything but the butterfly, and then inverse that selection to select the butterfly only. One click of the Magic Wand and a single menu command replaces many more moves and accomplishes the same task. It is not necessary to save one selection for the figure and one for the ground. One alpha channel will contain both. Any active selection can be inversed. Or an inverted version of any channel can be loaded as a selection by checking the appropriate box. Continually being mindful of positive and negative space will greatly aid you.

Selections are used to constrain corrections, to copy a portion of an image, or to mask out unwanted portions of an overlying image. Whether your vision is classically traditional or cutting-edge contemporary, you need to master selections. They're an essential part of anyone's digital technique.

You will find there are usually at least three ways to do the same thing in Photoshop. As long as it delivers equal quality, take the path of least resistance. If two paths are equally easy and effective, take your pick.

9. RESTORATION MAKING REPAIRS

To blend flawed areas into their surrounding backgrounds, traditional etching and spotting techniques typically have you use a brush to place ink of similar value over lighter flaws or work with a blade to scrape darker flaws off the surface of a print, thereby revealing the underlying emulsion or white paper base beneath. Analogous methods can be used to retouch film. In digital retouching, you have the ability to replace the damaged areas with fully textured photographic information without altering the surface of the image's carrier. In

1. In a seamless retouching job, no traces of the process are left.

truth, with a digital image there is no material surface. Therein lies great freedom and extraordinary capacities. The capabilities of digital retouching are so superior to traditional methods that you can easily get carried away. I advise erring on the side of efficiency without sacrificing quality. There are many techniques for digital retouching. Many save time and produce an acceptable result. A few offer superior results.

Would that there were a magic bullet for retouching. Alas, there is not. Looking for salvation, many turn to the Dust and Scratches filter (Filter: Noise: Dust and Scratches) and find

2. Retouching with hard-edged brushes can be difficult as the transitions they create are abrupt.

3. Retouching with soft-edged brushes provides smoother transitions.

4. Retouching at low opacities can cause an unnatural flatness.

misleading temptation instead. Dust and Scratches is a blur filter with threshold and radius controls. While removing dust and scratches, it blurs the image. In a majority of cases, this is an unacceptable trade-off. Consequently, in a majority of cases, you will not want to employ it. There are exceptions, of course, areas that won't be harmed from softening, such as very smooth or flat untextured surfaces or areas that are already out of focus. A clear blue sky will rarely suffer. Dust and Scratches need not be applied to the entire image. Often it is best used selectively, applied in local areas through selections.

Above all, remember that the computer simply isn't as intelligent as you are. And so there really is no substitute for careful work done by a skilled hand and guided by a sensitive eye. The basic strategy for retouching is straightforward. Replace flawed information with similar unflawed information. You find substitutes for the spots and lines or the dust, pinholes, scratches and hairs. The similar substitute information can come from the same image or another image. All that matters is that the replacement be similar enough to the replaced information that the flaws no longer distract the eye. Retouching is best when it remains invisible. It is one technique that does not want to call attention to itself.

Some sample, with the eyedropper, a nearby color or tone and use a brush to fill in the damaged areas. The result is usually unnaturally flat, without film grain, and you must take care to sample new colors frequently or you will not convincingly mimic subtle transitions within an image.

Some use the Smudge tool on Darken or Lighten mode (brushes may have multiple modes of operation) to smear nearby color or tone into the flawed area. This eliminates the need to frequently sample new colors or tones. You use Darken mode to fill in lighter areas only (lighter than the tone being smudged into the area), leaving equal or darker tones untouched. Conversely, you use Lighten to fill in darker areas only. The elegance of this method is that the effect is, in most cases, contained to the flawed areas alone and not to the surrounding areas. What's more, you can easily maintain surrounding subtle transitions in color and tone. The drawback is that the smudged information is blurred. It may be too soft.

There isn't a better tool for retouching than the Rubber Stamp tool (otherwise known as the Clone tool). With it you can avoid the pitfalls of all the aforementioned methods. Its flexibility is astonishing. To use the Rubber Stamp tool, move it to an area to be duplicated. Hold the Option key down (you will see the black triangle in the tool turn white — sample mode), and click. Let go. Next, move the tool to the area you would like to copy the information to. Click, hold, and paint (The triangle in the tool will be black — paint mode). A vector (an angle and

5. *Retouching with the Smudge tool can cause an unnatural flatness. The top stroke is a hard-edged brush. The bottom stroke is a soft-edged brush.*

6. *Retouching with a paint brush can cause an unnatural flatness and/or streaking. The top spot is a hard-edged brush. The bottom spot is a soft-edged brush.*

7. *Close repetition of the same information may create an unnatural pattern such as spotting or striping.*

distance between two points, the origin and the destination) is defined between the first option click and the second click. You will see a cross hair at the origin and the tool's icon at the destination as you paint. The angle between the two will be maintained until you define another (Option click). As you paint, you replace the original information with substitute information.

For a naturalistic look, you should avoid overt repetition of either large areas or small details. It is very easy to copy copied information as you proceed across an area. Soon a distracting series of stripes of similar information may appear. If you sample often, defining many varied angles and taking replacement information from many sources for a single area, you will avoid this. As a rule, randomized information without a strong pattern tends to blend into its surroundings. Any pattern stands out as order. Order gets our attention. And attention is exactly what we don't want to pay to the final results of most retouching. Pay attention to the way you retouch so others don't have to later.

You can choose between three graphic displays of any brush, including the Rubber Stamp tool (File: Preferences: Displays and Cursors): Standard (the icon of the tool found in the tool palette), Precise (a cross hair that displays the center of the brush), and Brush Size (a circle that shows the circumference of the brush used). I find the latter two most useful, and favor brush size heavily as I like to see where the edge of a brush is as much as the center. Often I "paint" with the edge of the brush rather than the center.

The Rubber Stamp tool, like any other brush, has the advantage of working in many modes, such as Darken or Lighten. Its opacity can also be reduced. Using a soft-edged brush will often help you to blend replacement information into its new environment. Essentially, the further out the replacement information is from the center of the brush, the more transparent it is. You need to handle the effect produced by the edges of large soft brushes and cloning at a reduced opacity with some care. Whenever you use a percentage less than 100%, the underlying information and the overlying information may blend in a way that softens the area, making it appear smoother and sometimes unnaturally flat. For this reason, I favor using an opacity of 100%. Yet, in a majority of cases, I favor using soft-edged brushes over hard-edged brushes. The edge of a hard brush tends to produce unnaturally pronounced transitions that are far more distracting than a little softening, which typically aids in producing more convincing transitions.

If replacement information becomes overly smooth and you would like to reintroduce the texture of film grain, the retouched areas can be selected and you can add noise (Filter: Noise: Add Noise) to simulate grain. (For the ultimate in flexibility you can add noise to a separate overlying layer filled with

50% gray and set to a mode of Hard Light. This way the noise can be masked and rescaled indefinitely.) Compare the Distribution settings Uniform and Gaussian on both the default and Monochromatic settings to find the most convincing effect. Remember, 100% is the only magnification factor that will truly display the level of detail that the image will have in its final destination, so check the effect at that magnification. In certain instances, to add texture, you can convert the image to LAB color which will allow you to clone the retouched areas from the L (Luminance) channel only. Or, you can change the mode of the Rubber Stamp tool to Luminosity.

You should check every image thoroughly. Sweep through an image systematically. At 100% magnification, start in the upper left hand corner (the white box in the gray bar at the bottom of the image should be all the way to the left and the white box in the gray bar to the right of the image should be all the way at the top). Check the window. Retouch if needed. Sweep to the right. Click once to the right of the white box in the gray bar at the bottom of the window. This will advance the display one screen length through the image. Check the new window. Retouch if needed. Repeat until you reach the right hand corner. Then click below the white box in the gray bar to the right of the image, lowering the view one screen length. Check the window and retouch if necessary. Then advance the screen to the left until you reach the left edge. Repeat this sweeping

8. An overexposed original.

9. The overexposed original multiplied. Highlight detail is increased. Shadow detail is decreased.

10. The overexposed original multiplied with a contrast mask applied. Highlight detail is increased without increasing the density of shadows. The subsequent application of a curve will achieve the proper tonal balance now that optimal information exists in both shadows and highlights.

process until you reach the bottom right hand corner. It's easy to miss an area of an image if you do not methodically check every portion of it. Systematically check every cell of the image at 100% magnification. Whether you work from top to bottom or from left to right, there's no substitute for this kind of thoroughness. Do it and there will be fewer unpleasant surprises in your future.

For the ultimate in flexibility, you may want to clone from an original image layer to a new blank layer. This way you can always return to the original untouched image, should you wish to improve the retouching, by making the retouching layer invisible. To do this, sample an area on the original image layer (Option click), create a new layer (I often name these layers "retouch" for easy reference), and clone to it (click and paint). Check Use All Layers in the Rubber Stamp tool's option palette so that you don't have to return to the original layer to define a new sampling point/vector. Still, if you're absolutely certain you want to remove a flawed area (dust or a hair or a scratch), there is no need to place the retouching on a separate layer. Save this for more substantial retouching. Keeping substantial retouching on separate layers provides a level of flexibility the History palette can't since previous states will not be saved after the file is saved and closed. Remember, you can also clone from one image to another, just as you can between separate layers. Sometimes you may find the best replacement information in another image.

While you can use the Rubber Stamp tool to duplicate large areas of an image, often it is more efficient to duplicate it in one fell swoop. Select the area, copy it, and paste it. This creates a new layer with duplicate information that can be repositioned, even resized or distorted. Copy a little more than you think you need, add a layer mask, and use a soft brush to create smooth transitions that can be indefinitely modified between the copy and the background.

It may produce an unnatural effect to have two areas of an image with identical information. In this event, use the Rubber Stamp tool on the copied information to redistribute a few of the relationships within that area and give it a unique appearance. A combination of the two methods, copy and clone, can give duplicated information the appearance of individuality.

There's a case to be made for placing this chapter after rather than before Sharpen. Unsharp Mask will often accentuate flaws in an image that wouldn't ordinarily be visible. After applying Unsharp Mask, you should make a second sweep throughout the image to catch this. If you save all your retouching until after applying Unsharp Mask, you won't be able to change the amount of Unsharp Mask you use. If you retouch first and sharpen later, you will. For the ultimate in flexibility apply Unsharp Mask to a duplicate layer or file. With the original information unsharpened you retain the option of returning to it to change the sharpening settings. I typically save at least two separate files of any given image: the first unsharpened and retouched in

11. An underexposed original.

12. The underrexposed original screened. Shadow detail is increased. Highlight detail is decreased.

13. The underexposed original screened, with a contrast mask applied. Shadow detail is increased without lightening highlights. The subsequent application of a curve will achieve the proper tonal balance now that optimal information exists in both shadows and highlights.

Photoshop format with separate layers; the second in TIFF format flattened, sharpened and retouched a second time. While this requires a two-step retouching process, the additional retouching you have to do after applying Unsharp Mask is typically minor. The extra time spent is well worth the flexibility gained. Whether you sharpen before or after retouching, do retouch after making substantial corrections, not before. Often retouching that was not apparent before you correct an image will become apparent after your image correction. When in doubt, save retouching for last.

For many forms of restoration you may not need to introduce replacement information, you may instead just make local corrections of tone and color. Stains, fading, decrease or increase in density, light leaks, lens flares, and Newton rings are just a few examples of the kinds of problems you can approach this way. I resort to replacing information when the damaged areas can't be repaired any other another way.

You typically repair imbalances in tone due to fading or overexposure and underexposure by applying tonal corrections to the image. For severe challenges a simple technique may dramatically resurrect information in thin or dense areas. Duplicate the image's background layer and change the mode of the duplicate layer from Normal to Multiply, to double the values (add density) of light images, or Screen to halve the values (subtract density) of the image in dark images. This doubles the file's size but there is a way around this problem. Create an adjust-

14. A poor retouching job. Traces of the retouching process are clearly visible: soft smudged color, poor matches in tone or color, the introduction of striped patterns, and unnaturally smooth areas created by soft brushes at low opacities.

ment layer (try Curves), make no correction, but when creating the adjustment layer, change its mode to either Multiply or Screen. This will produce the same effect without doubling your file size. You can multiply or screen an image any number of times to increase the effect. Add a layer mask to these adjustment layers and you can contain the effect to select areas of the image. Use a contrast mask as your layer mask and you can contain the effect to specific ranges of tone, for instance the shadows or highlights only. And remember, you can change the density and contrast of the contrast mask by applying a curve directly to further refine the adjustment layer layer mask.

Whether you choose to replace or correct, remember that you always have the ability to replace or correct information within a single channel rather than all three. For instance, the magenta component of a Newton ring or lens flare may be carried solely in the green channel; it alone may be retouched leaving the other two channels untouched.

It's far too easy to get heavy-handed, so I favor the lightest touch that will produce the desired result. When things are to be done artfully, finesse usually wins over brute force.

Some think digital sharpening is a cure-all that can remedy any lack of focus. Would that this were true. Alas, it is not. Understanding how digital sharpening works in Photoshop will help you to understand what it can and cannot accomplish.

Forget about Sharpen, Sharpen More, and Sharpen Edges; they are default settings of Unsharp Mask. With Unsharp Mask, you can do exactly what these others do, or you can do far more. Unsharp Mask in my experience offers greater flexibility and control.

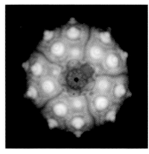

1. An out-of-focus image.

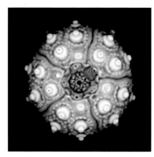

2. The out-of-focus image sharpened.
The results after sharpening will
rarely be as good as a focused image.

It may seem contradictory to call something that makes images look sharper "Unsharp Mask". This term has its origin in the traditions of prepress (offset printing). Traditionally, a light, soft (blurred, not sharp, or "unsharp") negative image (film) is registered with the original positive image (film) during exposure (typically of a metal plate but sometimes film or paper). Edges within the blurred negative spread in this process. The disparity between the soft edges and the sharp edges in the original intensifies lines throughout the image. The dark sides of lines get darker and the light sides get lighter. The result is an accentuation of edges, which makes an image appear sharper.

Though it is mindful of the same visual principles, digital unsharp masking works somewhat differently than traditional unsharp masking does. The Unsharp Mask tool does several things. First, it accentuates contrast on the pixel level: dark pixels become darker, and light pixels become lighter. Unless overdone, this does not affect the overall contrast of the image, but

it does make the image appear to be sharper since images with more texture and more contrast appear to be sharper. When this is overdone, the image may look overly textured with the introduction of a brittle, gritty pattern throughout, which is seen most prominently in smooth areas. Second, Unsharp Mask accentuates lines: it searches for broader areas where a light tone abuts a dark tone and makes the dark edge darker and the light edge darker. This also makes the image appear sharper. If this is overdone, you create unnaturally intense lines and halos.

The human eye actually works similarly to Unsharp Mask. The principles of simultaneous contrast are at work: in the presence of dark values, light values appear lighter and vice versa. This results in a virtual line between adjacent but differing values. The greater the difference in values, the greater the effect, known as the Mach effect. These differences are not physically measurable as they are artifacts of how the human eye perceives things. Nonetheless, you experience them. And it's lucky you do, since they help you to better discern the information you see. Under certain conditions, particularly when complementary hues abut each other, you will see a visual vibration (something the Op Art movement took full advantage of). These phenomenon may be related to the presence of afterimages. (Stare at a patch of color for an extended period of time, then move your eyes to a white wall, and you will see an afterimage of the color's complement. This effect happens with tone as well as color.)

You determine acutance, the physical measure of sharpness, closely linked to resolving power, by making quantitative measurements of edges with a scanning microdensitometer. Factors such as film type and development (including strength, length, and agitation) all affect an image's acutance. There is no substitute for actual acutance. Unsharp Mask will not increase it. Unsharp Mask will not make an image sharper; it will only make an image look sharper. There are certain inadequacies this tool cannot overcome. Although Unsharp Mask can make soft images look sharper, it cannot overcome a significant lack of focus. No amount of unsharp masking will cure motion blur. Here again, digital technique is not a substitute or a cure for a lack of traditional technique. But sharpening digitally can be a marvelous extension of how you might work traditionally. "Sharpness" is subjective. To the human eye it's a quality, not a quantity. And you can accentuate the qualities of an image digitally, including its "sharpness." While there are limits to what you can do, you are able to go quite far before you reach them.

Almost all images can use some sharpening. Even sharp originals properly scanned can use sharpening to overcome softening introduced by the limitations of camera, lens, film or CCD, and scanner.

Many scanners allow you to apply Unsharp Mask while making the scan. This may be a good time saver in situations that require high-volume output, but you can achieve better results. Knowing that I will be much more discriminating than the great majority of service providers and knowing that sharpening is one of the last techniques I wish to perform on an image, I request unsharpened scans from service bureaus.

Because every image is different, each will probably require a different amount of unsharp masking. Default settings rarely provide optimal results. Understanding the controls in Unsharp Mask will help you to determine your own optimal settings. There are three variables with Photoshop's Unsharp Mask: Amount, Radius, and Threshold. In all cases you get a stronger effect with higher numbers.

With the Amount setting you control the strength of the effect. The higher the amount, the more contrast you increase at the pixel level. Note that 100% does not represent the maximum setting which is 500%.

With the Radius setting you control the way Photoshop treats edges within an image, darkening the dark side (line) and lightening the light side (halo). The higher the Radius you set, the greater the line/halo accentuation; that is, the lines and halos grow wider. While Radius accentuates detail by accentuating line and halo, if you use too high a setting, you may subdue subtle detail. In these instances favor a lower Radius setting.

The Threshold setting suppresses noise. The higher you set the Threshold, the more noise you suppress. As you increase the threshold, subtler variations between areas of similar value are increasingly unaffected. The numerical value of a Threshold setting refers to the difference in values necessary in an area to be affected: if the setting is 10, then values must differ by 10 on a scale from 0–255 (RGB) to be accentuated. If noise cannot be adequately suppressed with the Threshold setting, you may want to resort to sharpening channels individually to minimize the amount of noise introduced by unsharp masking.

As sharpness is a visual quality, you determine an optimal setting for increasing sharpness visually. You should evaluate the effects of Unsharp Mask at a screen magnification of 100%, the only magnification that truly represents the level of detail an image is capable of printing. Any other magnification will not be as accurate.

To determine optimal settings for Amount, Radius and Threshold, start by overdoing it. Turn the Amount way up (400–500%) and the Threshold way down (0). Next, go to the Radius setting. It is the Radius setting that is most critical. It will make or break any attempt at sharpening. Amount and Radius both emphasize transitions, but they emphasize them differently. If you set the Amount too high the image will become noisy, even if the Radius is correct. If you set the Radius too high subtle detail will be lost, even if the Amount is correct. Set the Radius to just shy of the point at which significant detail begins to be subdued rather than accentuated. Use a lower Radius for images where subtle detail is important. As you increase the Radius you may need to decrease the Amount. You generally determine Threshold last. Set it to the minimum value necessary to subdue the exaggeration of unwanted noise. Don't mistake this with unwanted contrast brought about by the excessive Amount. Look for pronounced noise in smooth areas. The presence of smooth surfaces will suggest that you use higher settings. With small Radius settings, higher Threshold settings might unnecessarily subdue the overall sharpening effect. With higher Radius settings, you can use higher Thresholds without reducing the effect. You can combine very different settings to provide equivalent sharpness. There's no substitute for a little experimentation. Although some favor

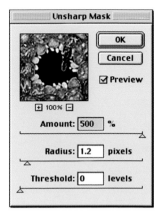

3. The Unsharp Mask dialog box.

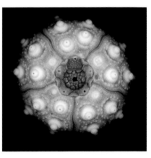

4. The unsharpened image. Detail is soft.

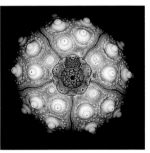

5. The sharpened image with a Radius setting that is too high. Note the exaggerated halos and lines.

more sharpening than others, I prefer to err on the soft side rather than the sharp side. Though some subjects favor more sharpening (rock) and others favor less (hair), this is largely subjective. Feel free to tweak any of the settings if this improves the image. After all, this is a visual effect, so make it pleasing to your eye.

When applying Unsharp Mask at 100% magnification, I routinely make a rectangular selection that encompasses a variety of textures within an important area of the image. Then I apply the Filter (Filter: Unsharp Mask) to determine the optimal settings. All the while I am able to compare the results with the adjacent portion of the image outside the area being sharpened, namely the unsharpened image. I apply the filter in the selected area. I then undo the change, deselect, and apply that level of sharpening to the entire image. You can do this by pressing Command F, which will apply the last filter applied at the last settings used. To apply the filter but bring the dialog box back up, press Option Command F. This saves time with larger files; however, with smaller files you can simply check the Unsharp Mask preview box on and off to see the image before and after sharpening.

Use as much Unsharp Mask as you can without making the image seem unnatural.

There are several telltale signs of oversharpening. Exaggeration of noise (grain with scanned film): random pixels will be accentuated making the image look grainy, for lack of a better word. Exaggerated contours: lines will seem too thick

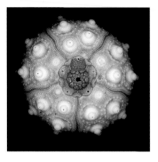

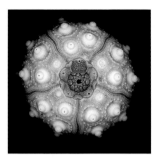

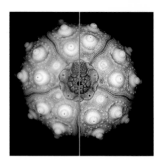

6. The sharpened image with the Threshold set too high. Note some areas of the image look flat and unsharpened while areas with greater contrast look too sharp and the transitions between them are too abrupt.

7. The sharpened image with optimal settings. Note the exaggeration of some unwanted detail; hair and dust now need to be retouched.

8. A larger comparison of the sharpened version and an unsharpened version can be seen side by side by determining settings inside a selection in an area of the image that represents the variety of textures an image contains.

or dark and halos will seem too wide or bright. Contrast shifts: stronger applications of Unsharp Mask can affect an image's overall contrast. Color shifts: as contrast is increased so does saturation, which can become unnaturally exaggerated. Intensification of unwanted detail: information not native to the image may be exaggerated, dust and scratches may become overly pronounced requiring extra retouching, or information native to the image may become overly pronounced, surface abrasion on metal or the pores and wrinkles on skin may become unnaturally apparent. Exaggerated texture: Unsharp Mask tends to make things look textured, sharp and sometimes brittle, which does not serve smooth or soft surfaces well. The silky fur and downy feathers lose their sensual qualities if they look razor sharp, rigid, and unyielding. It becomes that much more critical to get unsharp masking right when working large. Larger images show the effects of undersharpening or oversharpening more readily than smaller ones.

One technique for sharpening without accentuating unwanted detail is to apply smaller amounts of sharpening in several successive stages. Determine optimal settings for textured areas. Be conservative. Then divide the amount by four and apply the filter at that setting four times. You may even be able to get away with applying it a fifth or sixth time. The cumulative effect is less harsh when applied in successive stages.

Some problems are best solved by applying Unsharp Mask in another color space entirely.

The CMYK color space offers several advantages over RGB. The weakest channel in RGB is generally still stronger than its two counterparts in CMYK. If the weakest channels in CMYK are weaker than the weakest channels in RGB, they can be sharpened more. Sharpening in CMYK offers another distinct advantage over sharpening in RGB — the black plate. It can be sharpened without creating color shifts and without accentuating artifacts that may only be contained in the color components. Sharpening the black plate functions similarly to sharpening the L channel in LAB.

The LAB color space has three channels: two for color (A for magenta/green and B for yellow/blue) and one for luminosity. The L channel carries the tone. You can sharpen it and avoid unnecessary accentuation of noise, increases in saturation, and color shifts. As a result, you can apply more Unsharp Mask to a file in LAB than you typically can in another color space.

There are times when you may find that Photoshop will ask you to flatten an image when converting to another color space (from RGB or CMYK to LAB). This is only one of the reasons sharpening is one of the last steps I do. If you flatten and sharpen an image, save it as a new document, leaving yourself the option of returning to the original unsharpened image should you decide you would like to make changes in the future (including modifying the amount and kind of sharpening applied to it).

If you would like to apply luminosity sharpening to a file without changing modes, you can. It's a two-step process. Apply Unsharp Mask, then choose Filter: Fade. You generally use Fade to reduce the intensity of the effect of a filter by lowering its opacity. But you can also use Fade to change the mode of the filter. In this case you change the mode to Luminosity. (The same thing can be done with any filter. You can even accomplish the same thing with layers to provide future flexibility or selectivity. Duplicate the layer the filter is to be applied to. Apply the filter to the duplicate layer and change the duplicate layer's opacity or mode. This method generates a larger file, but it also provides the ability to change the opacity and mode settings ever after.)

Some problems are best solved by applying Unsharp Mask to select channels and not others. This is particularly appropriate when an image is dominated by a single color, particularly red, green, or blue. Generally the "weakest" channels are sharpened, and the "dominant" ones are not. The dominant channels are the ones that carry the lion's share of the detail, while the weakest channels carry the least. The darkest channels carry more information and are therefore more susceptible to creating unwanted artifacts when you sharpen them. If the image can be sharpened overall, the weakest channels can often be sharpened even more. In a portrait (Caucasian), the dark channels in CMYK are magenta (green in RGB) and yellow (blue in RGB). Avoid sharpening them. Instead, sharpen the cyan (red) and black channels. Here the CMYK space offers greater possibilities. You should be careful, but not necessarily avoid, sharpening the blue channel as you typically find the most noise there introduced by scanners or the CCDs of digital cameras.

Images will often appear more brilliant after sharpening. In some images this brightening will not be favorable. For such images, you can employ a complex method of sharpening. You need to create three copies of the image: the original unsharpened version and two versions sharpened in Luminosity mode. First, create a duplicate of the image on a separate layer. Second, oversharpen, not drastically but substantially. Third, fade the filter and change its mode to Luminosity leaving its opacity untouched. Fourth, turn the mode of the duplicate layer to Darken. Fifth, duplicate the duplicate layer. Sixth, turn the mode of the second duplicate from Darken to Lighten and reduce its opacity (determine the reduction visually). The effect dramatically reduces apparent shifts in tone while still allowing you to make an image appear substantially sharper. How often do I use this technique? Rarely. It's for extreme situations.

While I rarely use the Sharpening tool (a brush in the tool palette which has a Luminosity as well as a Normal mode) to sharpen an image in its entirety, it is useful for adding accents to an image. If there are small areas of particular interest in an image that could use sharpening (like pieces of metal, glass or jewelry, or specular highlights), sharpening them alone may make the image seem sharper overall. Accentuating them after the entire image has been sharpened may be the final added touch that makes the picture sparkle. You could do this by sharpening a duplicate layer and eliminating or masking out all but these small areas. You gain greater control of the sharpening settings and future flexibility but sacrifice simplicity and add to the file size.

Determining optimal settings is a purely visual process. Images differ so markedly in source, resolution, and kind that default numbers are only that, defaults. Textured images will support greater amounts of sharpening than smooth images. Similarly, textured areas of images will support greater amounts of sharpening than smooth ones.

Many caution against sharpening one area of an image without sharpening another or sharpening them differently. As a rule, I agree. If this is overdone, the two areas of the image will look as if they exist in separate realities, undermining the unity of the picture. The general practice of sharpening an image uniformly in order to accentuate noise or grain uniformly throughout the image avoids creating a distracting discrepancy within an image that might call attention to itself and undermine the distinctive qualities of the image. Now that you know the rule, you may want to break the rule deliberately. I make exceptions to this rule frequently. You could apply Unsharp Mask through a luminance mask modifying the effects in the shadows where excess noise is often found. Or, you could sharpen an image selectively by applying different settings to different areas of an image to increase its realism. I prefer to sharpen smooth and soft surfaces less than textured and hard surfaces. If both exist within a single image, I will often sharpen each area selectively. This accents the tactile qualities of the image.

Selective sharpening can impart a "super real" quality to an image. As long as the image remains believable, I value this.

There is a way to subtly reduce the presence of grain or noise in color images. It's related to sharpening in LAB color space. If you have taken the time to sharpen in LAB, you might also consider blurring the A and B color channels slightly. Artifacts that are carried in the color channels will be subdued or removed altogether. Blur them just enough to reduce noise. If you blur them too much, you will begin pushing color into areas where it is not wanted. Throughout this process the tonal relationships, carried in the L channel, will remain unchanged. In some cases, this effect is subtle but worthwhile. In other cases, it is dramatic. I have seen smaller format originals look like larger format originals. (It's a good idea to employ this method to remove the noise introduced into the Blue channel by many digital cameras.) Carefully managed, any channel in any color space can be blurred or despeckled to reduce noise, as long as it does not adversely affect image sharpness. There are even times when you should sacrifice a little sharpness to reduce noise.

With so many sharpening methods, it should be clear that no one method will be perfect for every image and the sharpness of almost any image can be improved.

11. OUTPUT I PRINT

Many think that if you make an image digitally you have to make a print on a digital printer. The reality is if you make a digital image you can print it in any way — all traditional, alternative, and digital printmaking processes are available to you. Digital images are not limited to digital outputting. The choice of how to make your print is yours. To make prints in the darkroom using traditional methods on conventional materials you need to make new film from your digital file with a film recorder. To make this new film you use an LVT film

1. The full-color image

recorder. (Kodak invented LVT — light valve technology. Think laser, which essentially replaces older CRT — cathode ray tube — film recorders.) You can also make contact negatives from offset lithography film for silver and alternative process printing (platinum, cyanotype, salt, gum bichromate, etc.). You can even use transparent materials for output on your desktop printers. And, of course, you now have a host of new digital printing options arise. Inkjet, electrostatic, and dye-sublimation are all printing options that employ different methods and different materials to reproduce images, but they all share one thing in common: all send a digital file to a digital printer to make a print. Film recorder technology has even been repurposed to expose traditional papers instead of film; a laser exposes the paper instead of an enlarger.

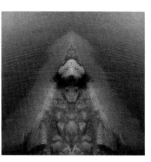

2. The Red channel.

3. The Green channel.

4. The Blue channel.

Some think digital prints are "fugitive," that they don't last. Some are; some are not. Some think that digital prints are not as archival, or long-lasting, as conventional prints. Some are; some are not. In a nutshell, the longevity problems arise because of two factors, the substrate used to print on and the pigment or dye placed on it. A paper free of residual chemistry, including acid left over from the process of making the paper, will last longer. Pigment lasts longer than ink, which is typically dye. Pigment has suspended particles of matter in it as opposed to colored globules of liquid. Pigmented inks are all the rage these days. Some feel they will replace silver-based prints. Pigmented inks are dye-based but incorporate finely ground pigments as well. The more pigment used in making the print, the greater the longevity. The challenge for most inkjet technology is to get permanent pigments ground finely enough so that the particles will not clog the nozzles that produce the fine spray of ink. In general, printers that use bigger dots can use larger particles of pigment, thus these put more pigment down on paper and the resulting images typically have greater longevity but also have more visible dots.

Rapid advancements have been made in this technology and so things continue to change rapidly. Be forewarned since there's a lot of hearsay. There are many misconceptions. Get the facts. One source is Henry Wilhelm, the foremost authority on the care and permanence of photographs. Check his web site, www.hwilhelm_research.com, for the latest information.

A glance at Wilhem's data will dispel a few misconceptions. Here are a few examples. C prints are more fugitive than Ilfochrome? Most are, but the Fujicolor Crystal Archive provides dramatically more longevity. Iris prints are more fugitive than traditional color prints? Iris prints are one of the most stable continuous tone print mediums, a few are as or more stable than Fuji Crystal Archive c prints. In dark storage inkjet prints are extremely durable because no residual chemistry is left in the substrate. Inkjet prints made with black ink or quadtone inks last even longer. Epson inkjet prints are extremely fugitive? With the right ink and paper combinations they can outlast all of the aforementioned, significantly. I have to struggle not to quote specific figures here, but I do so knowing that by the time these words see publication the playing field will have shifted slightly, while in a few years' time the changes will be dramatic. Huge advances in printing technology have been made in recent years. That rate of change is not likely to slow.

Assume that your digital image file is complete. You've determined the medium you wish to print on. You're ready to print. You select "Print," software and hardware kick in, and away it goes. But what's happening? Understanding what's happening will serve you well. Few output devices are true RGB devices; that is, they employ radiant light for the final product. Monitors (cathode ray tubes and liquid crystal displays) are true

5. *The Cyan channel.*

6. *The Magenta channel.*

7. *The Yellow channel.*

8. *The Black channel.*

RGB devices, and film recorders (cathode ray tubes and lasers) use radiant light to expose film. All other printers are typically CMYK devices, since they produce prints that rely on reflective light. There are exceptions. Durst's Lambda and Cymbolic Science's Lightjet 5000 machines make prints by exposing traditional photographic papers with lasers, just like film recorders expose film, and they use RGB files. But the prints they generate still rely on reflected light rather than radiant light for visibility. They do not contain a greater color gamut or dynamic range than all CMYK printers.

A printer may claim it's an RGB printer and in reality make CMYK prints. Generally, this means the conversion from RGB to CMYK is made by the printer as or just before it prints. It does not mean that the printer makes the prints with radiant light or that the resulting prints radiate light. Remember, RGB uses radiant or additive light and CMYK uses reflective or subtractive light.

When your image is converted from RGB to CMYK, it is transformed — substantially. It becomes apparent then that it is very important to understand how an image is converted from the richer RGB space with its greater color gamut into the weaker CMYK space with a more limited color gamut.

More and more, you see printers that are using hexachrome printing — that is, six-color printing. This is a modification of traditional four-color (CMYK) printing. Hexachrome printing adds two more colors. On offset presses, the additional colors are typically a bright orange and green. With Epson printers, they are typically more intense variants of magenta and cyan. The addition of the extra inks allows the printers to reproduce certain colors, very rich or saturated, that would otherwise be "out-of-gamut" or unprintable. Traditional offset printers will run a print through the press a second time adding extra density to ink to create a richer image. When a second run of cyan, magenta, or yellow is used, some previously "out-of-gamut" colors may be achieved. These principles are no less valid with digital four or six color printers.

With digital technology, you now find a closer marriage of the traditions of photography and prepress (offset reproduction) than previously seen. The one has in essence been an extension of the other. Throughout the history of photography they have never been entirely separate.

For many, the conversion to CMYK seems as simple as changing the mode of the file (Image: Mode: CMYK). Others are aware of what happens to a file when this is done. You need to know how to control that process to achieve optimal results.

Three important things happen when an image is converted to CMYK. First, the file is ripped. RIP stands for raster image processing. This is the process of turning pixels (squares) into dots (all manner of shapes, most typically round). Second, the image is compressed. The entire image is remapped proportionally. Colors in the gamut of the working color space

(RGB, LAB, etc.), but out of the gamut of the CMYK color space, are transposed into the new smaller output space. There are many ways of performing this calculation (perceptual, relative colorimetric, absolute colorimetric). Each form of calculation has its strengths, weaknesses and proponents. Third, three channels become four. A black plate, the K channel (they used K instead of B for black so it would not be confused with blue), is generated. A portion of the information found in the RGB channels, which become the CMY channels (they're complements — look at Color Balance for a visual demonstration of this), is used to create the black plate. Again, there are many ways of calculating this transformation (UCR or undercolor removal and GCR or gray component replacement) and different intensities (none, light, medium, heavy, maximum or custom).

The controls for this conversion are found in Photoshop under File: Color Settings: CMYK Set Up. You can specify the type (GCR or UCR) and amount (None, Light, Medium, Heavy, Maximum) of black plate generation. You can also indicate separate values by application of a custom curve for each of the channels: C,M,Y, and K. The black ink limit and total ink limit, the amount of ink that can be put on paper before the different colors begin to bleed into one another, can be altered (some inks are stickier than others and bleed less). Undercolor addition (UCA amount) compensates for loss of in density in neutral shadow areas by adding CMY back into those areas of the image (typically used with GCR). You can factor in the amount of dot gain, which compensates for how much the dots of ink bleed into the surface of the paper (some papers are more absorbent than others and cause ink to bleed more). Uncoated stocks such as watercolor paper bleed much more than coated stocks. Specify a higher dot gain and the image will be lightened, and vice versa, to compensate for the darkening effect that the dots bleeding will have on the image. You can even characterize the specific chromatic qualities of the inks (Ink Col-

ors: Custom) with CIE Yxy (CIE LAB) coordinates. These describe the specific qualities of the inks, for example, how red or green or dark or light a particular cyan ink is. This is for color scientists; the average user had best trust the results of measurements made with a spectrophotometer from a print made with the final output device. All of these factors can produce significant shifts in color and density. In short, they can alter your image significantly.

There are three ways to specify the CMYK setup: Built-in, ICC, and Tables. Built-in allows you to specify the settings manually. ICC enables you to use ICC profiles to do the conversion. You can specify a profile for the output device, a color management engine (most will use Adobe's Built-in), a rendering intent (most will use Perceptual, but Saturation, Relative Colorimetric, and Absolute Colorimetric are useful in specific applications), and you can enable (most will) or disable black point compensation. Tables let you save Built-in settings as ICC profiles. It also lets you load separation tables from previous versions of Photoshop or versions created by a service provider or tables found in another application.

Many printer software interfaces offer you the ability to control these variables. Here the printer offers to control the conversion rather than have the conversion controlled in Photoshop. With Epson printers, which take RGB files not CMYK files, in "Advanced" mode, find the "More Settings" and you will access a dialog box that will allow you to make changes to the CMYK conversion that the printer makes before printing. If your printer isn't printing perfectly, you can create and save a set of custom settings to tweak the printer's output in a consistent manner. (It's likely you will need separate settings for color and black-and-white output.) A custom adjustment layer in Photoshop could produce similar results; this time, you tweak the file before conversion to achieve better results. If you use Adobe PressReady, it is even possible to override the Epson conversion

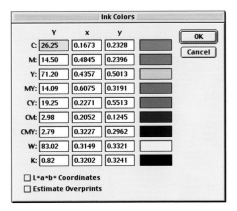

9. The CMYK Color Setting on Custom. You can
manually specify how CMYK conversions are made.

10. The Yxy coordinates specifying ink or pigment
characteristics. Typically ICC profiles set these values.

and send CMYK data, converted in Photoshop (Photoshop typically offers more control over the conversion) rather than RGB data to a printer.

The CMYK Setup is an important part of calibration. You are essentially doing the same thing when you manually create values for CMYK or generate profiles to control them. Either way you are specifying how files are converted to CMYK and how Photoshop will display CMYK information (in CMYK mode or with the CMYK Preview turned on) on your monitor (an RGB device which needs to be properly calibrated and have accurate CMYK Setup settings to make an accurate translation).

Accurate CMYK Setup settings are essential to getting an accurate preview of how files will look when printed in CMYK (softproofing). In order to do so you must constrain the display to what is printable as the monitor is capable of displaying a range of color and brightness that is unachievable in CMYK. The CMYK preview uses the CMYK Setup settings to do this. The settings also determine how Photoshop recognizes out-of-gamut colors. All Gamut Warnings are suspect if the CMYK setup is not set for the specific output device. For instance, Iris and Epson inks have a much greater gamut than offset inks. The defaults for Photoshop are for offset inks and are not as accurate for other types of inks. They will be overly conservative for inks that have a greater color gamut. Thus, you could expect to get a Gamut Warning where none was needed. If the settings are accurate (load an accurate ICC profile), you can trust your monitor. Then the preview works well and the Gamut Warning is useful.

You may want to bring out-of-gamut colors into gamut before making the conversion to CMYK. Select by Color Range offers a very nice feature as it allows you to select out-of-gamut colors only. Once you make the selection, save the selection as an alpha channel. Blur the alpha channel slightly because the edges created by Select by Color Range are typically too harsh. Then load the selection. With the Gamut Warning turned on, create a Hue/Saturation adjustment layer to reduce the saturation of the out-of-gamut colors. When the gamut warning indicators disappear, you will have reached the minimum reduction necessary, bringing colors down into gamut. Check the image critically after such a move. You may find you will want to make a subtle shift in contrast or color balance to compensate for the loss of saturation. Using an adjustment layer has a great advantage since it can be changed at any time in the future, leaving your original richer information untouched. Should new inks with greater color gamuts become available, or should

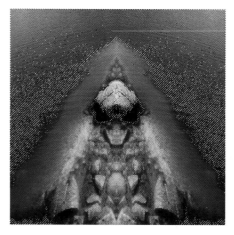

11. A selection made with Select By Color for out-of-gamut colors.

12. The out-of-gamut warning found in View. Out-of-gamut is determined by the values specified in the CMYK Color Settings, specifically the Yxy coordinates. Photoshop's default settings are for SWOP (Standard Web Offset Press). This warning will be inaccurate, overly conservative, for many digital printers. If you specify an accurate ICC profile for the output device, the warning will be accurate.

you decide to print to another output device that can take advantage of that richer information, you will not have removed it permanently. While it can lead to more predictable results, desaturating out-of-gamut colors before conversion has a disadvantage: the out-of-gamut colors may lose their relative relationship with the colors that are in gamut. The Perceptual rendering intent, used in a great many CMYK conversions, attempts to do this when an image's mode is converted. Regardless of whether the change is made before or after conversion, the image is changed to accommodate the narrower color gamut of the final output. Knowing what can occur, what to look for, and the various methods that can be used to control the transformation will serve you well.

All printing devices are not created equally. Each is unique. So it follows that the compensations necessary for each will also be unique. You will need to determine the specific conditions of your printer. If you are working with a service bureau,

the specialists there will be able to tell you how to configure the CMYK setup, give you an ICC profile or table to do this, or offer to make the conversion for you. As the conditions of a printer can change rapidly, you may be wise to do the latter.

If you are working with your own printer, you must learn to do this yourself. To perfect color management's capabilities you will need additional hardware (typically a spectrophotometer) and software to generate profiles from targeted output. Or, you can hire one of the many specialists who have arisen to fill the need for profiling services. They will profile a specific ink and paper combination printed on your printer.

This is an extreme distillation of a very complicated subject, a subject worthy of an entire book. And it's a subject that is constantly changing. To my mind, the definitive book has not been written. You may want to learn more. The struggle to reconcile the different opinions of knowledgeable professionals is worth the effort, even if it will not produce definitive answers.

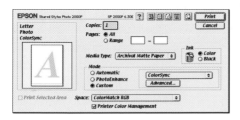

13. The Epson printing software interface.

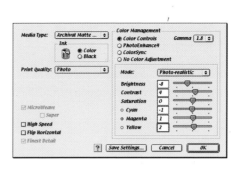

14. By moving to Custom and Advanced you can modify
the settings and further control the conversion to CMYK
and the process of RIPing the file.

Bruce Fraser and David Blatner's *Real World Photoshop* (which does the best job of making color science understandable) takes the new ICC color management route. Dan Margulis's *Professional Photoshop* (which does the best job of making classic prepress understandable) favors more traditional methods. All are highly respected professionals and deservedly so, yet their methods for dealing with the output of digital images differ. Neither system is perfect. Both systems require a breadth of knowledge. Those who sell color management would like you to think that it will solve color problems right out of the box. It will not. What's more, to fully take control of it, you will need access to additional hardware (spectrophotometers) and software (profiling), each of which typically costs more than Photoshop itself does (though this is changing rapidly), and understand the complexities of a Byzantine subject. Even then, if conditions change, you will need to reprofile, an arduous task (though it's becoming easier). Classic prepress methods require a first-hand knowledge of the final output conditions and the skill and experience to compensate for changing conditions, sometimes by the numbers rather than visually, which can only be acquired with time and patience. Both methods are capable of delivering excellent results. Which is best? The jury's still out. Many are not implementing the new color management; some

are. Neither method will eliminate the need for proofing. Both approaches need constant testing. Color management has certainly created more consistent color between separate monitors, applications, and platforms. It has reduced the number of proofs needed. It is far from perfect, but it is quite workable. I expect color management to improve, and to become easier and less expensive to control and to implement. At some point in the future it may be relatively invisible. Monitors, scanners, and printers may be self-profiling and able to implement color management without your having to dive headlong into it. The tide is with it. In the meantime, a knowledge of both will serve you well until the dust settles.

It takes a great deal of understanding and experience to control these factors skillfully. Whole books can and have been written on the subject. Even if you read those books, you would find that there is no substitute for experience. You do not need to know how to control every factor involved to produce quality images. It helps, but it's not necessary. You do need to know that these factors exist and how they function to better understand the process and communicate with those you work with or to solve your own problems as you encounter them. Half the battle is knowing the right question to ask.

12. OUTPUT II FILM

Film may be your final destination or your passport back to the conventional darkroom. You can make film from a digital file. LVT (Kodak's light valve technology) film recorders are capable of producing film that is every bit as good as traditionally captured film, and in some respects, better. Resolution for originals made with a film recorder are typically very high — at least 1500 PPI. It sounds daunting but remember film originals are typically much smaller than prints made from them, so file sizes (usually specified by a total pixel count rather

than megabytes or inches at a certain resolution) may be smaller than you think. Check with your service bureau (most will use a service provider as high-quality film recorders are extremely expensive) to make sure you are properly calibrated and that you have adequate resolution before creating files. Then treat the film recorder as you would any other printer. Remastering film with film recorders is typically costly and is limited in size, roughly $200 for an 8 x10 inch sheet of film. Once the film is output, treat it as you would treat any other film.

There is a more economical way to make negatives for monochromatic images: silver, platinum, cyanotype, or any number of alternative processes. Some of us, from time to time, use offset lithography film (the kind of film used for offset printing presses), typically for printing cards, posters, magazines, and books. Lithography film is significantly more economical than remastering with a film recorder, roughly $20 for an 8 x 10 inch sheet of film, and you can have film made in larger sizes. Though it is capable of producing results that look like continuous tone, this type of film employs a dot structure, most typically a halftone. As a result the negatives generated with this method are designed for contact printing and cannot be enlarged without the dots inherent in the film becoming pronounced.

Though it requires a great deal of testing of materials, once this is done, making film is relatively straightforward. The process is as follows.

1   Use your standard calibration settings.

2   Prepare all files as Grayscale TIFF files with a resolution of 400 PPI. Prepare them as you would prepare any other similar file.

3   Before sending them for output to film, apply a standardized compensation curve.

4   You may optionally place files into a page layout program such as QuarkXpress.

5   Specify a line screen ruling of 300 with an elliptical or round dot. (This is an exception to the rules, as normally you would prepare files at 600 PPI or twice the line screen ruling or lpi. Tests have shown little or no difference in quality between 600 PPI and 400 PPI files.)

6   Output the film.

7   Print the resulting film. Print for the minimum time to produce maximum black. Standardize your printing procedure by maintaining consistent paper, chemistry, exposure and development times. If your materials change, you will need to build another compensation curve.

There are a few pitfalls to overcome.

Film generated will not print like you see it on your monitor. To achieve this, you have to create a custom curve that will make a standard compensation (a Curve adjustment layer) for the discrepancy between what is seen on the monitor and what is printed. A precise curve will work for a majority of cases, but you may need to refine this for unusually challenging images. Once you apply this curve the image will not look right on your monitor. You hope that it will come out right once the resulting films are printed. So you must compensate by the numbers as you cannot trust what you see.

To generate this custom curve you have to test your materials.

Create a grayscale image with squares of tone that range from 0% to 100% that increase in density in increments of 5% (specify the percentages in the Color Picker and simply fill rectangular selections with the specified tone). Use the Type tool to note the numerical density of each square on the film. Use grayscale values. (The Info palette can be changed to display grayscale values. Use the submenu in the palette to find Palette Options. Or, on the Info palette, click the black triangle next to the eyedropper and select Grayscale from the dropdown menu.) Output that file on an imagesetter. Remember that not all service bureaus are created equally. Find one with a good reputation for quality and consistency.

Now, print the film you have generated with your desired paper chemical combination at a standard development time. Use the edge of the film to determine maximum black. You're testing the specific response of a film, paper and chemistry combination. Make sure you can repeat these variables since any subsequent deviation may render the tests inapplicable. If your paper chemistry combination changes you may need to change the films. You must isolate each of your variables to control them.

Use your test print as reference to create a custom curve that you apply to all subsequent images.

Measure (with the Color Sampler tool) and make note of the numerical values of a variety of tones throughout a photographic grayscale image you want to output. Visually translate the tones you see on your monitor into the values found on your test print. (Zone II may be represented by a 70% dot, Zone

III by a 60% dot, Zone IV by a 50% dot, Zone V by a 40%, Zone VI by a 30% dot, Zone VII by a 20%, Zone VIII by a 10% dot, and so on. These percentages are not exact and will differ based on your specific conditions.)

Compare these new numerical values with the numerical values used to generate the tones printed in your test print (squares of tone). Make special note of the ends of your scale, the points at which you cannot hold detail (white and black). For example, the paper/chemical combination I use for platinum printing allows me to hold a 3% dot and a 90% dot; a dot lighter than 3% will print as pure white and a dot heavier than 90% will print as maximum black.

Now create a curve that modifies the original values in the image to the projected values you have estimated. Using the Color Sampler Tool, you can allocate up to four separate measuring points and get numerical readings for each in the Info palette. Click to place a point. Hold the Shift key, click and drag to relocate a point. Hold the Option key, click and drag to delete a point. Note that each point will be numbered and have a separate readout. With these you can track the values of more than one area of a picture simultaneously. Place one in the highlights (quartertones), another in the midtones, and another in the shadows (three-quartertones). As you apply a curve as an adjustment layer, you will be able to see two values for each measuring point: the original value and the value as it is modified by the curve. The modified value should represent your visual estimate (based on your test strip) of the numerical values you need to achieve the desired tones.

If you guess correctly, the output will be correct. If you miss a little, you will need to refine your first assessment and generate another piece of film. Duplicate your first adjustment curve, turn the old one off, name and modify the duplicate appropriately, and make another test. Unless you're extraordinarily lucky, this will take several rounds. It can be an extremely frustrating

1. The image as seen onscreen before application of a custom curve and as a final print. It will print the way it looks on an LVT film recorder, which generates continuous tone film. It won't print the way it looks on an imagesetter, which generates halftones. It looks good but the offset litho film generated from this file will print poorly.

process to master initially. However, once you have the right curve, it will work for most subsequent images. After this initial period of adjustments, you'll find that working with new images will go much more smoothly.

As you work through this process take notes! I make multiple copies of an image either on a laser printer or a copier, and I consistently mark for easy reference the values of critical areas I find in the file that I use to generate each test print. I initially had to test an image over ten times. Even then, the curve generated didn't necessarily hold for other images. With successive refinements on multiple images, I now have a curve that works for a majority of images the first time. I test more than one curve at a time on a single sheet of film, usually two small versions of an image with two separate curves. I label each with a name (the image plus a, b, c, d, etc.) to note which

curve produced which film/print. Testing multiple versions of an image simultaneously saves time and materials. Again, finding the right curve becomes much easier if you take good notes throughout the entire process.

Once you find the right curve, apply it to a larger version of the image for final output. Simply drag the correct curve adjustment layer into the high-resolution file, placing it at the top of the layer stack. Flatten the image, save it as a TIFF file, and send it to the imagesetter for output to film. A specific curve can also be saved as a separate file (a very small file), kept in an appropriate folder for future use, and loaded into another image by opening Curves, clicking on Load, and selecting the saved curve. The two methods produce the same result.

It's a good idea to include a grayscale test strip in the border of your final image. It will help you assess the success of the

2. *The image as seen onscreen with a custom curve applied. It will print the way it looks on an LVT film recorder. It won't print the way it looks on an imagesetter. It looks bad but offset litho film generated from this file will print very well, and look like the image in Figure 1.*

conversion, determine printing times, and monitor changes in printing conditions.

There are two kinds of screens used in offset printing you should be aware of for this process: halftone and stochastic screens. A halftone screen places dots of varying size in a regularly spaced order. A stochastic screen places dots of the same size (typically smaller than the average halftone dot) in a random order. The random placement of the stochastic dot is less distracting to the eye than the regular placement of the halftone dot. The dot structure is more visible on coated paper stocks, such as silver gelatin paper. Uncoated paper stocks, such as the softer papers typically used in platinum printing, tend to obscure the dot as there is more dot gain. (The dot bleeds into the paper.) The dot structure is most visible in the highlights as only a very few widely spaced dots carry the information there.

Here again, stochastic screens may offer superior results as the dots are smaller. A higher line screen half tone dot may also do the trick. In darker areas of the image, the dots cluster — at times bleeding into one another — and are, as a result, less apparent.

There is less flexibility in printing offset litho negatives. Even given substantial over and under exposure, little change will be seen in the image. All you can do is produce a slight contraction or expansion of the dot size or fog the paper white to reduce its brightness. Print for maximum black. Should your chemistry change or you decide that a new interpretation of the image would be preferable, you will most likely need to make a new negative. The control is in generating the negative not in the printing. On the positive side, because offset litho negatives have so little latitude they print very consistently from session to session.

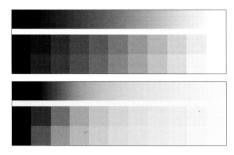

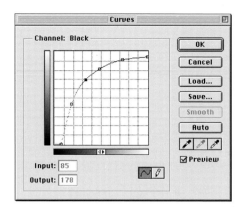

3. A test strip is generated and used as an aid for determining the correct custom curve. Here, tones are represented in 5% increments. Film is output on an imagesetter and a contact print is made. The resulting test print will demonstrate maximum and minimum printable percentages and which percentages will achieve specific tones. The first strips are what is seen on the monitor, the second are seen with the compensation curve and will print like the first. Inclusion of a graduated gray scale will help pinpoint uneven transitions.

4 . The custom curve used for a specific platinum paper/chemistry combination. The curve is built with the following input/output coordinates; 12/0, 46/111, 85/177, 126/208, 187/229, 255/246. You will need to customize a curve for your particular needs. A 10 (or more) point curve can be used for very precise control to target tone in 10 perecent increments. You might also include one point at both the minimum and maximum printable values.Either way, build smooth curves to avoid posterization.

Making digital contact negatives is similar to working in the traditional darkroom in some respects. You have to make a series of tests to control the final results. If your previous effort is not quite right you go back and test again until you get it right. The difference is that when you make digital contact negatives you make test negatives rather than test prints. If your film isn't right, no amount of darkroom wizardry will yield a satisfying print. The real control is in making the negative, not in making the print.

Never underestimate the value of working with a service provider who is consistent and does quality work. Inconsistent processing and dirty films are only two of the many factors that can impact the quality of the product they generate from you. If they're not consistent, your results won't be either. Without high-quality output from them, you will have a very difficult time achieving high-quality prints.

In an effort to exert more control themselves and to cut costs, some have used desktop inkjet and laser printers to output their films on various substrates such as acetate and mylar. Doing this is fraught with the perils of artifacting — banding, streaking, dust, noise — but it can be done.

For more information on this process, see Dan Burkholder's *Making Digital Negatives for Contact Printing*. His method differs slightly from the one I use.

To download grayscale test strips and compensation curves as starting points, see www.johnpaulcaponigro.com.

13. THE ELEMENTS OF PHOTOMONTAGE VISUAL SYNTAX

"To make others believe, we must believe ourselves." — *Gaston Bachelard*

Light, reflected light, color, atmospheric perspective, depth of field, linear perspective, texture gradient, overlap, scale, proportion, edge, noise, repetition, gravity, time. These are some of the fundamental aspects of an image that unite or separate the individual elements that

comprise it. They define relationships: relationships between individual elements and subsequently relationships between the image and the viewer. They are all part of an image's visual syntax. They are basic elements of visual language.

You might want to call these elements something else, and that's fine. Regardless of the nomenclature used, no one should be unmindful of them. A heightened awareness of each element in an image will make any work stronger. An understanding of these elements is necessary for all visual artists, not just those who are working with multiple images, but also those who are working with single images. Even the traditional photographer needs to be mindful of them, especially when making local corrections to an image.

You will inevitably begin to work with these elements, consciously or unconsciously. The more aware you become of them, the more you can control them. Ignored, they may become terrible menaces; attended to, they may become powerful allies.

DIRECTION AND
INTENSITY OF LIGHT AND SHADOW

No matter how complex the lighting situation, there is a consistent set of relationships within an image that defines the character of the light source or sources. Highlights within an image are generally generated from a single source, typically the sun, with an identifiable angle and intensity. So too are shadows. Shadows share a common density and will vary con-

sistently; their edges will grow softer and their densities lighter in proportion to the distance of the object casting them and the surfaces they are cast upon. They will grow lighter and darker depending on the intensity of the light casting them. There are many naturally occurring situations where multiple light sources are present. There may be reflected light, at times from multiple surfaces, or secondary light sources, such as fire. Whether it's found in the studio or in man-made environments, artificial lighting can become extraordinarily complex. While it may seem to work in mysterious ways, and it does, nonetheless, light works in consistent ways. If that consistency is undermined, relationship within an image is undermined.

When creating a composite image from multiple sources, the light within each piece must share similar qualities to enable an effective marriage. Create an image from multiple sources, where an object has a shadow cast upon it that falls in a different direction, does not conform to the object it is cast upon correctly, or has a different density or color than the shadows cast upon other objects throughout the rest of the image, and a unifying relationship will be disrupted. Those who do not make composite images will not be concerned with disparities in light but should be vigilant that local corrections do not create unwanted inconsistencies within the overall scene.

REFLECTED LIGHT

Light reflects off of surfaces consistently. A greater amount of light is reflected from shiny surfaces and a smaller amount from matte surfaces. A shiny surface, such as polished metal or a mirror, will change color entirely taking on the color of the surfaces it is reflecting. The color of a matte surface will only be modified, not transformed. Lighter surfaces are more reflective than darker surfaces. Make a portrait on a grassy lawn on a bright day and it is very likely that the face will contain green light reflected from the surface below it. Shadows in snow often carry the color of the sky above them.

If you introduce new elements into new environments, you should take care to make sure that the unity provided by reflected light is not missing. Traditionalists need to be mindful of making corrections that disrupt these shared relationships. As long as the changes made are made consistently, the picture will be consistent in its logic and thus be more convincing. Take care that shared light is not absent.

COLOR

Color has three basic components — hue, saturation, and brightness. Hue is the type of color (red, green, blue, etc). Saturation is the intensity of a color. Brightness describes how light or dark a color is. All three are interdependent. Change one and the others will change too, sometimes to lesser or greater degrees. Consider the complexity of color relationships between highlights, midtones, and shadows — one part the color of the object receiving the light, one part increased or reduced intensity of the light, and one part reflected light. Color is constantly changing as the position, intensity, and color of the light source changes. Despite its complexity, color changes in a consistent manner. As a result, there is a range of believability when correcting color (a larger range when working globally, a smaller range when working locally) or when combining color from separate sources.

Combine one element from a cold light source and another from a warm light source and the two will not appear to occupy the same reality; they will lack relationship. Similarly in a single image, if you correct one part of an image so that the light appears cold while the other remains warm, a disparity may be created that is too great to reconcile; the result may not seem realistic.

There are certain "memory" colors: sky blue, cherry red, lemon yellow, and flesh. All are very general specifications; they define a range of color rather than a specific color. Nevertheless, they are one factor in determining the realism of an image.

Different films see light differently. They impart different color biases to the information they record. Film, unlike our eyes, does not make compensation for different light temperatures. Film is optimized for a certain temperature (daylight, tungsten, etc.) and it will record all deviations from that temperature, whereas our eyes will adapt. (Many digital cameras have the ability to adapt to varying light temperatures, though some of these have difficulty handling mixed lighting situations.) As a result, the blue shadows seen in snow will look bluer on film than we remember them. It's not just that film may exaggerate the blue; some films will. It's also that our eyes will have adapted when looking at the snow and what is blue will seem less blue as a result. The question then arises: do you attempt to be objectively faithful to the situation or subjectively faithful to your experience of it. If the latter, what degree of subjectivity is desired? While it's true that the more subjective your approach to color, the greater your freedom; the situation may not be as open ended as you would think if your goal is to communicate with someone else. While color can be approached objectively, and it would behoove anyone working with it to know its science, color can also be approached subjectively, and it would similarly aid anyone working with color to also study its psychological dimensions (historically, culturally, cross-culturally, and personally). How you decide to correct color is in part a matter of your personal intention or philosophy.

ATMOSPHERIC PERSPECTIVE

The human eyes aren't far enough apart to see three-dimensionally at great distances. Binocular vision becomes monocular and the effects of parallax diminish as distance increases. Linear perspective and atmospheric perspective become essential for discerning spatial relationships. The principles of atmospheric perspective are relatively straightforward. Objects that are further in the distance appear to be cooler, less saturated, and contain less contrast. The effects of atmospheric perspective increase in climates where the atmosphere is thicker and decrease where it is thinner. In some cases where the buildup of atmosphere is very significant, objects may appear lighter as well.

Create a composite where an object that is to be read as far away has a higher saturation than the objects seen as being at a similar distance or than as objects seen as nearer to the viewer, and spatial relationships will be seen as inconsistent. Traditionalists routinely modify the effects of atmospheric perspective upon exposure with filtration. It is possible to modify those relationships after exposure. If you modify them, you should take care to do so consistently.

DEPTH OF FIELD

The human eye can focus at only one distance at one time. When we focus on objects very near to us, their background becomes out of focus and vice versa. This along with parallax, atmospheric perspective, scale, and overlap helps us determine distance relationships. The camera eye can have greater or lesser "depth of field" than the human eye. Whichever the case may be in a given image, the relative relationships of focus, how sharp or how soft, will be consistent. This consistency is linearly proportional. As long as that proportionality is maintained, the distance relationships within an image will be read as consistent.

One can control depth of field digitally to compensate for traditional limitations, to exaggerate spatial relationships, or to control the flow of the eye throughout an image. When compositing elements into new environments, their degree of focus should be based on the degree of focus found to represent similar spatial relationships.

LINEAR PERSPECTIVE

Codified during the Renaissance, linear perspective is a system developed for representing three-dimensional space on a two-dimensional surface. Straight lines appear to converge at a vanishing point, typically found at the horizon, as the distance between them, in reality a constant, appears to diminish.

To support the illusion of realism, transplanted objects should conform to the linear perspective of their new environments. You can make an exposure of the object at the correct perspective to begin with; alternately, you can correct the perspective digitally (image: transform: perspective or image: transform: distort). The latter has limitations. As our perspective changes, hidden parts of objects may be revealed. If those parts are not captured on film, no amount of correction will get them to materialize. Take an image of an object frontally. Then try and distort it so that it looks as if it was taken from the side. You can't do it. No frontal portrait is capable of producing a profile. The computer is marvelous at manipulating the information it is given; it is not as proficient at creating new information. Knowing what the computer is and is not capable of is a great advantage.

TEXTURE GRADIENT

Perhaps a separate category unto itself, perhaps a product of perspective, texture gradients also help determine space and distance. Close objects remain separate and distinct while objects further away tend to merge into a whole. Imagine a plain of sage brush: each plant is distinct before us but as the space recedes they merge into a single texture at the horizon. The texture gradient establishes a different visual rhythm, based on distance, even if the objects are the same.

OVERLAP

Another factor that helps us determine size is overlap. Objects closer to the viewer may overlap objects that are further away from the viewer, but it does not work the other way around. We have learned that when this happens the objects do not occupy the same space nor does one portion of an object replace another; we have learned that one is in front and the other is behind. Overlap is closely linked with scale.

This effect is so deeply ingrained in us that exceptions are rarely made unless it is for effect. The impossible cubes of M.C. Escher take full advantage of the disruption created when this rule is optically broken. Physically it is an impossibility. While transparency may challenge this tendency, we can almost always see a residual veil of the surface carrying the transparent effect.

SCALE

Objects closer to the viewer appear larger while objects further away from the viewer appear smaller. Two identical objects will appear equally large only if they are at equal distances from the viewer. Optical increases or reductions of size occur in direct proportion to the distance the viewer is placed from the object.

PROPORTION

Proportion can be thought of as a component of scale. Rather than relationships between separate objects, it can be used to describe relative relationships within a whole. If the distance from the ground to our navel is considered one unit, the distance from our navel to the top of our head tends to be .618 (the proportion 1 to .618 is the golden mean). Typically, with our arms hanging down, our hands reach to our mid-thighs. Longer or shorter lengths are atypical. We are more sensitive to the proportions of objects that we are familiar with. Objects that we are less familiar with offer greater latitudes.

EDGE

Light bends around the edges of objects. One can see the effects of light bending around objects in the soft outlines of shadows. Backlighting offers an extreme example where the outlines of the objects, sometimes in near silhouette, become very soft. Objects further from the viewer often have slightly softer edges than objects closer to the viewer. This can even happen with single objects — the contours close to the viewer will appear sharper than contours further away from the viewer. Part of this is based on how abruptly a given volume makes its transition from visible to hidden. Edges need to be handled sensitively to establish an optimal relationship between an object and its environment.

Far too often we see ultrasharp edges in composites. They look sharp, brittle, hyperreal. We also see the effects of edges that are too soft where the prior background of the imported element creates a divine and distractingly unreal halo. An awareness of the power of edge isn't just for compositors; the edge of a mask used for local correction should have an appropriate hardness or softness, or similar problems will arise.

NOISE

There is a relationship between resolution (the amount of information packed into a given area) and noise (the pattern not native to the information introduced by the structure carrying it, such as grain in film or pixels in digital files). Combine an image with great resolution and low noise (large format, less visible grain) and import it into an environment with lesser resolution and high noise (small format, more visible grain) and a disparity will be created. It will seem too sharp, too packed with detail, and lacking the noise found in adjacent areas of the image. Take an object shot with low resolution and import it into an environment with higher resolution and a disparity will be created. It will seem too soft, with less detail, and too much noise relative to adjacent areas in the image. Both cases are matters of texture. When texture doesn't match, the separate elements don't appear to occupy the same reality.

It may be possible to reduce the noise of the low-resolution image somewhat, generally not as much as we would like. It is, however, easy to accentuate the noise of a high-resolution image (Filter: Noise: Add Noise) to match the noise of a low-resolution image, though this is not always an attractive option. Unfortunately, in this case, the lowest common denominator often prevails. Those who don't composite need to watch this only when selectively sharpening an image.

REPETITION

Repetition is a clue to order. If repetition is created where no order is intended, it will be distracting. You may have seen the artifacts of a clumsy cloning job where the same area is cloned over and over again, sometimes forming stripes of similar information, sometimes creating many identical multiples of a single object. Symmetry is a form of repetition. Repetition is so formal that it calls attention to itself. It must be managed carefully. Its complement, variation, the absence of repetition, will make any repetition stronger.

GRAVITY

Although not visible itself, gravity affects us all. It determines up and down. It transforms matter. Some objects or surfaces are pliable. We are. Pliable objects display the effects of gravity. The visible effects of gravity need to be seen as if gravity is felt from a single direction for an image to be believable.

Objects imported into the new reality should also display the effects of gravity, effects consistent with those displayed by the other objects surrounding it. Imagine a figure with free flowing hair imported into a new environment. There are only a few possible angles that will display the effects of gravity before the prior effects of gravity become the presence of wind.

The shape of many objects, particularly living objects, changes under the influence of gravity. Think of the weight shift displayed by the human figure. We hold ourselves up against the effects of gravity, while a portion of us (often feet) becomes flat from supporting the weight of the rest of our bodies.

Place a new object onto a surface that is naturally yielding in a composite and the effects of weight should change the shape of the objects affected. A hand that touches flesh without that flesh giving way will seem to have made only a whisper of contact or the flesh touched will seem as hard as stone.

TIME

Also invisible and transformative, time binds things together. Like gravity, we can't see it but we can see its effects. We have learned to measure time in many ways. If we see one object in an image with more motion blur and the others surrounding it with less, we assume it is moving much faster than they are. If we see a clock at night that reads 10 a.m., we assume that the clock is mistaken, or broken, or the image is taken closer to one of the earth's poles during their winter season. Based on our previous experience, or what we have learned, we assume a great deal about the world around us and we expect images to uphold our expectations. We don't expect different historical eras, or the artifacts found in them, to coexist. We call them anachronisms. Granted, modern life is increasingly surreal. We are surrounded by anachronisms. Many conventional photographs derive their power from the effects of anachronism. But if they do so, in a majority of cases, the anachronism becomes the focus of the picture. The breach usurps the content of the image. Anythings out-of-synch stands out.

These principles can be employed equally by those whose aim is realism and by those whose aim is not. The conventional photographer and the photocompositor must be equally mindful of them. The montage artist will often employ them to different ends than the collage artist, but both will employ them. In both montage and collage, multiple sources are used to create a single image. In montage the disparity of the sources is invisible. In collage the disparity of the sources is visible, sometimes so much so that the whole is fractured into separate elements contained within a single area. In every case, unity and separateness are employed to create a visual statement. The elements of photomontage are part of the basic visual vocabulary we use to do so.

As a rule, if you are creating the illusion of realism, ask your viewer to suspend disbelief as little as possible. This rule, like any other, has its exceptions. You can make exceptions, and you can make them very effectively, but you would be wise to make them intentionally. Exceptions call attention to themselves. You can direct the viewer's attention to areas of importance by making exceptions, but if you overdo it the believability of your image will be disrupted. If not handled skillfully, the exception may become an intruder from another reality. The norm within an image is determined democratically, so to speak. If you change all but a small portion of an image consistently, the unchanged portion may appear to intrude on the whole. With knowledge comes freedom. Once you know the rules, you're free to break them. If you decide to break them, break them consciously and for effect.

Creating compelling images is often about striking up relationships. Strike up a compelling relationship between elements within an image and you greatly increase the chances of striking up a compelling relationship between the viewer and the image.

ADOBE PHOTOSHOP MASTER CLASS

CORE CHAPTERS

I Burn for You, The Sensual Land, 1997

I

EXTENDING FORMAT

A great plume of smoke trailed across the sky one morning, spreading from horizon to horizon. It slowly drifted and undulated through the vast blue empyrean above. The whole effect was breathtaking. Even lying on my back I could not take it in all at once. But, shifting my head, back and forth, I could. In my mind it was one great breath made visible. I was not content to break it into pieces. Fragments would not do. No one piece was as strong as the whole. It demanded to be whole.

My widest lens not being long enough, it took three shots to make one. At the seams of each exposure density varied slightly. A curve applied through a gradient mask provided sufficient compensation. I had not overlapped the separate images enough. A touch of perspective correction brought things into closer alignment. The remaining misalignment was removed by cloning information to restore a unified and unbroken field. In the end, it remained whole.

This photograph presents me with a wider view than I could see in any one instant but is faithful to the combined effect of my perceptions in several closely packed instants. In one sense, this image is super real in that it presents me with more information than I could see with my eyes at one time. In another sense it is surreal as the spatial relationships have been distorted in comparison to my perception and my physical or kinetic understanding of them has been removed from the final experience. The photograph presents more and less than my perception.

I find myself constantly struggling to expand the limits of my perception. The photograph is one aid in doing so. It holds single moments still for further contemplation. In those moments all things can be equally clear. Some photographs even represent what I cannot or could not see. Certain photographs can grasp both front and behind, both before and after, and place them side by side for simultaneous comparison. Photography expands my perceptual horizons. And yet, not being the same thing as the process of seeing, but rather a record of it, the photograph can never duplicate the seen or the experience of seeing. Instead, it offers a unique experience, with qualities all its own. There is always a gap between the original experience and the record. Some might see this as a flaw, an inevitable imperfection. I choose to see it as a powerful reminder, one capable of clarifying the nature of the observed, the observer, and the process of observing.

Some feel wide-angle vision is truer to human vision. With two eyes we scan the whole wide world, through time, continually updating the information we receive in a never-ending stream of sensation. While we mentally compensate for its effects, we see in dynamic perspective, where lines are slightly curved, rather than in linear perspective, where lines are perfectly straight. By comparison, the camera eye is generally single and fixed, capturing information in a single moment with a definite beginning and end. Many lenses "correct" perspective, making lines appear perfectly straight or "true". True to what? Our perceptions, our measurements, or our preconceptions? When talking of perception, the answer we fix on depends on whose vision we are discussing, as many individuals physically deviate from the norm. Some have greater peripheral vision, some less. Some have one eye. Moreover, even if our eyes were all the same, we would use them differently. Individuals fix their attention uniquely, some wide, some narrow. Few, if any, conform to the norm exactly; this depends on how tight the tolerances are set, but the abilities of the great majority hover around its assigned characteristics. As many have an urge to see more widely, they likewise have an urge to make images that present wider visions.

Photographers have been using a variety of techniques to create panoramic images since the invention of photography.

One way is extremely basic. Pull further away from the subject and crop. This method yields a smaller format, and grain or resolution can become an issue.

Extremely wide-angle lenses are available. These may cause some distortion. Straight lines become curved. The amount of distortion increases in proportion to how far away from the center of the image subjects are.

There are panoramic cameras which move, sweeping across a broad area to capture a single image. Typically these show less distortion. Some panoramas even show us three hundred and sixty degrees of space bounded by a border. Many find this disorienting, that the left side of a two-dimensional image could represent what's in front of us while the center represents what's in back of us and the right side represents what's in front of us again. To overcome this, a few such images have been presented as closed loops that the viewer must step into and rotate to see. However they are presented, they make intriguing images.

Another way of making panoramic images is to make multiple exposures of a single scene, print them, and by displaying them side by side present them as a single image. These diptychs and triptychs are a rich part of our visual heritage. We learn to read multiple images side by side as both separate and single instants. We mentally extrapolate what the image would be like without seams and without discrepancies in perspective. The resulting images are more challenging as they require greater skills of interpretation and selective attention. There are certain ways in which they better represent our visual process and our experience of the world, which itself is mentally composited from many separate instants and sometimes many angles. The work of David Hockney certainly makes this point by taking it to an extreme. We don't see his photographs as more real than traditional photographs made singly, but in certain respects Hockney's many photographs are more true to our experience.

If you have neither a panoramic camera nor a wide enough angle lens, but would like to make an image that encompasses more of what you see than your equipment will

1. North.

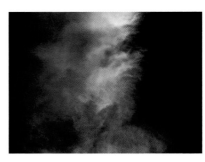

2. Overhead.

3. South.

4. North to south.

107

allow, you can resort to the method of taking several shots and compositing them into a single image, with or without seams and discrepancies in perspective. While this method effectively increases your format, providing a tighter grain structure or higher resolution, problems can easily arise if not carefully prepared for.

The primary problem is one of perspective. In a single image there is one horizon line and often a single vanishing point. If a single image is created from multiple images, each image will have a different vanishing point. As a result, information at the edges of the images may become misaligned. This is particularly apparent in photographing something rigidly geometric, such as architecture.

The effects of perspective between separate exposures can be minimized if the exposures taken overlap each other substantially. An overlap of twenty percent will work well for most focal lengths, but this figure will need to be increased with wider angle lenses, up to fifty percent in some cases.

You must be careful not to introduce other problems into an already complex situation. If you don't keep the camera parallel to its original position as it is moved or panned, additional rotation will be introduced. More cropping, possibly even cloning, will be necessary. While holding steady can be done with a hand-held camera if managed carefully, for best results use a tripod and a level, keeping the camera aligned along on a consisent plane of rotation. Center the point of rotation on the lens, rather than on the camera, or the tripod.

You may want to bracket exposures as tonal values may shift when the relative direction of the light changes. You can make adjustments through gradient masks to overcome the great majority of discrepancies in tone and color between separate exposures.

If discrepancies in perspective still persist, you can shift the perspective (Edit: Transform) of the individual images to realign the information at the overlapping seams. This will change the angle of the top borders, bottom borders and sides. Cropping may be necessary. In most instances you will want to use the perspective effect; however, there may be times when the distort effect (Edit: Transform) allows greater precision, although it is easier to get into trouble with it if you are not careful. In any case, it is a good idea to determine the vanishing point of the resulting image in advance and draw guidelines for reference while working. If you need a guideline that Guides will not provide, for instance a diagonal line, you can draw one on a separate layer with the line tool. Even a path can create a useful guideline.

Finally, if discrepancies still persist between the separate images, you can use the Rubber Stamp tool to redraw information along the seams. If your intent is to document a historical moment or a scientific fact, this method may not be acceptable depending on the type of information to be redrawn. If this is not the case, greater liberties may be taken. We are afforded greater flexibility with random patterns, highly textured fields, and organic information, such as texture on a rocky plain, particularly if the subject matter is unfamiliar. Rigidly organized or very linear subject matter is less forgiving. The traces of our work are better hidden in fields of disorder.

This technique is very difficult, sometimes impossible to employ if a fast moving object enters the scene. The same object may appear in both frames, or in two places at once. The time overlap between frames presents an obstacle that may or may not be insurmountable.

Your focus of attention, I do not mean where your image is focused but rather where you are looking, will alter the results. Keep your eyes fixed on the horizon throughout the exposures; don't simply move but rather rotate, and the horizon will remain constant while the information around it shifts. Keep your eyes fixed on a single point, the primary vanishing point, rotate and move so that the primary vanishing point remains constant in each exposure and information will shift around it. Your attention fixes things amid a set of constantly changing relative visual relationships.

You may or may not want to hide the artifacts of your working process. Some will want to hide seams and correct discrepancies between successive exposures. Others will not.

If you are aware of the technical problems involved in advance, you will be better able to compensate for them, both before and after the moment of exposure. Similarly, if you are aware of the visual problems involved, you will be better able to find new solutions. The new solutions may ultimately be as interesting, at times even more interesting, than attempts to make the new look like the old.

Not all extensions of format are panoramic. If a composite of multiple images results in a larger image than either of the images presented singly, format has been extended.

METHOD

1   Shoot a subject using multiple exposures. Rotate around the center of the lens, typically parallel to the horizon. Make sure there is adequate overlap between frames and that the base of the camera remains parallel in each exposure.

2   Composite the separate images. Make each image a separate layer in a single document on a canvas large enough to encompass all of them.

3   If necessary, make corrections to perspective (Edit: Transform: Perspective or Distort).

4   If necessary, make corrections to tone, color, and saturation with adjustment layers. Then employ gradient masks for smooth transitions.

5   If necessary, use the Rubber Stamp tool to retouch discrepancies that cannot be compensated for in another way.

Procession i, Elemental, 1999

II

SCALE

Optics can be deceiving. In *Procession i*, what seems massive is miniscule. The separate monoliths are a single pebble, no larger than a fingernail. I dwarf them/it, yet in this image they hover over a landscape dwarfing rocks that dwarfed me. When looking at this image we infer that the separate stones maintain a constant size and recede in space, not that rocks of varying size are slightly higher and lower than one another. Their linear placement helps reinforce this assumption but even if they were not placed linearly we would try to make this inference. If you look closely you will discover that we haven't got enough information to determine their exact sizes, so the best we can do is assume that they are of roughly equal size, an assumption that is confirmed by the close similarity of the two largest monoliths. This helps confirm relative scale within the image but it does little to confirm the scale of the objects relative to objects outside the image. Here we can only guess. Nonetheless, our guesses are limited to a general range. Everything in the image could be tiny, a collection of pebbles, but it's more than likely that it's relatively grand. A human figure might fit neatly on the small path in the dust, still it's fairly certain that it's not gigantic; the monoliths are not the size of skyscrapers. Overlap or abutment would help make relative size relationships more specific. Adding a recognizable object with an easily identifiable scale would give certain confirmation. Lacking that, we make an assumption, one that is easily called into question, to fix the relationships within the image or else the relationships remain fluid; they oscillate based on interpretation. As well as defining relative size, scale also helps define relative position. The placement of the monoliths relative to the ground is similarly ambiguous. The closer to us we imagine the monoliths to be the smaller they seem, the further away the larger they seem. Again there is a general range of possibilities but no one definitively fixed size.

I've always enjoyed distortions in scale. Whether they embody a subjective response, wish fulfillment, or optical illusion, all are interesting to me. While I spend a great deal of time ascertaining the objective sizes of things and the spaces between them, my experience of size always seems elastic. No size ever appears fixed. The further the object is from me the smaller it seems. The closer it is to me the larger it seems. I look to the horizon and see a tiny mesa. I drive towards it; it grows. Once I'm there, it's huge. Previously I seemed large, now I seem small. Is something large or small? Compared to what? From what perspective?

Scale helps define space. It's no mistake that I am fascinated by it. I spend hours looking at tiny details in nature. Isolated pockets seem like whole worlds unto themselves, worlds within worlds. I spend hours looking at the ocean, the desert, and the sky. These vast territories can seem abstract, flat, at times small. As I hold my hand up to the sky, it obscures a cloud or a galaxy. Alternately these places can seem overwhelmingly spacious, deep, and enormous. Physically enter any one of these places and the more that time passes the greater they seem. I dwarf and am dwarfed.

SIZE MATTERS

"Perception is relative: We see relationships."
— *Richard D. Zakia*

"Illusions are perceptual realities."
— *Rashid Elisha*

Closely linked with perspective, scale tells us not only about relationships in size but also relationships in space. Size and distance are intimately related. It is difficult to perceive one without the other.

The representation of three dimensions on two-dimensional surfaces has had a long and interesting history. The art of many primal cultures casts aside the effects of distance on size, maintaining instead the relative sizes of objects as seen at the same distance. It prioritizes one kind of information over another. Ancient Chinese paintings quite often downplay the effects of distance on size favoring vertical relationships to indicate spatial relationships. How far up or down an object lies on the page determines how far or how close it is meant to be read: higher signifies further away in space from the viewer. In ancient Egyptian images, size is used as an indicator of importance. The larger the object the more important it is. In their visual language it was clear to the reader, by convention, that smaller objects or people were not miniature but rather of a lesser status. Many such images relied on overlap to indicate position in space. Objects on top are read as being closer hiding portions of the objects they partially obscure, but they do not replace the unseen portions. Now, the dominant mode of representation, Western linear perspective, marries many of the conventions of the past. In linear perspective, a substructure of a grid is superimposed on images. A horizon line and a vanishing point are established at eye level. Vertical parallel lines optically converge at this point. The further away they are the smaller the distance between the two appears, yet it is still expected that an equal amount of space is contained between the two lines. Similarly the distance between equally spaced horizontal lines appears to consistently diminish as space recedes. Objects closer to the viewer overlap objects further away; the unseen portions are not replaced or eliminated but merely hidden. Closer objects appear larger, further objects appear smaller, but the objects that appear smaller may in fact be of equal or greater size than the objects that appear larger. The effects of time and motion add a fourth dimension to this system seen in moving pictures. Slow moving objects are interpreted as further away than fast moving objects.

Prior to global Westernization, linear perspective was not the most widespread visual vocabulary for representing scale. The now dominant Western method of representation is actually a relatively recent invention. For many the camera eye offers proof of its veracity and superiority. Yet it can be useful to be mindful that its strength is in making certain kinds of documents. It represents one way of seeing. It is not the only way. There are other ways of seeing. And there are other kinds of documents that can be made; they can even be made with a

1. Lacking comparison, scale is ambiguous.

2. Constant size and spacing, bases aligned horizontally. There is no reduction or recession.

camera. While there have been many vocabularies for representing space, scale has been a part of each. Even if it has been ignored, the omission is deliberate and intentional.

Comparison is essential for every system of representation. Without comparison there is little or no information to make a visual assessment with. Place an object on a blank background and there is no context to make a relative judgement about the object's size. We either accept the size of the image as the size of the object it represents or we make inferences. When we have nothing else to test our observations against, we are thrust into making assumptions about the object based on our previous experiences. Habitually we tend to filter our perceptions to organize them into a useful standard. To do so we make comparisons, inferences and assumptions. If we lack sufficient experience or information, the image and possibly even the experience remains ambiguous.

There's a lot of guesswork involved in seeing. Seeing may be a separate matter from perception. One offers processed interpreted information; the other offers unprocessed raw data.

There's a great deal of ambiguity in many relationships of scale. How many times have we guessed that something was big or small, been wrong, and had to readjust? We do it automatically. We cast aside the impressions that don't fit our current paradigm. Most of the time we're right. If we are left feeling uncertain, we make the best guesses we can but continually try to find more information to confirm or deny our suspicions. This is natural.

If we simply look at our raw unfiltered perceptions, the world may look surprisingly strange and simultaneously we may be surprised by how many things we take for granted and how many assumptions we make. It's magic when we deliberately break with our training and simply observe the optical

3. Overlap with equal size.
Less recession is implied.

4. Overlap with varying size.
More recession is implied.

impressions we receive without interpreting them. It can be very revealing to momentarily suspend and later to extend the process of perception and interpretation.

Ruptures in traditional representations of scale may create such momentary suspensions. Surrealists often capitalize on distortions of scale to shock the rational mind into a new way of thinking. The strategy still works. Ironically our world is getting more and more surreal. It seems we have to work harder and harder to shock these days. We're so used to being shocked, it takes a great deal more to shock us now than it did before. A common by-product of disruption is humor. The bizarre or fantastical can seem absurd. Nonsense can be funny. Nonsense can also be insightful. While certain disruptions ask us to reconsider our assumptions about reality, some reflect hidden connections, relationships that may be sensed but not yet articulated. This, unlike the disruption of convention, is one

kind of surprise that I think will never become dated, one we will never grow numb to or tired of, for it indicates the presence of insight which changes us.

It is interesting, perhaps even predictable, that reduction has not received as much attention as enlargement in modern times, at least not in the fine arts. In the crafts and in the lives of many young people, it has almost certainly received more attention. How many children favor life-sized or larger-than-life-sized dolls or doll houses? Miniaturization is a large part of our lives. Think of the drastic changes in size electronic devices undergo from year to year. Precedents aside, the psychological effects of such disruptions are indeed fascinating to observe.

It may well be that obvious ruptures of scale encourage entrance into imaginal realms. Children particularly appreciate ruptures in scale. Children value these internal realms far more than adults do. To my mind this is not lack of sophistication or

5. Varying size and spacing, bases aligned horizontally producing abutment. Reduction is implied.

6. Varying size, constant spacing, bases aligned horizontally. Reduction and recession are ambiguous.

maturity; it's an insistence on maintaining a rich and spirited life. Sure, there's danger in confusing the subjective and the objective worlds, but most children know the difference. Yet the boundaries between the two remain far more elastic for them. They dare to dream, to hope, to challenge limits, and in the process they usually end up looking at the world with more open eyes and have fresher outlooks.

What child hasn't imagined that he or she is gigantic (an elephant) or miniature (a bug)? I'm sure this impulse goes far deeper than a desire to be seen or not to be seen. In part it's a matter of establishing our objective relationship with the world. In part it's a matter of understanding the world sympathetically. In part it's a matter of exploring our subjective relationships with the world, how we feel or would like to feel about it. What if? What if can be a serious, meaningful, even insightful game. Sympathetic understanding aside, if we catch

ourselves in the act, a great deal may be revealed about ourselves and about what we assume about the world outside us. At times shocking, the gap between the desired and reality, the gap between the known and reality, the gap between appearance and reality is challenging, revealing, even astonishing.

William Blake remarked, "If the doors of perception were cleansed, man would see everything as it is, infinite." Fractal geometry reveals many truths that were previously sensed but not confirmed as well as many new insights and lines of inquiry. A river delta may reflect the structure of a tree. We are surrounded by a host of curious correspondences. Patterns abound. One of the interesting things about fractals is that the smallest parts of the geometric forms reflect the shape of the largest parts or the whole. At very high magnifications the structure of matter begins to resemble the heavens surrounding us. Macrocosm is contained in microcosm. Microcosm is

7. Varying size and spacing, bases aligned
horizontally. Recession is implied.

8. Varying size and spacing, bases aligned on
diagonal. Recession is strongly implied.

contained in macrocosm. Scale is a deep well to draw from.

Imagine the possibilities.

The methods for rescaling an image, or a portion of an image, in Photoshop are the essence of simplicity. Resizing things digitally is a matter of having more or less pixels. You can accomplish this in one of two ways.

One, scan an image or a portion of an image to the desired final size and composite it into another image, either the original image it was taken from or another image altogether. This is a matter of changing the resolution at which the scan is made, nothing more. Then simply make the two documents one by dragging the background layer of one into the other. You can predict how large the imported image is by calculating how many pixels it has and comparing it to the image it is imported into. (Import 1000 pixels into a 4000-pixel document and the new information will be 1/4 as large.) A file can only

have one resolution. A pixel is a pixel. In terms of size, all pixels are created equally.

Two, select and rescale the information within the selection outline (Edit: Transform: Scale). This will resample the selected portion of the image. Photoshop will perform complex averaging schemes to calculate a new pixel structure that resembles the original as closely as possible. In the case of reduction, little or no quality is lost. In the case of enlargement, past a certain point, quality will begin to degrade. You can avoid this by rescanning the image, or a portion of an image, at a higher resolution.

If you make an object larger, it will automatically obscure new areas of the image. No gap will be left. However, if you make an object smaller within a single image, a void will be left where the edges of the object previously lay. Two-dimensional images contain no information where objects overlap one

116

another. To maintain the illusion of realism, you must fill the void with acceptable substitute information that seamlessly blends in with the object's background. Very often such information will be found in adjacent areas of an image. At times similar information from another image may be an acceptable substitute. If you know at the time of capture that you intend to rescale an object, you may make another exposure of the information behind the object. Moving objects make this very easy to do as you can maintain the same vantage point and make a second exposure once the object has moved enough to reveal the information that was previously behind it.

Make a portion of an image or an object within an image larger. Make a portion of an image or an object within an image smaller. Make an object significantly larger than we are used to seeing it. Make an object significantly smaller than we are used to seeing it. Place two or more like objects together and significantly alter the scale of one or more of the objects. If scale is defined by comparison between an object and its environment, reducing the object or enlarging the environment (or vice versa) will accomplish the same thing.

While the method is simple, the potential locked within the visual strategies of altering scale are extraordinarily powerful and frequently overlooked. Enlargements and reductions within an image need not be obvious to be effective. Sometimes a subtle tipping of the scales produces significant results.

METHOD

1   Select an area of an image. Rescale it (Edit: Transform: Scale). Drag a corner out to make the selected area larger, and drag a corner in to make the selected area smaller. Hold the Shift key while rescaling to maintain proportion. To do so you must hold the Shift key before your first move as holding the Shift key afterward will simply retain the proportions of the newly distorted image. Hold the Option key to scale from the center point. Move the center point to scale from another point in the image.

It's likely that you will want to copy the area to be scaled onto a new layer. Simply copy and paste it. Then rescale this new layer, rather than the background layer. This will build in a safety net should you wish to restore the original image to its untouched state. And it's easy to compare the original version with the new by turning the new layer off and on, or bypass the clipboard.

No retouching is required if objects are enlarged. However, if objects within a single image are reduced, a gap of information will be left in the background. New information may be cloned into these areas from surrounding areas or from a separate exposure with similar information.

2   Alternately, copy new image material from another document into a final source document. (Click on and drag the background layer from one document into another. Hold the Shift key while dragging to place it in the center of destination document.) Use a layer mask to hide unwanted information. If you are sure you will never want to use the additional information, remove it; select and delete it, use one of the erasers or use the Extract command. I favor not removing additional information close to the boundary line of the object, preferring instead to hide it with a layer mask as I find edge treatment is more malleable this way and future freedom is preserved should changes become necessary. Rescale the resulting layer.

In general I favor scanning an image at maximum resolution and transforming images (or areas of an image) by reducing them rather than enlarging them. This avoids artifacts attributable to upsampling.

Sonata in Blue i, Elemental, 1998

I I I

PROPORTION

I find myself drawn to extremely simple compositions. This composition is bare bones simple. I think of it as a straight line. One less line and there would be no composition. I continue to do many preparatory sketches for this series. There is a set of drawings that consists of a single line that rises and falls, each marking a different set of proportions. Those same proportions are used in pastels where two colors are paired: often the same color but varying in tone, sometimes two colors made from the same underlying color, sometimes two very different colors. I'm particularly attracted to color unity, colors that are similar or share a common foundation. Small shifts in color can produce large shifts in emotion. For me this is the visual equivalent of searching for musical chords. Some of the first preliminary studies I keep on my piano where sheet music ordinarily rests. These images are visual sheet music. The series are musically titled: Sonatas, Nocturnes, Preludes, Etudes, Variations, Impromptus. I use the exercise and the pieces generated to watch my emotional response to these basic elements. I can't say what they mean. I wouldn't care to pin one meaning on them. Like music, blue is an experience, a state of being. So too is a set of proportions. I believe if a group of people were to share their associations that, among a set of unique and highly personal descriptions, many correspondences would nevertheless be found.

I experimented with many sets of proportions. How much sky with how much water? How wide, how tall? I experimented with traditional proportions — 1 to 1, 1 to 2, 1 to 3, the proportions of the Golden Section — then I let my intuition guide me. I placed all the variations side by side and looked for the one image that had the right ring to it. When an image works I often feel a vibration inside, the stronger the image the stronger and clearer the vibration. Finally I settled on this combination. I'm sure that without the presence of the streams of water and cloud I would have chosen a different set of proportions. They would change if the color or the combination of colors were different. The addition of each element modifies the total effect. Everything has its effect on the whole. Nothing is without significance.

It is, perhaps, not coincidental that these images are so much about proportion. A proportion will hold no matter how large or small it is reproduced. On a monitor (17" diagonally, 9.5" high, 12.5" wide representing the image at 72 PPI as a guide for a much larger 20" x 24" print at 300 PPI), I can directly experience proportion but I can't directly experience the scale of the final piece. I have to make an educated guess as to what its effect will be. Sometimes I will have to change the scale of an image upon seeing the first proof.

There's an impulse to strip things down to their bare essentials, to fundamentals, in much of my work. I've always been attracted to images that were at once literal and abstract. Any image is both. We "believe" in its depth (this is a knowing, if at times unconscious, suspension of disbelief), but we know it's flat. These surfaces are literal and abstract. The image would be even more abstract without pattern. I was attracted to the echo in the patterns between the heavenly and the oceanic.

They're so close in color they could almost be made of the same substance. I've seen many seascapes where the boundary between the two is imperceptible. The ambiguity is tantalizing.

Fixing the horizon line in an image is an interesting phenomenon. The horizon line is a virtual image like a rainbow. It moves as the viewer moves. It's never fixed. Consequently we have a difficult time proving it exists. But we experience it; we know our experience exists. We can't say for certain how real the world we perceive is, but we can say with certainty that our experience of it is real to us.

Is this image one photograph or two? Which set of proportions are the "real" ones? I think the questions are more important than the answers. They lead us to other questions. How do we know what we know? If the searching process continues, it helps the life of the image to continue. Once the question has been answered the searching often stops. Then the image has a tendency to become a solved equation rather than a living thing. I think it's important to make visible our assumptions, our questions, our interpretative processes. This fosters consciousness, a greater awareness of ourselves and the world around us. Knowing how the image was produced, I have an even greater challenge than the viewer to keep that process of searching alive. The process of communicating, sharing, the conversations I have with viewers, helps me do this.

Both the passage of cloud and water speak to me of the presence of the unseen. These are the residues of unseen forces. I continue to ask questions. What moved to create them? Did one force create them both? How separate are they? What's beneath the surface of the water? What's behind the blue veil of the sky? What's outside the frame? Are these all the visible traces of the breath of heaven? Reading the image is important for me. The psychologist James Hillman uses the phrase "animating the image." I think this is an extremely important process. Looking is a process for me and today's insights are enriched by tommorrow's. My vision evolves as an artist and so does my ability to see the world and my own work. I would not want to fix a single interpretation. I hope the viewer will continue the process of reading the image.

1. The proportion 1:1.618. Both sky and water are changed.

2. The proportion 1:1.

3. The proportion 1.618:1. Both sky and water are changed.

"You amuse me, you who seem worried that I impose impractical studies upon you. It does not only reside with mediocre minds, but all men have difficulty in persuading themselves that it is through these studies, as if with instruments, that one purifies the eye of the soul, and that one causes a new fire to burn in this organ which was obscured and as though extinguished by the shadows of the other sciences, an organ whose conservation is more important than ten thousand eyes, since it is by it alone that we contemplate the truth."

— Plato

Give a dozen highly accomplished photographers the same camera, the same film, and the same subject. At the end of the day, one thing, though not necessarily one thing alone, will surely separate their work — each individual will display a unique sense of proportion. Paul Strand had an indelible sense of proportion. Combined with an unusual sense of composition, many of his images are subtly and beautifully imbalanced, his classically straight images become unmistakeable. Forget the signature, the sensibility is the ultimate authentication; it leaves a far more lasting impression. One doesn't need to know how to read it to be affected by it.

Proportion has long been understood as a pillar upon which many of the arts are built. Music and architecture are two. A twelfth century reform movement, the Cistercian Order, combined both in breathtaking ways. St Augustine suggested that the two art forms responded to the same principles. Feeling that music and geometry were powerful meditative devices, St. Bernard put "Geometry at the service of prayer," declaring, "There must be no decoration, only proportion." Strict geometric proportions were employed in the construction of Cistercian

4. The proportion 1:1.618. The sky's proportion remains fixed.

5. The proportion 1:1.33. The sky's proportion remains fixed.

6. The proportion 1:1.11. The sky's proportion remains fixed.

monasteries and abbeys. Typically musical ratios were used: the octave (1 to 2), the fifth (2 to 3), and the fourth (3 to 4). The results are stunning "sounding boards" that are acoustically magnificent. In them the tiniest infant sounds like an angel.

Proportion asks the all important question of how much and how little. It's a measurement of relationship.

Proportion can be and has been redistributed in astonishing ways. Now there is one more way, a very powerful way.

What we do with this new-found power will depend on our intentions. Purists may simply be interested in making documents that are more objectively faithful to their original experience. They'll close the gap between the traditional photographic document and their perception. Others may be fascinated by the expressive potential of differing proportions. While some are dismayed by distortion within photographic images, others are thrilled by it. Think of the works of Andre Kertez and Bill Brandt.

It is wise to consider our intentions carefully. They determine the questions we ask, the answers we get, and ultimately the reality we participate in creating. Accepting conventions handed down by tradition, or not, is a choice which is best made consciously.

Anthropocentrism and familiarity can be our guides as to how much distortion an object will support before it no longer appears realistic. Man and familiar animals support the least amount of distortion. (Though many prefer it when their portrait is distorted very slightly to make them look thinner. Perhaps this is flattery, perhaps it is a compensation for the "ten pounds" the camera adds.) Man-made objects support more, particularly if they have not been the subject of widespread scrutiny. Unfamiliar terrains support the most, particularly those that are abstract and changeable, such as sea and sky. Of course, if you are willing to depart from realism, the possibilities are staggering.

There may be very good reasons why we accept many interpretations of proportion as realistic and prioritize other

7. *The proportion 1:1.11. The water's proportion remains fixed.*

8. *The proportion 1:1.33. The water's proportion remains fixed.*

9. *The proportion 1:1.618. The water's proportion remains fixed.*

elements before it. Motion makes our experience of proportion quite fluid. As we move, our experience of proportion is continually being updated whether we are conscious of it or not. Our experience of proportion is not as fixed as we would like to think it is. We fix it through observation. Strangely, once fixed we may trust our unchanging records more than our changing experience of it. We have a choice to anchor our point of view in measurement, abstracting a fixed truth, and let the chaos of our sensory experience operate on an unconscious level, or to make conscious our raw unmediated experience. The latter can be disorienting. It may lead us to a destination where cultural consensus is disrupted. Nonetheless, in this state of mind we may find fresh and compelling answers. Consider the "truth" of our phenomenological experience of proportion. Consider the potential of a subjective interpretation of proportion. Consider letting images be music to your eyes.

Cultivating a heightened awareness of the power of proportion will be a great boon to anyone who is visually oriented.

METHOD

1   Select an image (or an area of an image). Redistribute its proportion (Edit: Transform: Scale). Do not hold the Shift key while rescaling the image; doing so will maintain the current proportions. To apply a change, press Return, or to return to the undistorted image, press Escape instead.

In general scan an image at maximum resolution and transform images (or areas of an image) by shrinking them rather than expanding them. This will maintain the best possible image quality.

This technique is the essence of simplicity; its extraordinary power is, surprisingly, overlooked.

Ascent, Rites of Passage, 1994

IV

EXTENDING DYNAMIC RANGE

I had no intention of making a finished photograph when I made the basic exposure for Ascent. I was shooting transparency film and I knew I couldn't adjust my exposure and development times to maintain information in both the highlights and the shadows as well as I could have with black-and-white film. If I exposed for the shadows, the sky would have lost a tremendous amount of information. Similarly, I'd lose important information if I exposed for the highlights. So I made an average exposure. The highlights were too light and the shadows too dark. But I had no intention of making a finished photograph. I was making reference for a drawing. It worked well for that.

What I didn't know is that I would also make a finished photograph from it. I was able to do so by making two scans of the same original. The film had more information in it than was visible to the eye. A single scan would not have revealed all the available information. By scanning once for the shadows and once for the highlights and combining the best information from both, I was able to extend the printable range of a single piece of film and the range of capture of the scanner. Had the exposure been too contrasty for the film to capture the data scanning twice would not have worked.

I often say digital technique is no substitute for traditional technique. Why take the long and complicated way when the short and simple way will work? Yet on occasion the new freedom digital technology affords has saved an image or two, maybe three, or I should really say, it has made them possible. It has certainly changed the way I photograph. If I had known then what I know now, I would have made a very different exposure — actually I would have made two. Instead of exposing for the shadows and developing for the highlights, I would have exposed once for the shadows and once again for the highlights. Two pieces of film can, at times, do more than one. By combining the best information from both exposures, you extend the range of capture of film. You can do this for any type of capture, conventional or digital.

Now I use transparency film for all my needs. I expect one day soon I won't be using film at all. Yet I make a variety of types of prints — silver, platinum, giclée. Now, more often than not, I make multiple exposures to create a single image, even in situations where I intend to make a "straight" photograph. When the range of my materials fails me I take two shots, one for the shadows and one for the highlights. You can use one medium to overcome the limitations of the other. It reminds me of the saying, "Compromise is where one and one makes one and a half. Synergy is where one and one make three."

"The chief problem (of making a photograph) is to preserve the illusion of light falling upon the subject.
A print intended to convey an emotional impression may differ from a normal photographic record. You must
visualize the final expressive print, expose for the desired value of the shadows, and control the
high values by development."
— *Ansel Adams*

We have all encountered situations when the limits of our materials determine the information we capture, or force us to make a calculated sacrifice. This type of situation usually arises when the range of light we are trying to capture, sometimes color, is too great for the capture medium to encompass — eight zones for transparencies, nine for negatives versus all that our eyes can see. I resist using the word film and defer to capture medium, for there have been other forms of capture before film, paper and glass are two, and there are new forms arising that are likely to surpass and replace film in the future.

This disparity is in part due to the greater sensitivity of our eyes and in part due to the fact that our eyes are adaptive mechanisms that function through time. Our eyes scan an area over time and we form a mental composite of several instants which are continually updated. When we look into highlights our irises close down, and when we look into shadows our irises open up. Our eyes compensate for each unique lighting situation, even within a single scene, to give us a maximum of information. As a general rule, but subject to exceptions, the camera eye has only one view locked into one single instant of time.

Photographically, we then have to make a choice to sacrifice detail on one end or the other of the entire dynamic range, sometimes both. We "plug up" the shadows or "blow out" the highlights. Those who use transparencies favor underexposure

knowing that they can reclaim the detail found in shadows easier than they can reclaim detail lost in highlights. Those who use negatives favor overexposure knowing they can more easily reclaim detail found in highlights than they can reclaim detail lost in shadows. In both cases the densest areas record more information than the thinnest areas.

Traditionally photographers make adjustments to their exposure and development times to compensate for less than optimal lighting conditions or the responsiveness of their materials. Adding more or less exposure alone lightens or darkens the entire image and typically pushes information in one end of the dynamic range below or above the threshold of perceptibility. Making compensations in development times in response to overexposure or underexposure changes the relative distribution of tones and can push that information even further out of the range of perceptibility or preserve information that otherwise would have been lost with normal development — by overexposing and underdeveloping (less contrast, less separation, and more information on both ends of the dynamic range) or underexposing and overdeveloping (more contrast, more separation, and less information on both ends of the dynamic range).

This all boils down to where there is information on the film. When highlights are too bright on transparencies or shadows are too dark on negatives, there is a minimum density of information on the film, sometimes none. On the opposite ends of the scale, shadows in transparencies and highlights in negatives often have too dense a buildup of information in these areas to be adequately reproduced without sacrificing the quality of information in other areas of the tonal scale.

At least there is still information there. If the information lingers at the edges of the limits of reproduction, we can go to great lengths to restore it. A great deal of manipulation can be done after exposing the film, but if the initial exposure is not optimal you will have to work harder to achieve the best results and sometimes those results will elude you, particularly if you've lost information. At a certain point even virtuoso technique will not be able to overcome the limitations of a poor exposure. Once lost there is no reclaiming information. Capturing the maximum amount of information up front allows the greatest freedoms — if you have too much you can always push unwanted information out of the range of perceptibility, but if you don't have it to start with you're never going to be able to make it materialize magically.

If I must err one way or the other, I favor a lower contrast rather than a higher contrast exposure. I don't advise overdoing this as you will have to work hard to get adequate separation throughout other areas of the image, but favoring a lower contrast will preserve a maximum amount of information at the point of capture.

As an aside, one of the few filters I use when photographing is a Tiffen ultracontrast filter. I don't know of another manufacturer who makes a similar filter. Tiffen created it for the motion picture industry and repurposed it for the photographic industry. The name sounds like it would add contrast but it does exactly the opposite. It's for shooting in ultracontrast lighting situations and holding information in shadows and highlights that would normally fall out of the range of capture. When I encounter this type of situation, I consider using these filters to capture a maximum amount of information. In grades from one to five with increasing strengths, I find I use the greatest strength filters most often as the effect is somewhat subtle. It will not affect sharpness.

When working digitally, making a good scan is like making a good exposure. In the case of a digital camera, we simply scan the world before the camera not film; scanning film is essentially a second stage of capture. Often we scan a single sheet of film once with one software and then fine-tune the resulting single digital file with another software. Like a piece of film, a digital file typically has more information in it than is visible — there is additional information lingering in the brightest and darkest areas that can be made more apparent when we manipulate it after the moment of capture. Just as with working with film, when working with a digital file there is a limit, albeit greater, to the amount of manipulation we can perform to a single image with a fixed dynamic range. It's the end points of the dynamic range that are fixed: pure white (our white point or D-min) and pure black (our black point or D-max) are just that, pure, there is no information there and there is certainly nothing beyond it. Digitally or traditionally we are working with the curve (the relative distributions of tone within the total dynamic range). Because the curve in a digital file is not tied to materials and chemistry, but rather mathematics and electricity, you have a more fluid control of it. The digital range of manipulation may exceed traditional methods, but no amount of digital manipulation will restore what has been lost entirely. The closer we get to the farthest limits of our information, the more the quality of the information will degrade — artifacting will appear.

As with making any exposure, when scanning you must be mindful to capture the greatest amount of information throughout the entire dynamic range if you want to manipulate it later and retain the greatest amount of flexibility when

1. A normal scan. Shadows are too dark, and highlights are too light.

2. The normal scan darkened making shadows too dark while highlights remain on the light side.

3. A dark scan. Highlight detail is excellent. Shadow detail is lost.

4. No amount of lightening will adequately restore shadow detail.

5. A light scan. Shadow detail is excellent. Highlight detail is lost.

6. No amount of darkening will adequately restore highlight detail.

doing so. In this respect, digital exposures (scans) are no different than traditional exposures (film). Both place information within a given dynamic range. You capture a maximum amount of information digitally by applying an appropriate curve at the scan level using the scanning software. This is just like making compensations in your standard film exposure and development times. You then fine-tune the resulting digital file by applying a curve to it with image manipulation software. This is the same as any manipulation you might do to the print using filtration, paper, and chemistry. Like working with a well-balanced piece of film, in a well-balanced scan the quality of the information you will be manipulating will be that much better; it will allow you to go that much further, and you will achieve your goal that much easier. At a certain point even virtuoso digital technique cannot overcome the limitations of a poor scan. It's worth shooting a well-balanced piece of film, so it's worth making a good scan. Digital techniques are no substitute for learning good traditional techniques, but they can be a marvelous extension of them.

The entire range of manipulation, traditional or digital, is generally needed only for situations that are problematic: sometimes too flat, usually too contrasty. The flexibility of the digital curve may provide a greater range of manipulation, but sometimes even this is not enough for extremely difficult situations. In certain instances, generally arising from subject matter that has too great a range of contrast, no matter how hard you work, you will not be able to achieve optimal detail throughout the entire range of tones. But this does not necessarily mean a sacrifice must be made. In many of these situations, it is possible to extend the range of manipulation even further.

In extreme situations, even when a scan has been optimized for midtones, it may still not be possible to darken highlights and lighten shadows sufficiently. If a scan has been optimized for the shadows, it may be impossible to darken

("burn down") highlights convincingly. If a scan has been optimized for the highlights, it may be impossible to lighten ("open up") shadows convincingly. Just as with film there are limits.

If, however, you take two scans, one optimized for the highlights and another optimized for the shadows, and composite them into a single digital file, you will have optimal information throughout the entire range of tones. Two scans can have more information than one. By doing this, you functionally extend the printable range of a single piece of film.

We can take this one step further. We may still be limited by the range of capture of our film, but if we know in advance that we are going to be scanning twice to maximize the amount of reproducible information, we may make the decision to shoot twice. If you shoot two separate pieces of film, one with optimal information in the highlights and another with optimal information in the shadows, scan them separately, and composite them both into a single digital file, you have functionally extended the range of capture of a given film. Two sheets of film can have more information than one. Now we can choose the optimal information from each one and combine it into a single image. The very same principle applies to digital capture.

Most of us have heard the Zone System simplified as, "Expose for the shadows and develop for the highlights." Now you might extend this philosophy to optimizing multiple exposures for specific ranges of capture and later compositing them into a single image with a total range of information that was previously unattainable. Working digitally may change the way you photograph, even if your photographic intentions do not change.

This method works very well for images where the disparate information exists in discrete areas of the picture with simple boundaries or abrupt transitions, such as a bright sky behind a dark mountain or detail outside a window when photographing an architectural interior. For images that are highly

7. A composite of both dark and light scans revealing excellent detail in both shadows and highlights.

textured or contain long smooth gradual transitions between differing areas, it is much harder to employ this technique. The problem arises in creating a convincing transition of tones between areas that have been lightened and areas that have been darkened, which without a discrete boundary, such as a line, may look too abrupt. Backlighting can be especially hard to deal with. Take for example a forest canopy with bright backlighting. In this situation, the light is spilling around the edge of each leaf softening its contour. There is no longer an abrupt transition of tone between leaf and sky; instead we have a soft gradual line of transition. When we accentuate the relative values of the leaves to the sky, an unnatural boundary line can appear in the smooth areas of transition. Creating masks for these situations may be prohibitively arduous.

Often we would like our photographic images to represent all that we perceive, not less, and possibly more. Since the invention of photography, photographers have been trying to overcome the limitations of their materials to more accurately represent the full range of human sensitivity to the world. As early as the mid 1800s photographers, such as Hill and Adamson and Gustave Le Gray, employed similar techniques using multiple exposures. Today, despite our many advances in technology, the principle is no less valid.

It is ironic that despite its limitations, in many instances the camera can record much more than the human being is able to perceive. Photography employing a microscope or a telescope, stop action photography, infrared and x-ray spectrums all capture information the naked eye cannot see. Photographic vision is not human vision. They each have specific strengths and weaknesses. Engaging in the study of what they are can be highly illuminating and at times advantageous.

METHOD

1   Scan a contrasty original twice. Scan once optimizing detail in the shadows (apply a lightening curve with the scanner software). Scan again optimizing detail in the highlights (apply a darkening curve with the scanner software). Make sure that you do not change the cropping area or the resolution settings between scans to ensure that the two scans will align perfectly. Both scans should have exactly the same number of pixels. Save the two files, including the name "highlights" in one title and "shadows" in the other.

Alternately, scan two originals normally — one original optimized for the highlights and the other optimized for the shadows. Perfect alignment without some manual adjustment is nearly impossible in this scenario. Make it easy on yourself and scan both originals perfectly square so that rotation is not a factor when aligning the separate scans.

2   Composite the two scans into a single file. In Photoshop open both files. Drag the background layer icon from one document into another holding the Shift key down to center the newly dropped information and ensure proper alignment. If you simply drag one layer icon into another document, the two scans will not be aligned and you will have to spend an unnecessary amount of time realigning the two images. If necessary, crop or rotate after this step not before as aligning the two images will become much more difficult.

3   Select the portion of the image to be hidden wherever shadows are too dark or highlights are too light. There are many strategies for making such a selection. Different kinds of images will favor different strategies. In this case, where the mountains have a complicated jagged edge which would be arduous to select and there is fairly good separation between the mountain and the sky, a contrast mask is created. Duplicating a channel creates an alpha channel, creating a luminance mask as our base, letting the image do the lion's share of selecting itself. The contrast of the alpha channel is increased using Curves to provide maximum separation between the mountain and sky. The goal is to see no detail in the darkest areas (all black) and no detail in the lightest areas (all white). In most cases we will want to leave a little extra information in those areas only because pushing the information too far will degrade the quality of the transition line between highlights and shadows. Finally, with a brush the mask is retouched, eliminating any unintended selected areas. Our luminance mask has now become black-and-white without shades of gray.

4   Turn the alpha channel into a selection (Select: Load Selection: Alpha channel 1). Add a layer mask to obscure the information that is not optimal (Layer: Add Layer Mask: Selection). Your selection will automatically define the masked and unmasked areas of your layer mask. If the mask hides the wrong information, simply invert it (Image: Adjust: Invert). Further refine the layer mask manually with a brush if necessary. Use the filters Minimize or Maximize to contract or expand it. Use Gaussian Blur or Unsharp Mask to make edge transitions in the mask harder or softer.

5   Make further adjustments in tone or color to each scan separately (Layer: New Adjustment Layer: Curves and check Group With Previous Layer).

Posse, Allies, 1996

V

LOCAL CONTRAST

Posse snuck up on me. The stunning presences, within the series Allies, reminiscent of Native American totem poles, African sculpture, or Hindu figurines, had been pursuing me for months. There were, and still are, dozens waiting to find homes. While the majority of the images I had created featured solitary figures, I was drawn to explore the effects of many within a single image, group dynamics. I tried subtle variations of the same figure. Another image arose, Rainbow Warriors. I tried many different figures within the same image. Some worked together, others didn't. When the right ensemble gathered, Posse appeared. Both images were drawn from my old home, the New Mexico desert. Both images contained one shared figure. And the shared figure, appropriately, reminded me of the kachinas I read about, drew, collected, and watched in dances as a child.

I tried many landscapes. Few had the intensity to compete with figures. When I found this ridge I knew it had sufficient drama. It became clear that a land containing a sharp angular slope suggesting a possible impending descent was wanted.

I tried many skies. Many were too distracting. If the skies had a definite design, the image became too busy. I needed a single field, a ground without figure, to support the many figures hovering in the space above. Yet, a flat even sky was too simple. It offered too little support. Some skies contained too much color. A bright blue announced itself too loudly. Its dramatic contrast in color took attention away from what was already dramatic, form and light. Color in general was subdued and altered to produce unity and focus the attention of the eye on the essential elements.

An image can have too little or too much contrast. (Here I mean contrast between all elements within an image, not just tone.) Too little contrast and the message is unheard. Too much contrast and the message is obscured. In either case, the message is unclear. Most leading actors need supporting actors, all save the soloist need accompaniment. But, when supporting actors compete with main actors, the thrust of the drama is confused. Contrast needs to be placed in the most important areas. It establishes priorities. It is what we focus on. With this in mind I often downplay certain elements to let others shine. Yet, I didn't want the supporting elements to be silent. In them, I wanted a quiet life to simmer underneath the main action. They are there to echo, through similarity, and amplify, through contrast, the message. They reinforce the drama.

I found myself sifting first images and then elements. First one element, then another, a little to the left, a little to the right, a little darker, a little lighter, a little cooler, a little warmer. Seeing things side by side, simultaneous contrast, made things clear. Through successive iterations the image was refined. The proper balance was achieved. The image was sought and found.

I had to hunt this image down. I looked through the residues about me for the uniting presence within them. I tracked it. But did I find it or did it find me? The hunter can become the hunted. I don't think this simply means that the tables are turned. I think it means that to truly find something you must understand its nature so deeply that it becomes a part of you. Only then do you possess it. Only then does it possess you. Only when it possesses you do you possess it.

CHOOSE A PREFERRED SET OF TONES

"After silence that which comes nearest to expressing the inexpressible is music."
— *Aldous Huxley*

"All art constantly aspires towards the condition of music."
— *Walter Pater*

"Heard melodies are sweet, but those unheard are sweeter."
— *John Keats*

Is it coincidence that both musicians and visual artists speak of tones? Let us speak of images in terms of visual music. Orchestrating tone and contrast choreographs the dance of the eye throughout the image. Tone (overall lightness or darkness) sets the key, timbre, or mood of an image. Contrast (relative tonal relationships) sets its rhythm or pace. Ripe with overtones and undertones, both define character. Similarity and repetition (echoes) produce unity, field, ground. This is true no matter how varied the repeated components. It is reinforced as repetition increases. Variety produces divergence, individuality, figure. Contrast creates texture and delineates form. An object's appearance becomes increasingly three-dimensional as contrast rises, increasing depth. When contrast is pushed to an extreme, form breaks into abstraction, becoming flat.

Contrast is tied to atmosphere; typically the atmospheres in images with more contrast are transparent and more spacious while those with less contrast are translucent and less spacious. But this can be reversed; a uniformity of contrast may flatten the image plane while the successive reduction of contrast produces depth.

Our eyes are naturally attracted to contrast. Affecting con-trast locally, including making one area of an image lighter or darker, can deflect or draw attention to that area.

All of this involves visual composition, visual arrangement, visual orchestration. The arrangement of tones (contrast) produces a progression (scale). Each individual progression has unique qualities, a tempo if you will, with a unique pulse: adagio, moderato, allegro, vivace, or presto. As contrast is emphasized or de-emphasized, the visual rhythm of an image is transformed. Contrast creates counterpoint. Contrast could be thought of as volume: the more contrast an image has the "louder" it is, the less the "quieter" it is. Quiet/loud (piano/forte), soft/harsh (harmonious/dissonant), clear/muffled (chiaro/scuro), choppy/smooth (staccato/glissando) — these are but a few of the many words that could be used to describe the qualities, poles if you will, that images shift between as contrast is increased or decreased. The melody of a piece may be substantially altered through successive adaptation and variation. Orchestrate the perfect harmony between all elements in an image and you will find its truest voice. You may even find yours in the process.

Making changes to either or both tone and contrast may substantially change not only our experience but also the

1. The base composite.

2. The sky darkened through the gradient
mask applied to the sky layer.

content of an image; it can transform it. Ansel Adams'"Moonrise, Hernandez, New Mexico, 1941," changes time and atmosphere; its sky is dramatically darkened: it transforms late afternoon into evening. John Sexton's "Rock Shoreline, Dusk, Pemaquid Point, Maine, 1987," changes identity: three rocks are bleached white, rocks once integral parts of a unified fabric now stand out as radiant individuals. Paul Caponigro's "Apple, New York City, 1964," amplifies an implied metaphor: the edge of a solitary apple is darkened and nearly disappears into inky blackness making the clusters of white spots it contains seem even more like stars. The many masters of black-and-white photography have demonstrated time and again the importance of these two key elements: tone and contrast.

Strike a chord. Add trill, tremolo, arpeggio, grace note or cadenza and who knows what new harmonies will arise in your compositions? By scoring its contrast, an image can be accented, punctuated, syncopated, modulated. Its resonance can be greatly increased. Whether you favor the crisp runs of Vivaldi or the murky chords of Debussy, you will find realms of enchantment in tone and contrast.

But how should we proceed? Stravinsky said,"The trouble with music appreciation in general is that people are taught to have too much respect for music; they should be taught to love it instead." The same could be said for imagery. Master the Zone System; don't let it master you. Having first learned the formula, you may want to later abandon it. Practice controlled abandon. Improvise. Play adagio, moderato, allegro, vivace, or presto; simply play. There are many visual principles at work in imagery but there are only two rules — *a bene placita* (as you please) or *a piacere* (as you please). I follow Beaudelaire's admonishment, "Always be intoxicated. Never be sober. Never, ever, be sober. Use poetry, wine, or virtue, as you please." Let these wise words be your guide and find virtuosity in intoxication in all your visual performances.

Traditionally photographers "dodge and burn" selectively lightening and darkening; some even selectively develop, bleach, and tone an image to make local areas lighter or darker. During exposure, more or less light is given to specific areas of an image and as a result those areas become darker or lighter. Some photographers even dodge and burn with variable contrast filters

3. The bottom of the sky layer is flipped horizontally, making the left dark land edge stand out against the light sky and the right light land edge stand out against the dark sky.

4. The land layer's contrast is increased and saturation reduced. Then the land layer's edges are darkened through the mask.

when using variable contrast papers, altering not just the tone of the area affected but also its contrast. Color print materials don't offer as much flexibility as black-and-white materials do as it is difficult to shift tone without shifting hue. There are no such restrictions when working digitally. The curve (a map of relative tonal relationships) is extraordinarily flexible (it can be remapped). Moreover the masks you use to contain corrections to selective areas can be more precise and are easier to make and use (and therefore are more likely to be used).

For several reasons, I prefer dodging and burning using adjustment layers with masks rather than using the dodging and burning brushes found in the Photoshop Tool Palette. Very often the Dodge and Burn tools can be heavy handed. As their settings are tied to brightness controls, there is a tendency for the resulting corrections to produce dull, or gray, whites and blacks. Turning the tools' modes to Highlights or Shadows can help cure this problem allowing you to make more precise corrections. But, there are even more precise ways. Tying the correction to a curve in an adjustment layer allows maximum control through-

out the entire range of tones with the ability to preserve the character of whites and blacks. Should you wish to decrease the intensity of whites or to diminish the density of blacks, you can do so even more precisely with a curve. While it is easy to build up successive strokes at lower opacities with the dodge and burn brushes, it is equally easy to do with black and white brushes of varying opacities on an adjustment layer layer mask. What's more, both the curve correction and the state of the mask are indefinitely modifiable. With successive dodge and burn brush strokes, undoing and remaking successive stages would necessitate a Byzantine journey through alternate history states. If your History Palette were set at the default, you could only affect the previous twenty strokes. Hopefully, you would reset this number. You can also check the Allow Non-Linear History option to remove the strokes of your choice, but you must do so before making them and once saved their effects are permanent. There are no such complications or restrictions when using a layer mask. Using any painting tool, simply paint with white to reveal the correction and black to obscure it. Or, using a curve, lighten or darken the mask. Or, using a curve, increase its contrast. Or, using the adjustment layer's opacity setting, reduce the intensity of the effect. What's more, the kinds of corrections you make this way are not limited to tonal corrections. You can make any kind of correction available as an adjustment layer with this kind of selectivity. Think of dodging and burning with Color Balance or Hue/Saturation.

Here's a simple formula. Create an adjustment layer. For classic dodging and burning, select Curves. Focusing on the area to be affected, darken or lighten the image. The entire image will be affected. If you wish to affect the majority of the image, paint on the areas you do not wish to be affected with a black brush. You will be manually creating a mask for the correction on the adjustment layer layer mask, which is created automatically, unlike an image layer mask which has to be created intentionally. Vary the opacity of the brush to reduce the amount of the correction. If you wish to affect only a small portion of the image, fill the adjustment layer layer mask with black. This will totally obscure the correction. Then use a white brush to reveal it in selective areas. White reveals, black obscures. Again, use many strokes of varying opacities to obscure or reveal a correction to different degrees in different areas. If you make a mistake or go too far, reverse the color of your brush (use the icon in the tool bar or use the X key to reverse the foreground and background colors) and paint again. For smooth transitions, favor soft-edged brushes. If a mask is finished, but you'd like even smoother transitions, blurring the mask may help.

You may want to be very precise about the selectivity of a correction. To achieve this, you need to make a precise selection. All the methods and tools for creating sophisticated selections apply. Save the selection as an alpha channel for future use. Or, with the selection active, create an adjustment layer and an adjustment layer layer mask will automatically be created from the active selection. Both the alpha channel and the layer mask save the selectivity of the selection. One does so passively, the alpha channel. The other does so actively, the layer mask. Think of alpha channels, selections, and masks as different aspects of the same thing — selectivity. Alpha channels are used to store selections for future use; they are passive. We load a selection, turning an alpha channel into a selection, something active. Selections do not store. They constrain. They are active. If a selection is active when an adjustment layer is created, an adjustment layer layer mask is automatically created, constraining the correction made, just as if the correction were applied directly to the image through the selection, but with the added benefit of flexibility, as both the correction and the mask are infinitely and indefinitely modifiable. A layer mask is also active. It hides or reveals. An adjustment layer layer mask hides a correction. An image layer mask hides an image. (Image layers are not automatically created with layer masks. Layer masks must be manually added to image layers.) Alpha channels, selections and masks can be turned into one another. You could think of a selection as the intermediary state between an alpha channel and a layer mask. You could also think of a selection as the preliminary state of an alpha channel or layer mask. While one can turn into another, they all do fundamentally different things. An alpha channel is used to create or store a selection, a layer mask to reduce an image's opacity, and an adjustment layer layer mask to diminish a correction.

One of the most useful masks is the gradient mask. A gradient mask is typically created with the Gradient tool which paints a smooth transition from black to white or from one gray to another. Specify black as your foreground color and white as your background color. (The default blending mode will create a transition from the foreground color to the background color but the foreground to transparent mode is also very useful.) Activate the Gradient tool in the tool bar. (There are several types

5. The center of the mesa accentuated in contrast through the mask.

6. The mask created with a soft-edged brush.

of gradients available. Linear is the default and most useful. Radial is also quite useful.) On a new alpha channel, layer mask, or adjustment layer layer mask, click where black (hides) should be and drag to where white (reveals) should be. Any angle or position will work. A gradient will be created between the starting and ending points you specify. Do it again and you will create another gradient to replace the first. With a typical gradient mask on an adjustment layer, a correction is completely restrained in one area of an image (the area in which the mask is black), not restrained at all in another (the area of the mask that is white), and a smooth transition of increasing intensity is seen between the two poles. (A 0% mask density will allow 100% of the correction to be applied, a 25% density will allow 75%, 50% will allow 50%, 75% allows 25%, and 100% allows 0%.) A mask may also be used to hide image information on an overlying layer. If a gradient mask is used in a situation such as this, the

image will appear completely opaque in one area (white mask), transparent in another (black mask), with a smooth transition between the two. At times, it is difficult to control the placement of the midpoint (middle gray value) of the gradient exactly. There is an easy way to do this. Once a gradient is created you can control its transition of values by applying a curve to it. Darkening or lightening it will shift the midpoint. You can see this visibly if you look at the mask and image simultaneously (hold the Option and Shift keys and click on a layer mask or activate the alpha channel and highlight the eye in the Master Channel). For a slightly different effect, gradient masks can be used globally or locally. You can select an area and apply a gradient to that area to create a localized gradient mask. Any mask with a smooth transition of differing values could be termed a gradient mask, no matter how it is created.

While the curve can be used to isolate specific ranges of

*7. The highlights on the mesa accentuated through
the contrast mask.*

*8. The contrast mask derived from the green channel,
increased in contrast, and selectively
modified to fill the sky.*

tone, it is difficult to affect one portion of the curve without affecting neighboring areas or tones. Put another way, it is difficult to affect the eighth tones without affecting the quarter-tones, or it is difficult to affect the areas of the image at Zone V without affecting the areas in the image at Zone VI. For this level of precision, you can resort to a contrast or luminance mask. A luminance mask is a mask generated from the luminance values of the image itself. Where the image is light the mask will be light, where it is dark it will be dark or vice versa. A luminance mask made with the positive values of an image will affect the highlights more than the shadows. (Simply duplicate a channel to create one.) A luminance mask made with the negative values of an image will affect the shadows more than the highlights. (Simply duplicate a channel and invert it to create one.) These kinds of masks are not strangers to the traditional photographer. Cibachrome printers routinely need to create

them to preserve information in bright highlights or reveal it in heavy shadows. But the difficulty of creating them traditionally, with a precise level of density and contrast, and registering them with the original for use, is prohibitive to many. Consequently, they are used less often than they might be. When working digitally, luminance masks are extremely quick and easy to make and use. The simplest way to create a luminance mask is to duplicate a channel. Any one channel, or combination of channels, can be used to generate an alpha channel. Duplicating the Master Channel will create a mask that looks like the image would in grayscale mode. To be most effective, luminance (or contrast) masks generally need to have substantial contrast, therefore you may want to duplicate the channel with the most contrast in it. Click on the name of each channel separately to see which one has the greatest contrast, then duplicate it. Or, accentuate the contrast of an alpha channel with

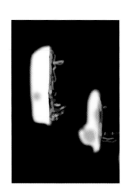

9. The figures introduced with contrast
set to a similar level as the land.

10. The figures darkened through the
mask, making them appear more
volumetric and affected by the light
source rather than being light sources.

Curves. The alpha channel can then be turned into a selection (by loading it), which can be turned into a mask (by filling the selection on a layer mask or an adjustment layer layer mask with black). Simply having an active selection before creating the adjustment layer will create an adjustment layer layer mask.

To create a luminance mask by combining a percentage of one or more channels into another, first duplicate the entire image, creating a new document. Have both original and duplicate open at the same time. Then use the Channel Mixer (Image: Adjust: Channel Mixer) on monochrome mode to specify a mixture in the new document. Make sure the total percentage of all channels involved equals 100% to avoid darkening (less than 100%) or lightening (more than 100%) the result. If you wish to darken or lighten the result, it is best to apply a curve to a version with a percentage of 100% or detail may be lost. Then duplicate a channel, any channel; they're all the same in the new document. Return to the original image and turn the alpha channel from the duplicate image into a selection in the original image (Selection: Load Selection and specify the

duplicate image as the source document and the new alpha channel as the channel).

Once a luminance mask is made you can change it to alter the way it constrains a correction, darkening or lightening it, increasing or decreasing its contrast, even inverting it, by applying a curve to it. (Corrections to alpha channels and layer masks cannot be made with adjustment layers; they must be applied directly to each.) It's wise to modify duplicate alpha channels should you wish to return to the unmodified original at some future point in time. You can see what the affect of a change will be interactively if you first apply the mask (to an adjustment layer or an image layer) and then apply a curve to it. While most masks want to have a fairly high degree of contrast you should be careful not to overdo it. The contrastier the mask the more judicious you want to be with the type of corrections made. An array of gray tones provide smooth transitions; eliminate them and transitions may become unnaturally pronounced. On occasion, a small amount of Gaussian Blur will cure this.

Once created, a mask, any mask, can be infinitely modified. The mask is essentially a grayscale image; anything you can do to a grayscale image you can do to the mask. (The same can be said for an alpha channel.) By selecting areas and filling them, or painting areas with a brush, select areas of a mask may be altered, allowing a very complex correction to be applied in a local area.

The kinds of corrections you can make here are extremely sophisticated. I caution against using the most sophisticated correction methods immediately. Start simply. For instance, build a sophisticated curve, specify a range of hues for Hue/Saturation, or use the right selective color correction tool. Very often a simple method will do the job and do it more efficiently. If the simpler method truly can't do the job adequately, then you have a good case for getting fancier.

Masking is certainly not a new principle since photographers have been employing these techniques with traditional materials for quite some time. Many printers routinely create them to help preserve information in bright highlights or to help reveal it in heavy shadows. Masking is the foundation of traditional unsharp masking methods. But, the difficulty of creating them traditionally with a precise level of density and contrast and registering them with the original for use is prohibitive to many. Consequently, they are used less often than they might be. The things that digital masks offer over their traditional counterparts are ease and speed of generation, modification, and use, which can result in greater precision. Combine digital masking with a flexible curve (not tied to materials and chemistry) and superior color correction capabilities (nonlinear, with independent control of hue, saturation, and lightness) and the resulting synergy can yield astonishing results.

METHOD

Dodge and Burn

1   Create a selection with any combination of selection tools.

2   Create a correction with an adjustment layer.

3   Refine the resulting mask as necessary.

You may find that increasing contrast increases saturation. It may also slightly shift the color balance. A successive adjustment layer may be used to overcome this. Load the selection of the previous adjustment layer layer mask and create a new adjustment layer to compensate.

Dodging and burning in LAB color space on the L (luminosity) channel only will produce no shift in hue or saturation. To achieve a similar result in another color space, change the blending mode of the adjustment layer to Luminosity.

Gradient Mask

1   On an adjustment layer use the Gradient tool dragging from black to white. The area of the mask that is black will show 0% of the correction, while the area that is white will show 100%, and a smooth transition between the two will be created. You can shift the midpoint by redrawing the gradient , unlinking and moving it, or by applying a correction to the mask to make it lighter or darker and thereby shift the midpoint of the transition.

Contrast Mask

1   Duplicate a channel, typically the one with the greatest contrast. Load it as a selection to affect the highlights more than the shadows. Or, load the inverse selection to affect the shadows more than the highlights.

Create an adjustment layer to apply a correction through the mask. Refine the contrast and density of the layer mask by applying a curve to it. You will be able to see the changes in the way the correction is constrained as you do so. To see the mask, hold the Option key and click on it. To see the mask and the image simultaneously, hold the Option and Shift keys and click on it. To disable the mask, hold the Shift key and click on it.

Dangerous Passage, Rites of Passage, 1994

VI

CONVERTING COLOR TO BLACK AND WHITE

Dangerous Passage was a compelling image. But something wasn't working. The thorns were red. The stalks were green. The water was blue. They were not subtle. The color was garish. In many ways, the color was too literal. The drama of the composition was competing with the drama of color. The two were at odds. Their moods were incompatible. One was harsh and edgy. The other was bright and cheery. Color was the problem. So I removed it.

I was astonished to see how much control could be exerted in the distributions of tone. The thorns could be dark or light or any shade in between. The shifts were not linear shifts where the entire image became darker or lighter. Specific areas became dark or light based on their color. There were three primary distributions of tone that I could choose from (based on the three channels of the document — Red, Green, and Blue) but I could also choose a blend of the three. It was similar to exposing black-and-white film with differing color filtrations but it was far more flexible and fluid. Best of all I could see the results instantaneously. The technique went way beyond dodging and burning. It was a form of tonal transformation, not augmentation. I was so impressed with the level of control, I stopped using black-and-white film altogether.

There were still many subtleties to be reworked. Where color, not tone, provided separation, things fell flat. What wanted to be read as separate merged, merged too much. Very often, color images converted to black-and-white need a little extra contrast. It was nothing a touch of contrast and a little dodging and burning couldn't cure. Now was the time for global corrections, akin to the corrections made in the traditional darkroom with variable contrast papers. The dodging and burning tools might have changed, but the practice was equally sound. Better still, the corrections were made to the image before printing, not to each print of the image.

In black and white, unity was achieved. There were no superfluous elements. A whole statement was formed. The message was clarified. The image carried a much greater weight. Less became more.

The image was somber in black and white. That much suited the mood. But it was ashen, cold, and remote. I missed the emotional power of color. So I put it back.

I converted the image back to a color mode and introduced new color into the image. I tried a variety of "toning" options: silver, bronze, and gold; white gold, red gold, and green gold. I ran tests on dozens of solutions. Looking at them side by side I felt the emotional impact of each color. Green was sickly, blue was ice cold, red was too hot. I would have thought that all of them were more appropriate than gold. I was surprised that the warmth of gold enriched the image. With its introduction, the image rose forward, rather than receding, yet the space within it remained clear and distinct. As a result it was less remote. Somehow, it was more present.

Later, as my technique evolved, I reconsidered the image. Over the years, I had discovered a greater degree of control in converting color to black and white. I could extend this new-found level of control to specific areas of an image and not others. Unfortunately, I didn't have the original full-color information in the composite. If I did, rather than recompositing, I would simply have returned to the original document and reseparated it. I had no choice but to recomposite the image. Now, I archive all my images in color, even those destined to become black-and-white images.

When I reconsidered the conversion, several things changed. The red thorns grew lighter. The sky grew darker. The contrast between the two made each even more dramatic. Many of the tonal relationships achieved would have been difficult to achieve by locally correcting them. Dodging and burning only go so far. The dynamic range of an area can be compromised or tonal transitions may take on an unnatural increase or decrease in contrast. When very substantial transformations of tone are needed, other methods are required to achieve optimal information throughout the tonal scale.

Very subtle shifts in composition were made. After all, the image was different now. The balance of elements needed to be shifted slightly to accommodate their new relative weights. Each new nuance demanded a counterpart in another area or aspect of the image. While new conversion methods provided the previous controls, this ability to fine-tune composition is clearly attributable to the fact that the image is a composite image. New methods offer new controls. Similarly, new kinds of images offer new kinds of controls.

Some think that digital printmaking is a matter of getting it right and then pressing a button. With the possible exception of printing an entire edition at one time, this is a misconception. No printmaking device is that constant. Digital printmaking is still just that, printmaking. As conditions change, adjustments must be made. Fears that an artist's interpretation of an image cannot evolve over time in digital printmaking are unfounded. Clearly it can. The West Coast tradition savors the famous line, "The negative is the score and the print is the performance." Whether you have a negative (traditionally or digitally created) or a digital file, every print is a performance. When do you stop? When the image can't be improved upon. In between performances, create the richest score you possibly can.

"... one sees differently with color photography than black-and-white ... in short, visualization must be modified by the specific nature of the equipment and materials being used."
— *Ansel Adams*

When shooting black-and-white film, many of us have, at one time or another, either experimented with or employed color filtration to redistribute tonal values within a given scene. The theory behind this phenomenon is fairly simple. The filter readily transmits its own color and resists its opposite color. Many photographers habitually use an orange or red filter to darken blue skies. With an orange filter, orange light is more readily let in and blue light partially blocked making earth tones brighter and blue skies darker — darker and brighter than the tones would appear if no filtration were used.

You can easily convert color images into black-and-white images digitally. Doing so offers an unparalleled degree of control and flexibility.

Aside from desaturating a color file, Photoshop has a standard method for converting color to black-and-white. It's as simple as opening a color file and converting its mode to Grayscale (Image: Mode: Grayscale). Photoshop performs a standard calculation converting the separate channels in a color file (three in RGB, four in CMYK) into one channel in a grayscale file. In RGB, Photoshop uses a mix of 59% of the Green channel, 30% of the Red channel, and 11% of the Blue channel.

In a majority of cases this method works quite well. Note that Photoshop favors the Green channel and think of green vegetation and green's opposite color, magenta, an underlying component in most flesh tones, two of the most photographed colors. Favoring the Red channel would produce flesh tones that would be too bright and foliage that would be too dark. Favoring the Blue channel would produce flesh tones that would be too dark and skies that would be too bright. When employing this technique you allow the default settings in Photoshop to determine the distributions of tone, defaults that work for a majority of cases. If, however, an image differs from the majority of cases, this technique may not be optimal.

You can be more selective. Every digital color image is a mix of a number of black-and-white images, or channels, of the same scene, perfectly aligned, but with different tonal values. If you look at the separate channels individually, you will notice that their distributions of tone vary markedly, especially in images with a variety of color. If you like the information from one channel only, you can override Photoshop's default conversion method. Simply target one channel only by clicking on it and then convert to grayscale. Photoshop will discard the other two channels. In many cases, one channel will have better information in it than the others or than the default averaging scheme supplies. I recommend you always check the channels separately before you convert color images to grayscale. You might be pleasantly surprised by another solution, one of your own choosing.

You can be even more selective. If you want to use a certain percentage of two channels, you can use Calculations to combine them into one new channel (Image: Calculations). In the Calculations dialog box, specify one channel in the first source and another in the second. Blend them using the Normal Setting and enter a percentage of the first channel that you would like to mix with the second. Specify Result: New Document. This way you will be able to go back to the original color file at any time. Unfortunately, there is no way to mix more than two channels at once using Calculations. To blend more than two channels, you have to calculate several times in a row. Even more unfortunate, you cannot see the result until after the conversion is made; you have to guess what numerical percentage will yield the best result before seeing it. Worse, if you decide you want to change the percentages or the component channels of the first blend after seeing the third or fourth in the mix, you have to start all over again.

Photoshop has a feature called the Channel Mixer (Image: Adjust: Channel Mixer) which is more intuitive. It functions much like Calculations, allowing you to blend a percentage of the separate channels into each other or to make an entirely new channel, even in a new document. But, unlike Calculations, you can see the results generated as you specify percentages of each channel. Among other things, it can be used to make high-quality grayscale conversions. Check Monochrome and specify a mix of any percentage of multiple channels. Specify a combined percentage that is greater than 100%, and you will lighten the image. Specify a com-

3. The image with default conversion to grayscale — 59%/30%/11%.

1. The full-color image.

2. The image desaturated.

bined percentage that is lower than 100%, and you will darken the image. The same will happen if you specify a higher or lower Constant percentage. I recommend using neither in a majority of cases as they function much like Brightness, reducing dynamic range by graying whites and blacks. Instead use Curves after the conversion. When you have achieved the desired result, you will have generated a black-and-white RGB file. To make it a grayscale file, simply change modes.

There is an even more powerful way. Like the Channel Mixer, it allows you to see the changes you are making as you are making them. You can blend more than two channels and have the ability to see the visual effects of changing select percentage values as you change them. What's more, you can change the order of the blends and their percentages at any time achieving a maximum amount of control and precision. This method is slightly more time consuming, but it allows unparalleled flexibility and precision.

You can turn the individual channels into layers in a separate document and then selectively modify their opacities to achieve an ideal mix. Simply go to each channel separately in the original full-color image (click on it), select it (Select: All), copy it (Edit: Copy), create a new document (File: New: OK), and paste the copy into the new document as a layer (Edit: Paste). Repeat this process moving on to the other channels in the original document, copying them and pasting them into the same new document. Note each channel has now become a separate layer. If your original document is in RGB with three channels, you will generate a new grayscale file with three layers, each with one channel. The difference between channels and layers is that channels compose a single image and layers are entirely separate images stacked on top of one another. Name each new layer appropriately. (Double-click on its icon and give it the name of the channel that generated it.) Then, turn down the opacity of the top two layers until a desired mix has been achieved. Highlight the layer to be affected, and in the Layers palette, use the Opacity slider to lower the percentage, or type in a percentage value.

Note that changing the order of the layer stack (click on a layer and drag it below or above another) will alter the effect. This is because the bottom layer is being seen through translucent overlays of the other two. If you copied and pasted as recommended, the three separate components of the image (channels that become layers) will be perfectly registered. The bottom layer will, as a rule, always want to be at 100% opacity. If all the layers have a reduced opacity, you will be blending them with a percentage of background white, creating a light veil over the entire image.

You will have to determine an ideal order for the layers based on the nature of

4. The Red channel.

5. The Green channel.

6. The Blue channel.

the image. In general, place the layer with the most useful information at the bottom of the layer stack and use low opacities of the other two layers. When you've achieved a desired result, save the file. It can be used later if you decide to modify the image further as it has all the flexibility of separate layers.

For greater control in fine tuning your image, you can always change the tonal scale of an individual layer by applying a curve to it (Image: Adjust: Curves). For maximum flexibility, use an adjustment layer grouped with that specific layer to apply a curve. As an adjustment layer, the curve correction can be turned on and off or reduced in opacity at any time.

You can refine this even further. Add layer masks to the top two channels and selectively modify local areas by painting them with varying opacities of black. By doing this, you are modifying the opacity of the layer selectively, showing more or less of the information of that layer in local areas. Unlike channels, layers can have varying opacities in different areas. Hypothetically you could see 11% in one area, 22% in another, 44% in another, and 88% in yet another. It's entirely your choice.

Remember this only works for color images, as a black-and-white or grayscale image has only one channel. Even if you scan a black-and-white image in RGB, the resulting three channels will be identical and it would be pointless to use this method. This method will work equally well in RGB or CMYK mode.

The control and flexibility afforded by this method is absolutely phenomenal. It is, in my experience, unparalleled. I know of no way to achieve it with traditional materials. With enough patience, you could probably figure out how to do it, but the work would be so backbreaking that few, if any, would use the technique. Once the concepts behind this method are grasped, the technique is simple and highly effective. It offers an unequaled level of control over tonal distribution when converting color to grayscale based on human decisions, not the limitations of materials or the default choices made by machines. (Remember, shooting black-and-white film is one way of making this conversion.) This method allows you to see the results of your choices immediately with the added ability to interactively experiment with the results. There's absolutely no guessing about the final results. What you see is what you get. And, should you choose to, you can make another decision in the future.

For this reason, you may choose, as I have, not to use black-and-white film, even if you want to make black-and-white images. Shooting in color gives you more freedom, flexibility, and control. It is truly exciting! Think of the possibilities the next time you photograph.

7. 50% Red with 50% Green.

8. 50% Green with 50% Blue.

9. 50% Blue with 50% Red.

METHOD

Change Mode (Three Channels at 59/30/11)

1   In Photoshop open an RGB file and convert it to Grayscale (Image: Mode: Grayscale). When the Discard color information dialog box appears, press OK.

Change Mode Selectively (One Channel)

1   In Photoshop open an RGB file and look at the channels individually. In the Channels palette, click on one channel and then another. The eye (what you see) and black bar (what you're affecting) will be on that channel only. Compare the varying tonal distributions between channels.

2   Highlight the channel with the most pleasing distribution of tones and convert to Grayscale (Image: Mode: Grayscale).

Calculations (Two Channels)

1   In Photoshop open an RGB file and use Calculations to blend two channels into one (Image: Calculations).

2   Specify one channel in the first source and another in the second source and blend the two using Normal mode and a desired percentage of the first channel, creating a new file by specifying Result: New Document.

3   If results are not optimal, repeat and modify the percentage appropriately.

Channel Mixer (All Channels)

1   In Photoshop open an RGB file and use the

10. Red, Green, and Blue blended selectively using layers and layer masks.

11. A graphic composite of the layer masks used.

Channel Mixer to blend two or more channels into one (Image: Adjust: Channel Mixer).

2 Check Monochrome. Specify a combined percentage of all three channels that equals 100%. For greater control, use a curve afterwards to lighten and darken the image rather than a percentage higher or lower than 100% or increasing or decreasing the Constant percentage.

3 Convert the black-and-white RGB file into Grayscale (Image: Mode: Grayscale).

Turn Channels Into Layers (Three Channels Selectively)

1 Open an RGB file and highlight the first channel. Copy it (Select: All, then Edit: Copy). Create a new document (File: New: OK — Photoshop will automatically create a document the same size as the information copied into the clipboard.) Paste the copied information into the new document (Edit: Paste) and a new layer will be created. Name the layer appropriately. If you copied the Red channel name it Red. To change a layer's name hold the Option key and double-click on the layer icon or go to Layer: Layer Properties.

2 Repeat step one for the second channel.

3 Repeat step one for the third channel.

4 Using the Opacity slider, turn down the opacity of the top two layers until a desired percentage is achieved. This works just like the Channel Mixer only with layers instead of channels.

5 Refine this further by adding layer masks to the top two channels. (Layer: Add Layer Mask: Reveal All) and use a black paintbrush to paint away select areas. To reduce the effect of the mask, turn down the opacity of the paintbrush. Make sure you are painting on the layer mask and not on the image — you will see a mask icon, not a paintbrush icon on the targeted layer. (If you paint on the image, you will replace photographic information with the newly painted marks, whereas, if you paint on the layer mask, you will simply hide or reveal the image where the marks are made.) Layer masks are extremely flexible as changes can be made at any time. Create a mask by painting with black, remove a mask by painting with white. You can use brushes with varying opacities. You can even apply corrections to masks either globally or locally.

Voyage of Grace, Rites of Passage, 1994

VII

MULTITONE

Of all the images from my series Rites of Passage, which explores a variety of digital equivalents to alternative processes, Voyage of Grace had the best chance of standing up as a color image. The original image was full of autumnal colors from the Scottish Highlands. The fern and heather had turned brown and the trees had turned brilliant colors. One was bright red, another was orange. Still the image improved with loss of color. While the colors within the image were comparatively unified, a few elements stood out more than the rest distracting attention from the main theme, disrupting the flow of the image. When asked to share the same color, a greater harmony was established. The content of the image followed a single course. All subthemes, tributaries, merged into the dominant stream.

I used the dominant hue of the color version as my guide and inspiration. I created a duotone that approximated its color. It was good, but I felt it could be better. So I turned the duotone back into a full-color image. The original color was not reclaimed. Once lost it can never be recovered without returning to the original. But now that it was once again a color file, I could color correct the image as I could any other. A slight shift, adding magenta into the shadows and yellow into the highlights, created a subtle split-toned effect. The space became clearer. The light grew golden. Everything was rendered in bronze. The image seemed to trace its origins to another time and place. It was an ancient land.

I tried a variety of options: a warm red, a cool red, a heavily split-toned effect. It was wonderful to be able to compare so many solutions in minutes which ordinarily would have taken hours or weeks and very possibly many different media. There were many dead ends, but they provided visual confirmation that this was indeed the solution that was right for this image. In the end, one of the more subtle solutions proved best.

Matching the proper material to the image was as important as selecting the appropriate color. The tactile qualities of surface are extremely important, but often overlooked. It would not do to print this image on plastic or with metal. It was rough and natural, soft and atmospheric. Printed on a heavy, fibrous watercolor paper, it retained a sensuous, velvety luster much like the land it was drawn from.

This was done some time before the introduction of multitones to inkjet printers, so it was printed in CMYK or four standardized colors. Today, it would be possible to create a custom ink mixture and print a true multitone, two or more custom color mixtures, that would come close to its present rendering. Carefully managed, this would increase the longevity of the print. Managing the golden highlights would be no easy task, but I would not want to say it is impossible. Still, it is likely that some sacrifice, or better, some further translation would have to be made. The task is to sacrifice the less important for the more important.

"This ponder well, the mystery closer seeing;/ In mirrored hues we have our life and being."
— *J. W. von Goethe*

"…white and black are not true colours, but, one might say, moderators of colours …
Furthermore, you will not find any white or black that does not belong to one or the other of the kinds of colours."
— *Leon Battista Alberti*

Look at the finest black-and-white reproduction you can find. Chances are it was printed as a multitone. Multitone: the term applies to images made with more than one ink. Two, three, four, five, or six inks do more than one. Created for the printing press, multitones are being repurposed for many new printing devices.

A duotone is printed with two inks, generally black and a second color. Tritones use three inks, quadtones four, and so on. All are multitones. The term duotone is commonly used loosely to describe all types of multitones and, even though it is at times innaccurate, it enjoys the benefits of familiarity.

The purpose of multitones is threefold — to extend dynamic range by providing richer blacks (more ink) or smoother transitions in highlights (a lighter ink) and on occasion to impart coloration to an image (a different color ink). Multitones need not look colored; they are highly efffective if only used to provide richer black-and-white reproduction.

There are several kinds of multitones: a halftone printed over a solid tint; a halftone printed over a high contrast line or bitmapped image; a halftone printed over the same halftone (the dots from each halftone are registered); and a halftone printed over a different halftone (the dots from each halftone are offset from one another).

"Fake" multitones (the first) color an image by laying a flat tint of color over a black-and-white image. An equal amount of additional ink is distributed throughout the entire tonal range. As a result these kinds of multitones darken highlights as well as shadows. True multitones (the last) distribute color nonuniformly throughout the image based on the tonal relationships within it; typically the amount of additional ink is greatest in the densest areas of the image and least in the thinnest areas of the image. If more additional ink is distributed into the midtones, the image will carry a stronger color. If less, the additional ink will add less color but still deepen darker areas of the image. Either way, as little additional ink is distributed into the highlights, these areas remain bright and clean yielding more apparent contrast. Even better, some multitones replace black in the highlights with lighter additional color creating smoother and cleaner highlights.

PMS or Pantone multitones use custom inks mixed to match an industry standard with readily available specifications and printed samples. The Pantone matching system (PMS) takes the vagaries of verbal expression (Exactly how much yellow is in crimson?) and provides printed reference for all to see along with numerical specifications for how to mix the color using a combination of fourteen primary ink colors. Be mindful that

1. The grayscale image.

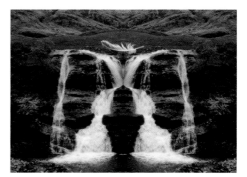
2. Duotone preset 464.

simulating PMS colors with process colors (CMYK) is problematic. A solid color looks different than simulations of it using a combination of four separate inks with white paper showing through. As cyan is a comparatively weak blue; the blue end of the spectrum suffers most (green through purple). Most PMS swatchbooks have two versions of the same color: one for PMS inks and the other for process inks demonstrating the closest match. When talking with a printer, be sure you specify the correct one.

Some multitones are created with more than one black ink, a range of grays, often one cool and one warm, are typical variations that allow fine control over subtle tonalities. At times a light gray will be used. The lighter gray will be used to carry detail and transitions in highlights, again for a finer, smoother look than if they were carried predominantly with black ink.

Multitones can even be created with metallic inks. Nearly impossible to calibrate your monitor to, or to proof, often requiring additional passes through the press with high dot gain and longer drying times, these are the most challenging types of multitones to create and reproduce.

Process multitones use the same cyan, magenta, and yellow inks found in four-color printing. It is possible, and not uncommon, to create a process quadtone that looks like a black-and-white or monochromatic image using the four inks found in four-color printing. The difference between a quadtone and process (CMYK) printing is not the number of inks used but generally the kind. While quadtones can be created using cyan, magenta, yellow and black, they are more often created with black and three custom mixed inks, three different grays or three different colors, for instance. Quadtones are generally the richest multitones as the combination of four inks (it is rare that more than four inks are used) provides the richest black and smoothest tonal scale.

Even though many inks are used in its creation, multitone typically appears to have only one channel. In truth it has as many channels as inks but each channel is based on the same information, the base grayscale image. Custom curves are created for each channel which, when applied to the base grayscale image, create variations of it and thus varying ink distributions: one may be lighter, another darker, another contrastier, another flatter, yet all have a common foundation. Each ink-specific curve changes the ink's distribution in response to the base information, or the single grayscale channel.

To create a multitone start with a Grayscale file. Only Grayscale files may be converted to Duotone mode. Files in other color spaces must first be converted to Grayscale before

3. Duotone preset 144.

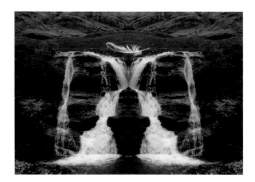

4. Duotone preset 478.

being converted to Duotone mode. One of the keys to making an excellent multitone is to start with an excellent Grayscale image. Next, change the mode to Duotone (Image: Mode: Duotone). The resulting dialog box will ask you to specify a duotone parameter. Photoshop provides preset duotone preferences. Created by Stephen Johnson, they are quite good. To use them, simply click Load and then find the preferences (Photoshop: Goodies: Adobe Photoshop Only: Duotone Presets: Duotones: pick one). Once loaded these settings can be further modified. You can create your own by clicking on the color box to specify color and clicking on the curve box to specify how it will be distributed throughout the image. Each set of boxes can specify a different color and a different curve. Again, the curve for each ink tells Photoshop how to distribute the ink throughout the tonal range of the image by referring to the original grayscale channel and making compensations based on that curve. Many types of inks may be specified. Subdued colors, often earth tones, are favored over brilliant colors which because of the addition of black never print at full purity. For this same reason be mindful when selecting additional colors that the results will be darker than the additional inks specified. When building a custom curve for a duotone setting, specifying highlight and shadow density is relatively straightforward

as you are setting minimum and maximum printing densities (determined by the press). Start with a baseline of 0/3 (black/additional) (K/X) for highlights and 90/90 (K/X) for shadows on standard offset presses. Better yet, rather than relying on general defaults, consult with the printer to find out his/her specific press's requirements or measure your press or printer's response to differing densities. After that, ink densities throughout the rest of the curve are specified based on the ink colors used. If the additional ink is dark, the curve will likely be lowered in the midtones to avoid excessive density overall. If the additional ink is light, the curve will likely be raised in the middletones to provide adequate density. If the additional ink is of medium value, a straight curve might be employed. (Note the curve in Grayscale and Duotone mode is reversed from RGB; that is, highlights are represented at the bottom left and shadows at the top right.) Curves for additional inks in tritones and quadtones will typically be lowered in each, sometimes with addtional lowering of black as well to avoid excessive density overall. Creating a process multitone can be as simple as changing modes from Grayscale (or Duotone) to CMYK; typically you will want to favor a heavy black plate generation (GCR) with images of predominantly neutral color.

You can view and edit the channels in a multitone file

5. Duotone preset 159.

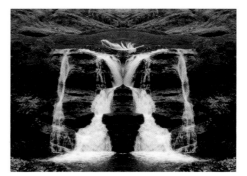

6. Duotone preset 506.

separately by converting its mode to Multichannel (Image: Mode: Multichannel). The resulting file can then be output to film and/or printed like any other multitone.

There is no substitute for experience. Build and test curves to get the feel of it. Since the Photoshop presets are excellent, use them as your guide. By looking at printed results and comparing the curves used and the resulting dot densities, you will develop an eye for multitones. It is extremely wise to stay in close contact with your printer throughout the entire process. There is no substitute for the printer's experience.

Calibrating monitors for duotones is no easy task and neither is proofing. The problem lies in the fact that custom colored inks are a challenge to simulate with red, green, and blue phospors on monitors and with CMYK inks in proofs. Correct separations settings used within Photoshop (ink limit, dot gain, the effects of paper color, color animation tables, etc.) help monitor display to be more accurate but will not ultimately cure this fundamental discrepancy. Monitors, proofs, and printed pieces are just not the same thing, but though not perfect, monitors and proofs can provide useful reference. While on-screen, Photoshop handles this fairly well. Press proofs, proofs made on the printing press with the inks to be used for the final print run, are expensive. There is a book available that has the same image printed with the various duotone settings in Photoshop on an offset press with the specified inks — Duotone Guidebook (New England Book Components, 1994). It's an excellent reference if you bear in mind that changes in paper stock, the physical conditions of the printing press, and even the daily relative humidity will have some effect on the final result.

Some use this technique for affordable reproduction of their work. Some use it as a means to better reproduction of black-and-white images. Others use it as an expressive wellspring for creativity. Multitones can be used as starting points for further refinement of an image. It's a simple matter to move from duotone mode to another color space and from there use the color correction tools available to further alter coloration within an image — either globally throughout the entire image or globally throughout a single range of tones, or locally in selected areas. Be mindful that the resulting image will have to be printed as any other full-color image would be. This method offers an astonishing range of options and controls for image making. The results can be very impressive.

7. *Duotone preset 478.*
Less black, more brown.

8. *Duotone preset 478.*
Slightly more black, slightly less brown.

9. *Duotone preset 478.*
More black, less brown.

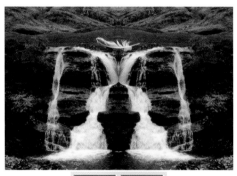

10. *Duotone preset 478.*
Still more black and less brown.

METHOD

Multitone

1   Convert a Grayscale image to Duotone mode (Image: Mode: Duotone: Load: Adobe Photoshop: Presets: Duotones). Use a preset as a starting point.

2   Alternately, build your own settings. Modify an existing setting or start from scratch. To change the color of the ink specified, click on the color and select another color. To change distribution of the color, click on the curve and enter new values.

3   If desired — convert the image to a color mode (RGB, CMYK, LAB) and use a color correction tool to further modify coloration, mindful that the resulting image will need to be output.

4   The image may be selectively toned by making a selection and creating a color correction adjustment layer.

Journey to the West, Rites of Passage, 1995

VIII

ONE SOURCE, MANY PATHS

This image, Journey to the West, could have stayed as it was. It was so blue it looked like a cyanotype right from the start. Yet it was at odds with the other pieces in the series, Rites of Passage. They contained a wide range of color — some looked like warm or cool toned silver prints, some like platinums, others like ziatypes of varying hues — but all were monochromatic and the palette was subdued. They pushed the envelope of "gray." This one was decidedly full-color. And yet it didn't seem that it was very far from finding unity with the rest of the series. It didn't contain a great variety of color; it was a symphony of one color — blue.

I tried a variety of options: converting it to black and white, creating a duotone, color correcting a black-and-white version, even "split-toning." Well past resolving the issues of composition, tone, and contrast, I kept two questions in mind. Which blue? How much blue?

It was when I was trying a "split-toned" version, giving highlights and shadows differing colors, that it occurred to me. The image was already split-toned; it was naturally split-toned. The shore had a magenta undercoloring, the waves had comparatively neutral white caps, and the waters were a warmer blue than the horizon. Atmospheric perspective was already working dramatically within the image: warmer colors were up front, cooler colors were in back. The space was deep, not flat. Picking another set of colors would have reduced it. If I subdued the intensity of the color, all those relationships would be preserved.

It was the simplest solution of all and the most effective. It also yielded the most complex visual effect. The range of colors was more complex than any cyanotype or split-toned image could ever achieve. What's more, the colors were not arbitrarily assigned; they had a preexisting set of relationships between them which even when subdued remained intact. It would be a challenge to maintain those exact relationships even if I painted them in. It was a wonderful discovery. The world can tone itself. Since then I've become fascinated with subdued color images. A new body of work arose to explore this — Allies.

Black-and-white imagery involves a significant transformation of the world; it's less representational. Some say they dream in black-and-white, some say black-and-white images are more dreamlike. Others say they are nostalgic. They are certainly otherworldly. They evoke another place, another time, or both. Whatever connotations we bring to them mentally, just as significant are the emotional responses they evoke. These are impossible to define specifically, yet all we have to do is look at them to feel their power. They offer a decidedly different experience.

Merging full color with black and white is an emotional union for me. Subdued color images are still otherworldly and yet they have not lost color's ability to move us emotionally. It's not surprising that I'm attracted to subdued color as much of my prior work was tinted drawing. To some, subdued color images are reminiscent of tinted drawings or hand-colored photographs. Yet they're richer and more complex.

I'm particularly attracted to color unity, colors that are similar or share a common foundation. Without the presence of other very different colors to compete with, the subtleties of their differences can be more fully appreciated.

Small shifts in color can produce large shifts in emotion.

I am often asked why I choose to work in both color and black and white. Actually, I work along the spectrum from full color, through subdued color, to toned black-and-white images (those tinted with color), to very neutral black-and-white images. I find that working in one way sharpens my perceptual skills, not just in that one way but also in other related ways. Aristotle said that to be a great tradgedian you had to be a great comedian and that to be a great comedian you had to be a great tradgedian. I take his point. To truly understand something you need to know about what it stands in relation to. Often, some of the strongest relationships are found in opposition. So I watch the pendulum swing within my work. After going through a period of working with color I return to working with very nuetral black-and-white imagery. After working in black and white for a time I return to working with color, very strong color. After working with calm unified fields of color I move to working with intense color variety. I am constantly watching my visual progression. It is a powerful indicator not only of where I have been and who I have been, where I am and who I am, but also of where I am going and who I am becoming.

While all of these ideas and techniques are in operation as I work they are not the primary impulses for making the decisions. The image before me is. In deciding whether an image should be in color, subdued color, or black-and-white I always ask the image first. I listen to the work. It has a life and a voice of its own. In it I hear the voice of the other, that which is not me, and the voice of the other me, that which I have yet to become aware of. Amid its voice is my as yet unheard voice.

This is my discipline. After all the preparation, I abandon myself. I abandon myself to find the world. I abandon myself to find myself. I abandon myself to the process of watching and listening. I've found that the more I do this the more my understanding of the world and of myself grows.

"We are constantly taking information given in one form and translating it into alternative forms..."
— *George Miller*

She'd spend days on press, he'd spend days in the dark-room, making sure it was just right. In watching my mother, Eleanor, oversee the production of fine art books and in watching my father, Paul, use a great variety of papers, developers, and toners to produce fine art prints, I was sensitized to the powerful effects small amounts of color had within black-and-white images. For all the trouble they went to, they must have been chasing something important. They didn't have to tell me what it was. I could see and feel it. The emotionally expressive potential of color is highly compelling, even (one half of me wants to say especially) in images that are not full-color.

Later I saw a number of Alfred Steiglitz's platinum prints and was impressed by the variety of color they contained. Their range was entirely different than what I saw in my father's dark-room. From then on my interest in alternative processes continued to grow. I kept looking. Each had a unique sensibility. The same image could speak differently depending on the material that gave voice to it. Much much later, I was exposed to Tillman Crane's survey of alternative processes. Seeing a host of alternative processes side by side, yet unified with a common vision, confirmed my suspicions. For some of us one material (I use the word material rather than medium deliberately) won't do. Thankfully we have many.

In the world of black-and-white printing there are warm and cold toned papers. Here tone refers not to value, how light or how dark, but to color. There are also many toning solutions that impart a color to them: brown, sepia, blue, gold, selenium, even polytoner. There are essentially two categories of toners for the traditional darkroom: dyes which stain the print and chemicals which react to the metals comprising the image. A great variety of colors can be imparted to black-and-white images. Change the metal involved in making the prints and the variety increases. Platinum, palladium, salt, orotype, cyanotype, gum bichromate, the list goes on.

While the range of color achievable is impressive, it is not always easy to achieve and each has limits. It's difficult to control the specific color of a cyanotype; it's blue, but achieving a specific blue, a red-blue or a green-blue, is taxing. The chemical reactions involved determine the resulting hues. Some yield better blacks than others so a trade-off between dynamic range and color is sometimes made.

More difficult to achieve is the creation of a high-quality platinum print from a color transparency or a negative. The film type shot usually determines what kind of print is made. Translation from one film type to another is certainly achievable though tedious and costly and may involve loss of quality with successive generations. This is something digital technology changes.

Wide and narrow are relative terms which depend on comparison. The range of toning options afforded by traditional and alternative processes is wide in comparison with the limitations of a single material, in comparison with the painter's palette their range is relatively narrow.

Digital technology offers an unprecedented degree of control over color in photographic images. This applies not only to full-color images but also to mono-chromatic images. I use the term mono-chromatic since speaking about color in black-and-white images can be somewhat problematic. All blacks are not created equally — some are brown, some are green, some are blue. There's no limit to the variety of hue that can be found within black and white, or gray. Now an even greater variety can be imparted to photographs.

When I was introduced to Photoshop, achieving a wide range of toning options was one of the first things I began to explore. I quickly saw that I could create the visual equivalent of a variety of traditional and alternative process prints with great flexibility and freedom. I could even exceed their color limitations and in some cases obtain richer blacks.

There are many ways of imparting color to black-and-white images digitally. While each one can be used to create similar results to the others, each also offers a unique set of possibilities. Subtle nuances can make all the difference in the world, they can make or break an image, and so it behooves you to become familiar with the various methods before settling on one.

Black-and-white images are generally Grayscale files. That Grayscale file may or may not be created from a color image. You can convert a Grayscale image to a color space (RGB, CMYK, LAB, etc). This creates a neutrally balanced color file and still

1. A full-color version.

2. A black-and-white version.

3. A duotoned version.

looks black-and-white. Once in a color mode, any of the color correction tools (Color Balance, Hue/Saturation, Curves, etc.) can be used to tone an image. Color Balance is very intuitive, and with it, subtle and complex relationships are easily achieved. Hue/Saturation's forte is control over the intensity (saturation) of color. Check the Colorize button in Hue/Saturation to create stronger, and somewhat simpler, effects. The most complex, Curves, offers the ultimate in control. (For added flexibility make all corrections as adjustment layers.)

You can create a multitone. While duo-tones, tritones, and quadtones are intended for offset printing presses with custom ink mixtures, the files generated to do this in Photoshop can be easily converted to RGB-files by simply changing their modes. You must start with a Grayscale file to create a multitone. Once a Grayscale image is converted to Duotone mode it can be converted to a color mode. Once in color mode it can be printed just as any other color file. It can also be color corrected. Though they are not the most intuitive toning solution, multitones can be interesting starting points for further toning.

Digital images can be "split-toned". The term split-toned usually refers to images in which highlight areas carry different hues than shadow areas. Traditional methods of split-toning employ specific paper/chemical combinations (silver chloride papers are favored). Two things happen in split-toned images. One, spatial relationships are accentuated. Two, emotional response is altered: two colors carry more complex emotional connotations than one as each individual color suggests an emotional response and it can in turn modify an emotional response to another color. Traditionally split-toned images offer a limited range of color choice while digitally split-toned images offer an unlimited range. To split-tone an image digitally, use Color Balance. First check the Highlights button to tone the highlights and then check the Shadows button to tone the shadows. Tone each in a complementary manner. Color opposites tend to produce the greatest separation. Or, use Curves. In separate channels (Red, Green, or Blue), increase (raise) or decrease (lower) one area of the curve only (the quarter tones or highlights), then produce the opposite shift in the same channel or in another channel. You may find yourself building "S" curves for one, two, or more channels. It is more than likely that after such a correction you will want to return to the Master channel to make a correction to counteract any resulting shifts in tone or contrast.

Even more complex tonings can be achieved if you start with a color original and take out most of the color — but not all of it. Use Hue/Saturation and lower the saturation to a pleasing level. (Making a

4. *A black-and-white version toned with Color Balance.*

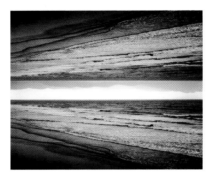

5. *A black-and-white version split-toned with Color Balance.*

6. *A color version desaturated.*

maximum reduction in saturation will create a neutrally balanced or black-and-white image.) To some this effect will look similar to hand coloring, but the color relationships involved will be much more complex. With this technique the world tones itself.

All of these options can be used in combination with each other both globally and locally. Selectivity affords even greater choice. The possibilities are limitless. Now instead of asking, "Can I do it?" you may ask, "When should I stop?".

With greater control over color comes greater control over emotional response. The many moods of color can be brought to monochromatic images to great effect. It is even possible to achieve, in certain cases, an extended dynamic range digitally as new print materials may hold a richer black than some alternative processes. You can make any kind of print regardless of the capture type (transparency, negative, CCD) of the primary exposure. Once the digital file is created, it can be duplicated and/or repurposed to any material. You need not sacrifice quality. Carefully managed digital output can equal, at times even exceed, the quality of traditional prints.

There are ways to make negatives for traditional and alternative processes from digital files, but they do not offer the control of color discussed here.

What these equivalents can never replace is the purity of the visual effect of a given material. There is no substitute for platinum or silver, only equivalents. Each has unique qualities that cannot be duplicated by any other material. Silver, for example, holds light in a unique way. Its tones, its scale, its depth may all be duplicated, but the tactile qualities of the visual sensations it offers cannot. Digital equivalents can duplicate the look but not the feel. However, the new feel may also be quite compelling.

These new "toning solutions" are designed to make color prints. Color prints are generally significantly more fugitive so we sacrifice permanence for a greater possible range of expression. There are many kinds of color prints that can be made: c (chromogenic), Ilfochrome, carbon pigment, giclée (inkjet), electrostatic, etc.. Each has its own unique qualities which can be put to good use. Think of these not as substitutes but as new possibilities.

A relatively new development in the field is the introduction of quadtone inks for digital printers. You can find these for a range of printers from the desktop (Epson) to the service bureau (Iris). Here we're back to the notion of multitone printing (duotone, tritone, quadtone). More than one ink is used to print an image offering richer blacks, smoother transi-

7. An alternate color variant.

8. An alternate color variant.

9. An alternate color variant.

10. An alternate color variant.

tions, and optionally, color. Typically the inks used are a combination of blacks and grays, some warm and some cool. These inks last significantly longer than full-color inks and can be printed on a wide variety of surfaces (watercolor paper, canvas, silk, mylar, etc). It's a time of great transition. It's a time of great invention. Watch carefully and you'll see that a great deal of the new is simply the old transposed.

It may be that one day in the not too distant future what are now considered traditional processes will be considered alternative processes. On the other hand, the advent of digital technology may encourage a resurgence in the use of alternative processes. Personally, I hope so, since they are a rich and wonderful part of our visual heritage. This has certainly been the case for me. Along with these digital equivalents I have also been making traditional platinum prints from digital files. I plan to use silver again. Finding replacements for the traditional is a move I think should be made only out of necessity, say when the traditional is no longer available. I'm much less interested in finding replacements for tradition than I am in seeing tradition evolve. One limits while the other expands our horizons. Think of the endless possibilities.

METHOD

Multitone

1   Change the mode of the Grayscale image to Duotone (Image: Mode: Duotone). Load the duotone preset of your choice. (Presets are located in Photoshop under Presets.) Or create your own.

2   To print the result on a color printer, convert the mode from Duotone to RGB.

Tone

1   Tone by making a color correction. Create a Color Balance, Curves, or Hue/Saturation (Check Colorize) adjustment layer. A combination of many adjustment layers may be employed. adjustment layer layer masks may be added to apply a correction in local areas only.

   Try many variations to confirm your choice.

Split-Tone

1   Create a split-toned effect by making differing color corrections to the shadows and highlights. Use Color Balance. Check the Highlight button and make a correction. Then check the Shadow button and make a different correction. Mix a compelling color combination. Or use Curves. Raise the curve of a single channel (Red, Green, or Blue) in the highlights and lower it in the shadows. Alternately raise the highlights in one channel and lower the shadows in another. In either case, return to the Master channel to compensate for shifts in tone or contrast appropriately.

Reduce Saturation

1   Create a complex toning solution by opening a color image, creating a Channel Mixer adjustment layer with Monochrome checked, and reducing its opacity. To reduce the images saturation a Hue/Saturation adjustment layer may be used similarly. The underlying color in the original will tint the image with a variety of colors based on the original color relationships.

Small Green Island, Elemental, 1996

IX

COLOR ACCURACY

In Small Green Island, the color was beautiful just as it was.

The luminous greens of the seabed shimmered with golden light undulating across them. The yellow light was echoed in the ochre kelp pods that drifted to the surface sparkling as they bobbed in the light. The blue shadows in the depths echoed the blue highlights on the water's surface and the blues found high in the air. All the colors shared components with some other color in the image. Each was different, yet they all related harmoniously. None of the colors were at their purest, yet they were rich. It was a subtle symphony of color.

All the colors within this earthen palette grew cooler in shadowy depths and warmer in the bright shallows, grew cooler and less saturated as they receded into the distance and warmer and more saturated as they approached. The cool color of the water progressively altered the appearance of what was seen through it. The cool colors of the sky above progressively altered the surface of the water and what was seen through it. The light was gradually filtered as it passed through the depths and as the surface of the water receded.

A sheet of light grew from the horizon and disappeared at my feet. Faraway, I could not see the ocean depths, only the light from above was visible. Nearby, the surface was so clear it was almost invisible. Faraway it was filled with pale shades of white, uniform, without texture, without form beyond the flat plane of the surface. All this was gradually reversed as distance was decreased. Nearby, it was rich with saturated colors, varied, with texture, and with depth and volume beyond the flat plane of the surface. Two states existed, surface and depth. Typically you could only see one or the other at one time. Here I could see both simultaneously. One was visible where the other was not and vice versa. Both were surely present in each location, but I could only see one aspect in one area at one time from one vantage point. To see another aspect I would have to shift my perspective, both in space and time. What I saw was relative to a location and moment. It always is.

I shifted my perspective to find the sky in the final composite. The two images, the oily water suggesting a starry night sky, and the beds of kelp reminiscent of clouds drifting across an evening sky, came from the same geographic area. They were a few hundred yards from each other. They found unity in color. Green, both blue and yellow, provided the dominant color chord for the image uniting the upper surface with the lower surface. They found unity in form. Water was everywhere. Yet the water suggested air in both places. The two planes shared a common metaphor.

The transparencies were fairly accurate. The moments were fairly clear in my mind. I had my records and my memories to guide me. In comparison to my memories the film was a bit contrasty and a bit saturated. But I hadn't remembered the complex undercolorings, the immense variety of subtle colors in the original scenes. My memory had served me. My memory had failed me. Knowing that, I was then faced with the challenge of deciding when to regard and when to disregard it. Prior experience helped guide me. I'm familiar with the general response of the film I use. I'm familiar with the general topography and conditions of the area. I have many kinds of memory to serve me.

Photographs are a kind of memory. Photographs are representations of memories. Often we don't realize how important the memories of their makers are in establishing our relationships to them. Part of their authenticity is derived from the testimony of the witnesses who made them. It's that testimony that would stand up in a court of law more strongly than the data in the document. Clearly the two are inextricably linked. When a photograph's maker is gone, what happens to that testimony? How often do we presume too much?

This photograph is a representation of a memory and a feeling. While it is part fact, it is also part fiction. It is only partially objective, it is clearly subjective. Though it may not be as clearly stated in many photographs as it is here, I think most photographs are. The larger metaphor this image portrays, "as above, so below," once latent now overt, suggests a relationship that cannot be grasped from one vantage point at one moment in time. It can only be found in the comparison of many memories — some above, some below, some by day, some by night.

Just as when I am painting, I watch for the point at which too much work makes an image lose life. I watch for the point at which excess manipulation or addition produces an adverse shift in an image. I am always on the lookout for a quality of freshness, something to be preserved within the document recorded and something in my subsequent activity with it to be introduced. It may sound strange for an artist who does the kind of work I do to quote Theodore Roosevelt, "Leave it alone. It cannot be improved upon." While I allow myself to take liberties with my material, some call it artistic license and think this makes a work better, there are also times when I want to be faithful to the original event. Others think this discipline makes a work better. Neither is necessarily so. It depends on your point of view. Seen from different perspectives, both may be true. This image finds a balancing point between the two. I recognize the impulse to accuracy and the impulse to expression as two poles within a spectrum of many available responses. For me, no one answer will do for every instance. I prefer to be mindful of the larger field of possibilities. It helps me cultivate a larger awareness, both of myself and the world I live in.

Would that I were a plein-air photographer. If I could see the recording at the moment of exposure and compare it to the scene at hand I would be able to achieve greater accuracy. That day is coming — soon. On that day, will I more strongly defer to document than memory? Will that always be wise?

"What we see changes what we know. What we know changes what we see."
— *Jean Piaget*

"Color is one of the great things in the world that makes it worth living to me and as I have come to think of painting it is my effort to create an equivalent with paint color for the world — life as I see it."
— *Georgia O'Keeffe*

"Truly color is vice! Of course, it can be, and has the right to be one of the finest virtues."
— *James Abbot McNeill Whistler*

"Color is my day long obsession, joy and torment."
— *Claude Monet*

For some it's the Holy Grail. It's been going on for a long time, but the search for color accuracy continues to bedevil us. Color is a chameleon.

The Impressionists championed *plein-air* painting, favoring direct observation and color accuracy. They attempted to paint not what they knew but what they saw. It's interesting to note that prior to that a majority of color was painted from memory rather than direct observation. It's equally interesting to note that even the Impressionists were known to finish a few canvases in the comfort of their studios where direct observation was no longer possible. Is it coincidence that this movement arose at a time close to the invention of photography? Their preoccupation with "getting it right" is still with us today. Perhaps more so in photography than in painting.

Photographic documents are thought to be more objective and factually true than their manually rendered counterparts. We admit that our capture devices (film or CCDs) are limited (the range of tone and color able to be captured photographically is far less than the human eye can see) and often impart biases to the information they render (such as shifts in color). Quite often, our capture devices are built to operate under specific color temperatures. We can go to great lengths to stabilize lighting conditions in artificial environments, but in natural settings the temperature of light is ever changing, and our capture devices aren't usually optimized for all situations.

If our capture devices impart biases, at least they do so in a relatively consistent manner. They are not nearly as changeable as we are. It is certainly far harder to establish a consistent baseline between individuals with different eyes. "How red is red?" Show a group of people the same color. Then take it away and get them to reproduce it, in any medium. The range of responses is truly astonishing. This is true even among skilled professionals. Knowing the biases of our capture devices or materials, we interpret the information they render. Often we do so based on our previous experience. In a majority of cases, this means based on memory. It rarely means based on comparison with the thing itself. To complicate matters further, the human eye is an adaptive mechanism (as conditions change so does its response, and it tires requiring variety and rest to refresh it) and vision necessitates cognitive interpretation to be understood and translation to be communicated. Roughly 70% of our sensory receptors are located in the eyes. What we see is a distillation of over seven billion sensory impressions a second. We are highly selective. Our selectivity complicates the process of interpreting the data our eyes render, because it has already been interpreted, and the interpretation is being constantly updated. But, without interpretation, the information would not be as useful to us. Interpretation allows us to see the same object as red by day and by night (or under both tungsten and flourescent light) even though our optical response to it differs. This leaves a great deal of room for the influence of subjectivity. Amid the complex variables of the limits of our capture devices and the materials we use to reproduce the information found, the differences between unique individuals who adapt and update, the disparities between conventional and personal interpretation, and the limits of the language (linguistic or numerical) used to describe the phenomenon of color, color accuracy begins to seem something akin to perfection, something to be strived for, but ultimately, never truly achieved. Instead, it is approached by degrees. Lifetimes have been spent studying the complex phenomenon of color and it could be rewarding to anyone to spend part of a lifetime studying color. Understanding the problems involved will benefit you immensely.

Some trust the human eye more than the camera eye. Others trust the camera eye more than the human eye. Both sides make compelling arguments. Whichever pole we lean towards, we must acknowledge that understanding color accuracy is not simply a matter of understanding the responses of the materials we use to light, it's also a matter of understanding how our eyes respond to light.

For both the calibrationist (those who think that a monitor's radiant light can truly represent a print's reflective light with the help of profiles) and the numerical analyst (those who think you can't trust a monitor and so make corrections numerically based on their previous experience of output conditions), I give you the work of Josef Albers. Anyone working with color will benefit from exposure to his work *Interaction of Color*. Put very simply, he demonstrates that our experience of color is relative. Our perception of color changes in response to the colors surrounding it, simultaneous contrast. Put the same color in the midst of two very different colors and it will appear to be different, sometimes dramatically so. A few underlying principles can be noted: a light color will make a dark color look darker and vice versa; a cool color will make a warm color look warmer and vice versa; complements make each other look particularly intense; a small amount of color in the presence of another color will appear more intense than a large amount. No amount of numerical measurement has ever been able to accommodate these phenomena; it is not measurable, it is experiential. Greek temples were not built perfectly square, the columns not perfectly straight; instead, they were built to compensate for the optical distortions produced by linear perspective or our visual response to things. In them, lines appear perfectly parallel but are not. We need to make similar compensations to reproduce color. Perhaps this is one of the reasons why there is still an art of color. Color has steadfastly resisted becoming pure science. I do not mean to diminish the positive contributions of the color scientist or the methods of the skilled color professional. I simply mean to point out that color is an extraordinarily complex phenomenon. It's a phenomenon where you can't eliminate the human factor. After all, we can't say with any certainty that color exists in the external world.

What we can say with certainty is that color is our response to stimuli we receive. Color is a response. Color is a physical, cognitive, and emotional response.

Black-and-white image makers, don't think you're exempt from these problems. Similar phenomena occur with tone. Our job is in one respect more complicated than the colorist's. We must make the translation from color to neutrality. Neutrality is not an absence of hue; it is an unbiased hue, one that contains an equal balance of all colors. Black, white, and gray are all colors, very specific colors.

If accurate representation is achievable only by degrees and is so subjective, why try so hard to be objective and make color accurate when you will never achieve perfection? Perhaps it is like Olympic sports. Perhaps the perfect score is only the last best score achieved. Ultimately there is no perfect score. (And this does not mean that some scores are not better than others.) We are continually raising the bar, the goal. And in striving we amaze ourselves and each other.

There are benefits to achieving color accuracy. Peel away the veils of color afflicting an image and an optical purity will be achieved which will allow all the colors within it to seem maximally intense, creating an apparent increase in saturation and spatial relationships throughout the entire image. The image will seem more clear,

2. Highlights set with white point eyedropper. An inaccurate specification can lighten the image adversely and lose detail.

1. Shadows set with black point eyedropper. An inaccurate specification can darken the image adversely and lose detail.

3. Color balance set with Gray Balance Eye Dropper. Just as an accurate specification can remove a color cast, an inaccurate specification can create a color cast.

more present, more real.

Solutions for color accuracy with Photoshop can range the gamut from simple to complex. Start simply. Before progressing to the complex, see if a simple solution will do. Strive to correct an image in as few steps as possible. Favor efficiency. Think globally before you act locally. If a color imbalance exists, it usually exists throughout the entire image. You may only notice the cast in a specific area, but when you remove it globally, you may find that doing so has improved all areas of the image. If you first correct the cast locally, through a selection or with a Selective Color correction tool, you may fail to notice its presence in other areas. If you do subsequently notice the same imbalance in those areas, you will likely have to make an additional selective correction to all the other areas, save the first corrected area. Things can become complicated quickly. It takes discipline to keep things simple. If, and only if, a simple solution will not do, progress to a more complex solution. (Much of this is covered in Calibration, Tone, Color, Comparison, and Output.)

Set the highlights (white point eyedropper or better yet the white point slider in Levels), set the shadows (black point eyedropper or better yet the black point slider in Levels), clear color casts in neutral colors (neutral balance eyedropper), and often the rest will fall into place. It helps to know the numerical values for the colors you target

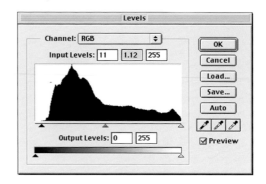

4. Black point and white point set with the Levels Master channel. Move either the white point or black point sliders too far and detail will be lost.

5. The Levels diagram.

customized for the output device you use. Typical numerical values for black (5/5/5 in RGB — 63/52/51/95 in CMYK — 98 in Grayscale), white (250/250/250 in RGB — 2/1/2/0 in CMYK — 2 in Grayscale), and middle gray (128/128/128 in RGB — 44/33/32/11 in CMYK — 50 in Grayscale) vary from printing device to printing device. (The CMYK figures given are for SWOP or a generic representation of standard web offset presses, which are quite different from inkjet printers.) If you want to precisely control results, you need to know how these values will print out on the device you intend to use. One device may be capable of holding discernible detail with a 2% total dot in the highlights, where another will need a 16% total dot. One device may need a value with 10% more magenta than another to reproduce the same blue. Even if your devices are not calibrated and you are not employing color management software, if you build your file with the numerical values needed to generate a specific response on your output device you can achieve accurate color. Do you need to memorize the numerical value of every possible color to achieve color accuracy? No. But it helps to know the numerical values of certain important colors. Photoshop provides for the use of up to four separate simultaneous color measurement points in the Info palette.

(Using the eyedropper, hold the Option and Shift keys and click on the areas to be measured to add or subtract a point. Hold the Command and Shift keys and click and drag to reposition one.) The numerical readouts in the Info palette can be reset to any combination of color spaces. (In the submenu find Palette Options. There is also a submenu under the eyedropper in the Info palette which enables you to see readouts in one of several color spaces.) You might use one point each for shadows, highlights, neutrals, and a memory color (such as fleshtones or sky blue) respectively.

A great deal of color correction can be done by simply clearing casts in areas that are neutral (such as a graycard). If these areas are truly neutral, it is fairly likely that all the other colors within an image will fall into place along with the neutral colors. Neutral colors are also excellent areas for detecting subtle color casts that might not be as apparent in more richly colored areas. However, an image may not contain neutral grays. In this event you will need to use other visual cues as guides. Despite their wide range of hues, we are exceptionally sensitive to the color of fleshtones, so look for color casts there and balance them so that they appear natural and pleasing. Yes, this is subjective, but our sensitivity to these color families aids us in

6. Black point and white point set by establishing a full dynamic range in each channel separately.

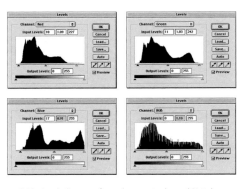

7. The Levels diagrams for each separate channel. Note how different the separate histograms are.

our quest for accuracy. You can also use memory colors to guide you. Corporations spend a great deal of money controlling the color reproduction of their logos to establish their colors as memory colors. Sky blue, cherry red, forest green, the list could go on. They're all colors that are easily recognizable and it is relatively easy to establish a consensus about what they should look like because of the consistency and frequency with which we have seen them. Again, this is somewhat subjective, but these colors narrow the range of our responses. With them in mind we can work within tighter tolerances.

The colors of highlights will often give away a color cast. So too will shadows, but they can also be misleading as they may contain a great deal of reflected color. They are not always good points to set a gray balance, but they are good reference points for comparison during color correction. In ambiguous situations an imbalance in color can be perceived in mutual relationships. It's a good idea to keep all of these footholds in mind, comparing one to the other, when correcting color. Working to make sure all of them seem right can be a juggling act.

If a perfect balance can't be achieved, sacrifice the accuracy of the least important color or areas of color that offer the greatest flexibility (colors that are not memory colors, the colors of objects that are not readily identifiable, or the colors of objects that routinely appear in a variety of hues).

This methodology works well for a majority of cases. But like autoexposure which can provide excellent exposure readings for many situations, it helps to know when exceptions are likely to arise. For every rule there is indeed an exception. They even say exceptions prove the rule. For instance, clear the color cast from a scene shot in early morning or late afternoon light and the golden or rose colored light you so patiently waited for and were thrilled by may be removed. You have to be simultaneously aware of all the variables, play them against one another, and know when to make exceptions and sacrifices. There's no substitute (or software package) for experience. It is the only "magic bullet."

It is extremely helpful to try variations of a single image. Look at several versions of an image side by side (onscreen or in prints). Nothing jars us out of our perceptual biases or proves a point so quickly. Simultaneous comparison is essential to achieving optimal color accuracy. There are many ways to facilitate simultaneous comparison. For instance, use Variations or create low-resolution duplicates of an image and view them side by side. Comparison breeds experience. As a discipline,

8. *After black and white points are set with levels, fine tonal and color correction is made with curves.*

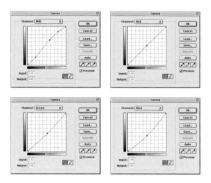

9. *The curves used.*

I will not finalize an image until I have tested at least four variations after I have done the lion's share of color correction. I insist on proving to myself that an optimal color balance has been achieved. I find I often have to fine-tune the results I thought were good to make them even better. I find the discipline is worth every effort I make. It keeps me sharp. I find when I look more closely at my images, I look more closely at the world. Truthfully, that's where I find the greatest rewards.

You may feel you have achieved accurate color on your monitor, but will you be able to achieve it in your output? Calibration and characterization are critical. This includes viewing output under optimal light temperatures. Color accuracy extends to output as much as to the monitor. Check the Gamut Warning to see if any colors are out-of-gamut or too intense to be printed accurately. I don't recommend making these kinds of corrections to your image permanently as the gamuts of printing media are constantly improving. Instead, make a flexible correction. Make a selection for out-of-gamut colors (Select: Color Range), then make an adjustment layer for Hue/Saturation to reduce the saturation of the selected areas. Or, simply reduce overall saturation to preserve relative relationships in saturation. Remember, the Gamut Warning is set to the gamut of offset presses until you load another profile. Similarly, colors — even very specific ranges of color — that have suffered in translation and are no longer as brilliant as they once were can be intensified using Hue/Saturation.

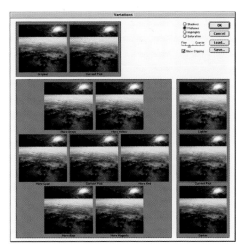

10. If an accurate color balance has been achieved, the surrounding versions found in Variations will all appear to contain a color cast.

METHOD

1   Create a Levels adjustment layer. Using the Master channel only, drag the black point slider to the right until it touches the point on the histogram at which information begins. Then drag the white point slider to the left until it touches the point on the histogram at which information begins. Then use the midpoint slider to establish an overall tone (dark or light). Use the gray balance eyedropper to set the gray balance by specifying a neutral color.

If a color cast persists, it is likely that the neutral value specified was not truly neutral or that an imbalance exists within the image itself. If a better neutral value cannot be found, let your eye be your guide and remove the color cast by going to the appropriate channel and sliding the midpoint slider up or down appropriately. Alternately, if you have known numerical values for a memory color that exists within the image, defer to them and drive those areas to those values.

This method may accentuate existing color biases within an image. In instances where this bias is desirable, such as an image made under the influence of warm evening light, this is the method to use.

2   Alternately, create a Levels adjustment layer. Proceed as above with one exception. Set the dynamic range in each channel separately. Use the submenu to activate the lowest channel first. Set the black point and white point. Repeat for each channel above it. Then return to the Master channel and use the midpoint slider to adjust the overall tone.

This method achieves a very neutral color balance. It's great for color correcting a strong unwanted color cast, such as daylight film shot under tungsten light. Be careful. It may wipe out wanted color casts such as early morning or intentionally introduced artificial light.

3   Create a Levels adjustment layer to set dynamic range with the Master channel (as in method 1). Then create a Curves adjustment layer for very fine tonal and color correction. While setting dynamic range is best done with Levels, very fine tonal and color correction is best done with Curves. Treat Curves as you would Levels, with one exception: instead of three points of control, you have an almost unlimited number with which to pinpoint corrections. The most complex color corrections can be made with Curves as they enable the removal of a color cast from single ranges of tones (such as the highlights or the shadows) without affecting the other tonal ranges. Before building a complex curve, check to see if a simple correction in the midtones will work just as well.

Rosa Celestia, Elemantal, 1996

X

COLOR EXPRESSION

This image has two titles, Rosa Celestia or Mandala in Silver and Gold. It belongs to two bodies of work: my work before it and my work after it. It changed me. Surprises often become the start of something new. I find they contain the seeds for a new series or a new subset of an existing series. A latent theme is suddenly made visible. Rosa Celestia is one of those images for me. It's the seed syllable that arose spontaneously and generated my series Mandala. Like a stone dropped in water, it changed nothing and everything. It left ripples in me. Its vibrations continue to expand.

This image announced the blossoming of an interest in abstraction within me. The Mandala series is my most abstract photographically based work to date. This work led to other works. I might not have begun the later musical series (Sonatas, Nocturnes, Etudes, etc) had I not first made this image. Both share an intense interest in color (hue, saturation, brightness, and proportion). Both share a similar meditative quality.

I was entranced by the play of light in water when I made the initial exposures. Time did not seem to move as it ordinarily did. The world grew quiet. I was absorbed by beauty. I had no idea what I was going to do with the images. I simply made exposures as a sign of recognition, recognition of beauty.

Later as the image confronted me, I found it contained even greater beauty. Symmetry revealed a hidden dimension within it. It tuned the frequency of the vibration. I've found a similar pattern in many of the symmetries I've created with nature. This leads me to think that it is somehow indicative of a deeper order to be found within nature.

I wanted the image to be as spacious and literal as it was geometric and abstract. After many experiments, I chose the proportions very carefully. Changing proportion provided relief, amplifying the contrast between the upper and lower halves. It transformed a repetition into an echo. I weighed dozens of variations side by side, registering the effects of each individually before choosing one. I discovered I could, and may, make many separate images from the same material.

The image revolves around many polarities. Literal and abstract, spacious and flat, ephemeral and permanent, far away and near, visible and invisible, light and dark, cool and warm, saturated and subdued. The image has another title for me personally — particle/wave. Two more poles. Paradoxically, light is both. Color is light.

The secondary colors are important. The yellow light on the surface of the lower portion suggests a unity, a shared existence, relationship. It helps unite the total space. The purple undercoloring strikes a complex chord within me. Ordinarily, I would not have paired orange and purple. I would have paired gold and purple or gold and orange. Gold seems to be the unifying note.

I have no idea how I arrived at the final color combination. The original image was sand colored. Perhaps I took my cue from the subject matter. Cool liquid was filled with warm fire. Perhaps I took my cue from its undercolorings and overcolorings. Every color has another color under or over it. If color is a vibration, like sound, it too contains undertones and overtones. Perhaps the choice was completely subjective. Like sound, color combination is a matter of harmonic resonance. To arrive at this combination, I let the vibrations color produced within me be my guides. I let my instincts guide me.

Color is what I can explain least and continues to fascinate me most about this image. To this day, I still have no idea why I chose these colors. I have no idea what they mean. I only know that they move me — in specific ways.

While I don't know what these colors mean specifically, they do elicit many strong associations within me. I suspect that if a group of people were to offer a number of adjectives in response to specific colors, many correspondences would be found. I believe there are three levels at work simultaneously when we respond to color — universal, cultural, and personal. A particular individual's response to color is a unique combination of all three levels. Yet, we share similar responses on at least one, sometimes two, and more rarely three levels.

I've come to know more and more about this image the longer I have lived with it. Yet it still remains a mystery. The fact that I can't explain it, yet it still moves me, tells me the work is alive. I continue to look and be fascinated by it. I see more every time I return to it. It has become a well to draw from.

SUBJECTIVE COLOR

"Merely copying the object is not art.
What counts is to express the emotion called forth in you, the feeling awakened ..."
— *Henri Matisse*

"The chief aim of color should be to serve expression as well as possible ... I discover the quality of colors
in a purely instinctive way ... My choice of color does not rest on any scientific theory;
it is based on observation, on feeling, on the very nature of each experience."
— *Henri Matisse*

"... instead of trying to reproduce exactly what I have before my eyes, I use color more arbitrarily
so as to express myself forcibly."
— *Vincent Van Gogh*

"Color is the keyboard, the eyes are the hammers, the soul is the piano with many strings.
The artist is the hand that plays touching one or the other purposively, to cause vibrations in the soul."
— *Wassily Kandinsky*

While the finest examples of photography have certainly proved the art of transcription, the finest photograph is no mere copy. Photography is our paragon of objective representation. Yet many still say that photographs are artistically inferior to paintings as they involve less interpretation. While the one has held the lock on scientific accuracy, the other has held the keys to expression. Some say this is particularly true for color photography as the methods of converting color to black and white offer the possibility of transformation and significantly more control. Color photography has been described by some as "merely descriptive." To my mind, its finest examples lay waste to such a claim — Porter, Haas, Eggleston, Meyerowitz, Dow, Burkett, and the list goes on. But if there are still any lingering doubts remaining, digital color should put these concerns to rest — finally.

Until recently it has been far easier to transform color with paint than it has been photographically. Not anymore. Digital color is extraordinarily fluid. It, unlike traditional color processes, offers independent control of color's three primary components (hue, saturation, lightness) and nonlinear color correction (the ability to transform specific colors or ranges of colors independently of others). To my mind, it's a revolutionary, or better yet evolutionary, development that has been overlooked amid the excitement of digital imagery's more flamboyant possibilities. (None of these are necessities for making digital images.) It has not been celebrated to the degree that it should be. As

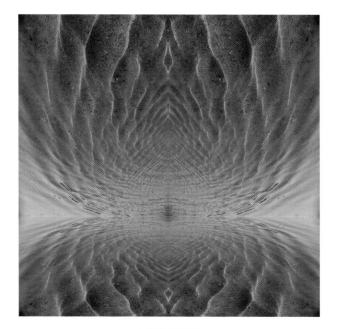

1. The root image.

with any crossroads there are many paths to choose from. This wonderful new control can be placed in the service of color accuracy. Or, it can be placed in the service of color expression.

To be effective, color transformation must be handled artfully. An image can quickly become imbalanced. Radically transform the color of one object so that it is no longer representational and attention may be driven to the new relationship. It may dominate the picture. Then the object becomes an intruder that steals the show rather than an actor in a larger drama. Radically transform all the colors in an image and color itself may dominate the image. Color may become the primary impulse, subordinating all other themes. Skillfully bypassing novelty and artifice and placing them in the service of a clear vision, you can use these tendencies intentionally.

Color can be transformed radically and still appear to be representational. Optimally, factors of familiarity (we are used to seeing the new color with the object or we have no familiarity with the object and any color seems possible), color relatedness (the hues share a common color component, are of similar value, or are of similar intensity), and color sharing (reflection) are kept in mind. Find the right balance of these factors and the color transformation can shape the content of the picture, subtly or dramatically. The transformed object continues to interact with its environment more or less democratically.

As leader of the Fauves (wild beasts), Matisse championed the power of color. Unlike the Impressionists whose color was tied to the objects and atmospheres they painted (accuracy), the Fauves gave themselves liberty to use color free from representation and thereby increased their access to its emotional potential (expression). Color became their primary concern while other concerns took secondary roles. Color was championed for its suggestive (connotative) rather than its descriptive

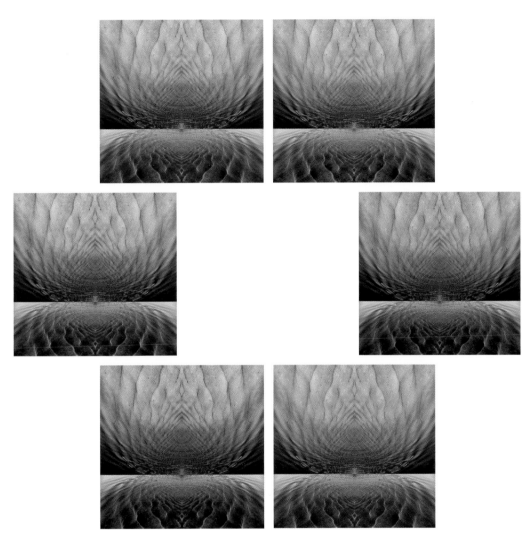

2. Variations of the final image arranged around a color wheel.

3. Variation 1.

4. Variation 2.

(denotative) qualities. In this realm only a poetic description of color can do justice to color's true power; scientific description falls comparatively mute.

Color's meaning? Try and pin it down. It can't be done definitively. Useful generalizations can be made and overturned. Yet, it may still be useful to make such observations. We may learn as much from our failures as from our successes.

Color is language as well as light. Color is communication. It may be an expressive poetry. It may be the latest fad. It may be a sacred language used to describe the divine. It may contain the revelations of scientific inquiry. It may be a navigation device. Color has been used in applications as varied as evaluating personality and stimulating biologic growth and physical healing. Color has many dimensions. A survey of Faber Birren's monumental study of color (*Color* is one of more than three dozen books) would increase anyone's appreciation of its many aspects: cultural, personal, optical, medical, psychological, etc. A great deal of food for thought is in store for anyone who becomes enchanted with the realm of color.

One can easily become entranced with color. Salvador Dalí observed, "Imagine a piano having seventy five thousand different sounds. That is the situation of the painter." Color is music. Certainly there are many kinds of music. And so it follows that there are many kinds of visual music.

While there are no set rules for color combination, the principles of consonance and dissonance apply. Similarity produces harmony; dissimilarity produces tension. Whether color relationships are derived from similarity or contrast, either is ultimately all about relationship. Relationship shapes quality of interaction.

Success can often be found by doing more with less. A great variety of intense colors within a single image is exceptionally difficult to control. As the strength of the color rises, images tend to become more decorative. Here color can be exciting and yet serve little else. When it is truly effective, color's deep connection to our emotional and psychological natures is revealed. There is no substitute for depth. Lacking this depth our "poems" will be filled with exciting words but no meaning.

Compare the works of Albers and Rothko. Both painters stripped their images down to rectangles of color and revealed the power of pure color. Both were exceptionally sensitive to the effects of color. One's intent seemed to be optical, the other's expressive. I find Albers' work fascinating, but I am truly moved by Rothko's work.

To my mind, color is best used to describe an object or quality of light optically or to generate a specific emotional

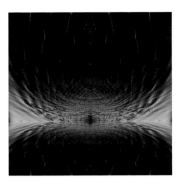

5. Variation 3.

6. Variation 4.

state. While one method looks outward and the other inward, both require a great deal of study and above all observation. If either is entered into lightly, the resulting work generated is usually similarly light. However, I do not wish to devalue responses born of innocence or generated spontaneously. I've found that no matter how trained or untrained the eye, the liveliest response in the artist generates the liveliest response in the viewer. I value living color over calculated color.

Does this mean anything goes? Yes. No. Maybe. Probably not. Incredibly, at one time or another, all these answers are correct. Don't expect an answer from anyone else. Find one for yourself. The color that interests you most will likely interest others most. Along the way you may find the answers others have found to be equally fascinating.

Wonder, study, love — to me this progression seems the only path to find the true heart of color. There are no definitive answers. But there is truth to be found in the experiences you collect along the way. That there is no answer beyond being does not mean that profound meaning cannot be found in color's depths. Try putting meaning to a passage of music. Does your love have an answer? It's more likely that it is the answer. Here words fail us. However, our awareness does not. It can be intensified. What riches lay in store for us. We have only to awak-

en and continue to be awake to receive them.

There are a variety of tools used for transforming color: Variations, Color Balance, Levels, Curves, Channel Mixer, Hue/Saturation, Selective Color, or Replace Color. Each can be placed in the service of objectivity or subjectivity. Variations and Replace Color are the only corrections that cannot be made with an adjustment layer. There are ways around both of these problems. Multiple low-resolution copies can be viewed simultaneously, enabling the great advantage of simultaneous comparison that Variations offers and adding a level of sophistication it does not allow. The Replace Color tool is essentially a combination of Hue/Saturation controls with the selectivity of Select by Color Range. You can first make a selection using Color Range and then create an adjustment layer for Hue/Saturation to achieve the same results. You cannot subsequently change the selection as easily, but the increased flexibility of being able to modify the correction indefinitely outweighs the inconvenience of having to make a new selection.

Color Balance (tied to the RGB color space) offers the most intuitive and straightforward color solutions. While the tool does not offer the sophistication of Levels or Curves, it accomplishes many of the same things with a simpler interface. Still, it would behoove anyone to become comfortable with Curves as

7. Variation 5.

8. Variation 6.

it offers the greatest sophistication. Though they are capable of making very strong color departures (especially in varying color modes), transformations made with these three tools tend to be more subtle and naturalistic.

Hue/Saturation (tied to the HSL color space) offers tremendous power but less subtlety. It offers the greatest possibilities for color transformation as the Hue slider's effects are very strong. Often they can be so strong that they will overwhelm subtle nuances in color relationships. You can restore some of these by making subsequent corrections to highlights and shadows independently. Be very cautious with the Lightness slider. It reduces dynamic range and can have an adverse affect on image quality if the image area affected contains significant contrast or texture. Tonal corrections are better made with Curves. Hue/Saturation is indispensable when it comes to one component of color. It is the only tool that allows inde-

pendent control of a color's intensity or saturation. This makes it a critical color transformation tool.

Selective Color (tied to the CMYK color space) and Channel Mixer both offer a tremendous degree of sophistication with their ability to affect both tone and hue simultaneously in complex ways. Working with the black component of an image in Selective Color (or with Channel Mixer in CMYK mode) often allows you to achieve certain pastels or shades (whiter pale colors and grayer darker colors) as no other tool does.

Past a certain point it is senseless to describe the effects of each tool with words. It's like trying to describe the sound of a digeridoo to someone who has never heard one. Words can suggest or point the way but they cannot be as specific as practical experience. I recommend spending a few minutes making transformations with each tool to translate your understanding of the effects of each into a feeling for each.

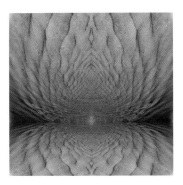

9. Variation 7.

10. Variation 8.

METHOD

1   Transform color globally. Create adjustment layers for color correction. Use Color Balance, Curves, Hue/Saturation, Selective Color, or Replace Color. Any one can be used in combination with another or with a group of other corrections.

2   Transform color locally. Some methods allow you to make corrections to specific ranges of colors (Hue/Saturation and Selective Color are two). To further localize corrections create layer masks. Gradient masks create smooth transitions from one area to another. Luminance masks are very useful for constraining corrections to specific ranges of tones, particularly highlights and shadows.

3   To drive one component (H, S, or B) of all the colors in an image toward a single value, pick a color and fill a new layer with it. Then turn the layer's blending mode to Color, Hue, Saturation, or Luminosity. Lower the opacity if necessary. Add a layer mask as desired to restrict the effects of the color overlay.

Try solving various color problems. Change a color's kind, its tint or hue. Change a color's value, its lightness or darkness. Change a color's shade, its whiteness or blackness. Change a color's saturation or intensity. Invert the tone; use Curves to make the white point the black point and the black point the white point. Invert the colors; slide their hues around the color wheel to their complements. Use Hue/Saturation to shift the hue one hundred and eighty degrees. There is a variety of ways an effect can be achieved and each solution offers a different set of possibilities.

Compare many variations. Find the one that moves you most. Don't worry if it remains a mystery why. Take comfort in a true feeling.

Oriental, Allies, 1998

ATMOSPHERIC PERSPECTIVE

Oriental, the title of this image, was not plucked out of thin air. I have always been particularly attracted to Asian callig-raphy and painting. Ancient oriental paintings rely on overlap and atmospheric perspective rather than linear perspective to depict the recession of space on a flat plane. I particularly like the way they treat morning or evening mist over mountains. One abstract shape precedes another, successively growing paler, and each is paler at the bottom and darker at the top. You can see the atmosphere. It is so thick it begins to hide the objects within it. Without the objects in it, you wouldn't see the atmos-phere as clearly. The lack of clarity the atmosphere brings to the objects within the scene reveals the invisible. It reveals space.

This is a reversal of Western tendencies. More often than not, we try to minimize the effects of haze to make objects within that space appear more clearly. While it increases clarity, many times this reduces space. When skillfully applied, at-mospheric perspective allows us to maintain clarity and increase space.

Atmospheric perspective helps describes spatial relationships, usually those involving great distances. When I demon-strate this technique, I mention other ways of treating spatial relationships — linear perspective, tonal sequencing, scale, overlapping planes, texture gradients. Atmospheric perspective can be coupled with any or all of these for even greater effect.

I use atmospheric perspective in so many of my pictures that when it came time to demonstrate the principle in words, I had a hard time singling out one image. What's more, generally I accentuate atmospheric perspective subtly. In a majority of my images you wouldn't know that it had been accentuated, but you'd feel it. Space is extremely important in my work so this technique is one of my cornerstones. Needing an image that demonstrated the method dramatically, I created a new one.

I had been planning to do an image like this for quite some time. As I sorted through my sketches, making new ones all the while, I remembered how much the Scottish Highlands look like woven tapestries in the autumn. They are at once flat and spacious, abstract and literal — like many of my images. With this in mind I began to shape an image that worked in a simi-lar way. I decided to create a desert tapestry, placing one dune in front of another in succession. A procession of earth emerged.

The subject of Oriental is so organic that the effects of linear perspective are nearly invisible in it. Like oriental paintings, the image relies on overlap and atmospheric perspective to describe space. Saturation is successively reduced and color is made progressively cooler, increasing space. The atmosphere remains invisible, but its presence can be felt.

In the full-color version, the image recedes from saturated color to less saturated color. In the final version, the image re-cedes from color towards black and white. Subtlety won out again. While I liked the full-color version, I liked the subdued color version even better. Reducing saturation equally throughout the entire image diminishes the intensity of the effects of atmospheric perspective, but it is still present. However subdued, you can still see and feel it at work.

The Great Sandunes National Monument, where the initial exposures were made, shares similarities with both Scottish highlands and Asian mountains. They are abstract and spacious. There, one mountain of sand precedes another. It is difficult to determine the scale of the dunes. As you walk out into them they seem to grow larger. They shift. New dunes become visible. The wind sighs and sand drifts across the plains and into the air. Its breath is made visible.

One cannot say this image objectively represents the place the exposures were made, nevertheless there are many ways in which it is true to the place. There are times when fiction can reveal the truth of our experience better than nonfiction.

While the image contained no symmetry, either in the environment or in the sculptural objects within it, the image seemed to belong with my series, Allies. Aside from the fact that it favored a subdued color palette, I couldn't tell why at first. It seemed to mark the emergence of a new theme within the body of work. It is only as I write this that it becomes clear to me. It is a constructed land that suggests an organic, living entity. Its themes and methods are very much the same as the other pieces in the Allies series.

I thought I was creating an image for one series (Elemental) but it ended up being for another (Allies). Such a shift does not indicate a lack of clear intention but rather a flexibility, a willingness to listen to the work. You have to listen to the work to keep it alive. In the end, the image became more mine than I had imagined. Sometimes you have to abandon yourself to find yourself. Preconceptions cannot lead you to your true voice, only the experience of it will. Though it may sound strange at first, when you hear it you will know. Time and again it has been the exploration of the unknown that has clarified and drawn me back to something I know so well, my own vision.

*"The painter can suggest to you various distances by a change in colour produced
by the atmosphere intervening between the object and the eye."*
— *Leonardo Da Vinci*

In the history of art there have been many responses to treating spatial relationships to give the illusion of virtual space within the two-dimensional plane of an image. Artists in the Orient tended to stack elements on top of one another, linear perspective was invented during the Renaissance (Giotto being one of its earliest practitioners), atmospheric perspective soon followed (masterfully employed by Leonardo Da Vinci), later Modernists departed from the desire to portray illusionistic space in favor of more subjective spatial treatments (as in the Cubist paintings of Pablo Picasso and Georges Braque or the photocollages of David Hockney).

Atmospheric perspective has been a part of the Western canon of representation and realism since the Renaissance. The principles of atmospheric perspective can be stripped down to a few essentials: warm colors tend to approach (rise forward or appear closer) and cool colors tend to recede (fall backward or appear further away); saturated (intense) colors tend to approach, less saturated colors tend to recede; contrast is reduced as the distance increases. Or, veils of atmosphere successively accumulate.

It is now possible to accentuate or reduce atmospheric perspective and in so doing expand and contract spatial relationships within a photographic image to an unprecedented degree and with an unprecedented degree of control.

One of the extraordinary advantages working digitally offers color photographers is the ability to control hue (color), saturation (intensity), and brightness (tone) as independent components. This, along with the ability to redistribute relationships in a nonlinear fashion (that is, blue separate from red and green), heralds a dramatic evolution in color photography.

This technique is extraordinarily simple, which is perhaps one of the reasons it is so often overlooked. We simply modify saturation and hue selectively and consistently throughout a given image making planes closer to the viewer more saturated and warmer, and planes further from the viewer less saturated and cooler. On occasion you will also want to slightly reduce contrast in planes that are intended to be very distant from the viewer.

In some cases when an image is composed of a single receding plane, this can simply be done by applying a Hue/Saturation correction through a gradient mask. In other cases you will have to determine the individual planes within an image and modify them selectively. Individual gradient masks can be tailored to individual planes for even more convincing results.

By allowing ourselves to accentuate the visual cues within an image, we enhance the expressive potential of our visual vocabulary. For control of spatial relationships, this technique belongs right next to depth of field; it can be marvelously paired

1. Atmospheric perspective is not accentuated.

with it. Subtle modifications of these two elements alone, saturation and hue, are often enough to yield dramatic results.

We have all seen glaringly obvious examples in advertising where Advil pills and Coke cans are portrayed with bright saturated color in subdued, monochrome, or black-and-white environments, dramatically directing our eyes to the product. This could be seen as a kind of atmospheric perspective rendered with a sledgehammer, but I hesitate to make that case as it is so dramatic it seems to transform rather than augment. The technique is a powerful way of directing the eye's attention. It creates a hierarchy of the information in the picture. As a rule our eyes gravitate towards saturated color, towards sharply focused detail, and towards areas of contrast — a black spot on a white field, a white spot on a black field, a red spot on a green field, a saturated green on a less saturated green field, a sharply focused area in a softer field. By accentuating elements in one area of the picture and deemphasizing them in others, you can direct the flow of the eye, the viewer's attention.

What we don't often see is a more judicious application of atmospheric perspective. Often it is forgotten. If our aim is an illusionistic accentuation of existing relationships and this technique is convincingly employed, we generally won't notice it; we'll feel the difference without seeing it as obvious.

If you want a photograph to maintain its realism, you will most likely want to employ this technique judiciously. If the relative saturation and color balance of the separate planes is not handled smoothly and somewhat gradually, the effect will seem false, forcing the separate planes into different color realities. Thus a straight picture may very well look overly manipulated or even like a composite if you're not careful. Subtle accentuation of relative relationships can produce relatively dramatic results without having to resort to exaggeration.

2. The fourth dune from the front is placed as the middle plane. All elements behind it are reduced in saturation and cooled in hue. All elements in front of it are increased in saturation and warmed in hue.

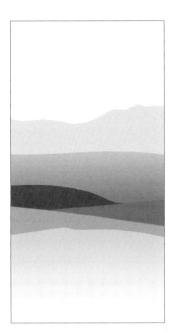

3. A composite of the separate masks made to affect the separate planes. Corrections have been made in varying intensities with them.

You can go one step further. A hierarchy of spatial relationships can be created or accentuated by placing background values darker and foreground values lighter (or vice versa) relative to each other.

You can go one step further still and accentuate spatial relationships even more by digitally controlling depth of field — blur the background and sharpen the foreground or vice versa.

Modifying atmospheric perspective is not new in photography. A host of photographers use and have used polarizers and/or red, orange, and yellow filters with black-and-white film to reduce haze; both methods modify spatial relationships in a given scene by reducing the effects of atmosphere. This has been much more difficult for color photographers — until now.

Those with more conventional tastes need not revolt. They will no doubt want to employ this technique with more discretion. After all, different film types distort atmospheric perspective as a result of their hue or saturation characteristics. Certainly Velvia is much more saturated and represents colors differently than Kodachrome. Those with a penchant for the utmost in accuracy might want to compensate for this, perhaps even digitally. Others may want to accentuate atmospheric perspective dramatically for expressive ends.

Controlling atmospheric perspective isn't just for those who want to augment existing spatial relationships within a single image; it's also for those who wish to create convincing ones in constructed images. Disregard for the effects of atmospheric perspective can be dead giveaways of compositing and undercut or destroy the illusionistic qualities many strive for.

Regardless of your aims, you should never forget atmospheric perspective. It is a powerful visual tool.

4. The saturation of the sky and furthest dune have been left untouched. Everything in the plane in front of them has been increased in saturation and warmed in hue.

5. A composite of the separate masks made to affect the separate planes. Again corrections have been made in varying intensities with them.

METHOD

1   Make selections of the planes within the image to be separated and save them for future use. Use the Lasso tool to make a rough selection, then use the Quick Mask feature to refine it with a brush; black hides and white reveals the areas to be affected. Once the quick mask is made, switch back to a selection and save the resulting selection (Selection: Save Selection) for future use.

2   Repeat this for each plane that will be affected separately.

3   Load the selection of the furthest plane (A) and create a Hue/Saturation adjustment layer to substantially reduce the saturation of that area and shift its hue towards the cooler end of the spectrum.

For correcting color, I often prefer Color Balance or Curves over Hue/Saturation as the resulting modifications are more subtle and convincing. But to employ this, you must make another adjustment layer with the same selection. Used judiciously the Hue slider in Hue/Saturation will do a fine job. Hue/Saturation color shifts are stronger, simpler, and can destroy subtle undercoloring in substantial color shifts. Unless you're treating a flat color or tone without texture leave the Brightness slider alone, it will destroy your dynamic range.

4   Load the selection for the next closest plane (B). Once again, using an adjustment layer, reduce saturation and shift hue cooler, but less substantially than the furthest plane (A).

5   Leave the middle plane (C) alone. (If you have an even number of planes, shift all the planes one way or another; if you have an odd number, as a rule, leave the middle plane untouched.)

6   Load the selection for the next closest plane (D). Using an adjustment layer, subtly increase its saturation and shift its hue warmer.

7   Load the selection for the closest plane (E). Using an adjustment layer, substantially increase saturation and shift its hue warmer.

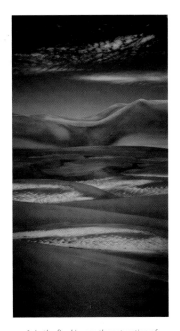

6. In the final image the saturation of the entire image has been reduced. The intensity of the effect is subdued but still present.

8   Optionally, to further refine each adjustment, gradient masks can be created that allow smooth transitions within select areas of an image, in this case each separate plane. This can be used as an alternative to a single gradient for the entire image area and in certain cases can be more convincing. Highlight the adjustment layer, hold the Option key, and click on it. This will show you the mask that isolates each correction. Use the magic wand to select the white portion of the mask. Then use the Gradient tool to create the gradient within the area of the mask constrained by the selection by clicking at the bottom and dragging to the top with gray as your foreground color and white as you background color. A lighter gray will allow more of the correction, a darker gray less. You can use curves on the mask itself to trim the blend or lighten or darken the mask, but remember to do this with the selection active. Finally, hold the Option key down again and click on the adjustment layer to return to viewing the image rather than the mask. If at any time you want to see the mask and the image simultaneously, hold the Option and Shift keys before clicking on the mask.

When working on composites there will likely be no reason to make complex selections; simple gradient masks on each adjustment layer grouped to each individual layer will suffice if the densest and thinnest portions of the mask are precisely placed.

You could do this without the use of adjustment layers by simply making selections and applying Hue/Saturation corrections to the background layer, but a great deal of flexibility would be lost. When you use adjustment layers, you can change the values of the correction at any time (double-clicking on the adjustment layer will bring up the correction which can then be modified if desired) or even turn down the opacity of the adjustment layer to reduce its effect. It is critical that relative relationships between the planes be seen simultaneously to determine optimal correction values, thus the ability to modify each correction at any time is a great boon.

Nocturne iv, Elemental, 1998

XII

THE LANGUAGE OF NIGHT

There was a galaxy spread before my feet. But, it was day. I knew what the metaphor was in Nocturne iv; I had only to heighten it. I had been pursuing seascapes, studies in proportion and color, visual equivalents of music: sonatas, preludes, etudes, and variations. It was time for a nocturne.

Generally my preliminary studies, in pastel, contain only a little variation. They match two tones and two colors. This helps strip the image down to its bare essentials making visible the dominant relationship without a great deal of distracting variation. Everything is played against those two notes. They set the key of the piece. But here the textures are equally, if not more, important to the colors. Both are united by a heavenly tapestry.

It was relatively easy to turn day into night. The sky grew darker and less saturated. Following my instincts, I reorchestrated the foreground leaving a luminous glow. Maintaining this luminosity forced me to include more light in the sky than I had anticipated. I had to readjust. The hour quickly approached dawn. The long smooth variations of the sky are deceptive. They seem small at first, side by side, but when you compare the darkest value to the lightest value, you'll find there is quite a broad range of tone and color. Is the sky many colors or many variations of one? Here it contains the purest color, though not the brightest value which is found in the foreground, forcing the eye to travel from one to the other. In the sand, a rich burgundy provides a secondary dominant chord. It transforms into blue as it grows closer to the waves and the sky. The wetter sand reflects the sky more, the drier sand less. By day the blue sand was very pale; here it grew rich and saturated. If all the elements were to share a single reality, I had to balance them, each according to the others.

If I had shot this at night the waves would likely have turned to mist. The long exposure needed would render the water as pure motion. There would be a definite horizon line but the water's edge would be anything but definite. It would be soft but not still. It would have been difficult to simultaneously freeze the waves and maintain the stars. Two shots might have sufficed, but the high speed necessary for freezing the motion of the waves would have left them so dark their color would be lost. Rather than deferring to the vision of the camera eye, I was now able to render either what my eye saw or what my mind's eye could envision.

Viewers who are familiar with our constellations are sometimes disoriented when looking at this image. In this particular case, the constellation has no heavenly equivalent. It is created. It sketches patterns that softly echo those found below it. (As above so below. As below so above.) It is a counterbalance, no more. Those who know our constellations in the heavens above may take these stars as a clue that the image has been altered. Quite often I like to leave traces of the process as clues for the viewer in this game of looking.

A LANGUAGE OF DARKNESS

"In a dark time, the eye begins to see."
— *Theodore Rothke*

"Black is the queen of all colors."
—*Matisse*

You will be richly rewarded studying the language of night.

Night's cloak transforms our visual world. As the heat of the day recedes, colors cool favoring the blue green end of the spectrum. We no doubt label these colors cool in part because of night's embrace. At night saturation is subdued. For lack of light, intense colors cannot shine at full strength. As in descending through watery depths, light dwindles, color dims, and finally disappears from sight; not gone, but out of sight, it can be brought back by the introduction of light. There are rich colors in the blacks of night: slate, indigo, Prussian blue, even green. A thousand subtle shades of charcoal make night a burnt land. At some point our eyes fail us and night becomes a void. At times this is terrifying; at times it is deeply relaxing.

With our defenses diminished, in a time typically ripe with dreams, when creatures hidden by day appear, our irrational or subconscious aspects rise. Night is full of mystery. It can be unnerving or tranquil, suggestive with new stimulation or calming with diminished sensory input. Its "void" can be full or empty.

Night is evocative; it hides rather than reveals. Its province is sanctuary and suggestion. By limiting our scope it can intensify the experiences that emerge from its veil. In darkness' isolation, tiny nuances bloom, pockets of light become whole worlds.

Certain hours are bathed in moonlight. The stars recede, their chorus dimmed. The inky shadows recede. All is bathed in silver. The land blossoms with muted colors.

We usually say we see in full color, not in black and white, often overlooking the subtleties of the subdued land of night we enter at day's end. Our language being loose and flexible, we might well describe night as black, not blue or green. There is some debate about whether we see in color at night. Our eyes have two kinds of receptors, rods and cones. One set sees well during the day in full color while another sees better at night but with much less color sensitivity. While our color sensitivity is clearly diminished in low-light situations, it is also equally clear that we have some ability to see color at night. The core of the debate surrounds how much, not if, we see color at night. Some choose to defer to film to render color at night. But, all films do not render color equally. Achieving accurate color at night is extremely difficult. Wherever you choose to enter the debate, however you choose to meet the challenge, great fascination results from looking closely without language, and without habit at the life that washes over us. A life examined yields untold riches.

I've long been interested in the challenges of making images of the night. Painting the night presents a number of difficulties. If you take your canvas and paint into the night, it is difficult to see the specific color of the paint you are using. If

1. Day.

2. Day turned to night.

you take light with you, your eyes adapt to the light you carry with you and you can no longer see into the night as clearly. At times, you are thrust into painting from memory. Many of my drawings are filled with the magical realism of impossibly starry skies hovering over moonlit landscapes.

Photography at night is typically very challenging. For lack of light, fast films with pronounced grain or very long exposures are favored. We can bring portable light sources to push back the darkness. We may favor making images found amid man-made light sources — be it the campfire, the lone street-light, or the constellations of a slumbering city.

Hollywood has been using filters and underexposure to simulate night for ages. They film night by day. It is possible to simulate night's glamour. Think cool. Think muted. Think dark. Night has many colors. Find one and follow its siren call.

I remember seeing varying reproductions of a painting by Fredric Remington. Luckily, I had seen the original. It was a night scene with snow painted in a symphony of muted greens. In one reproduction, the snow had been color corrected to white. (It was not a bad assumption by the color corrector but you know what they say about assumptions.) What was green and riveting was transformed to flat ash; the painting fell apart. This made quite an impression on me, that night could be green. I've never seen a night as green as Remington's, but having seen his, I now know to look for the green in night.

There is a prejudice rampant within photography that good photographs have a plenitude of detail throughout an image. This can sometimes be an overabundance. Some of the more compelling images I have seen contain only a sliver of detail. The little that is shown would be drowned into silence surrounded by a wealth of detail, but surrounded by hushed, mysterious darkness it becomes radiant.

The primary decision is not only what, but also how much to show. The inky shadows of night may have no discernible

3. Lens flare rendered with a paintbrush.   *4. The Photoshop lens flare 105mm prime.*   *5. The Knoll lens flare 105mm prime.*

information or they may be pregnant with hushed whispers. Under the moon's gossamer gaze, a full range of detail may be present depending on how full or how hidden it is. There is an enormous variety of nocturnal light and with it comes enormous flexibility in creating nocturnal images. Often, we are so used to the notion that we can't see at night that we don't see, or rather we fail to look carefully. Look carefully, you'll be amazed at what you see.

Dusk and dawn are two of the most favored times of day. Photographers go to great lengths to chase the waxing and waning of the day. Often the light is soft and warm. These are the "magic hours." At their far reaches, our tools can sometimes fail us when the film is too slow or the light is moving too fast forcing us to capture a longer period of time than we would

like. If we think creatively, we may well be able to bring the experiences we had in these magical moments back to light.

"It is easier to destroy than create." The maxim holds true here. One can subdue diurnal light and make it look nocturnal convincingly. The reverse is extraordinarily difficult.

It's appropriate to ask a few questions here. What are your intentions? Are you making a purely aesthetic image meant to evoke an emotional response? Or are you fashioning a document that records the way the human eye sees? Or are you creating a record of the way the camera eye sees, perhaps more than the human eye, perhaps less, perhaps just different? Are all these elements at play? Answering these questions will help you determine what practice is right for you.

Don't forget night's companions, stars.

6. The Knoll lens flare Six Pointed Star 2.1.   *7. The Knoll lens flare Quntum 5.1.*   *8. The Knoll lens flare Vortex Bright.*

METHOD

Night

1   Use an adjustment layer, creating a Curves correction, to compress the dynamic range by lowering the white point. (There is rarely a white point in night images unless it is a product of specular highlights, the stars, perhaps the moon, or an artificial light source.) Further darken the image by lowering the midtones. If less shadow detail is desired move the black point to the right. You may well want to prioritize a range of light by building additional contrast in that area of the curve steepening it. Which range of light you choose is generally based on the subject matter and will vary from image to image. If a color shift is desired make an appropriate correction to individual channels.

2   Use an adjustment layer, creating a Hue/Saturation correction, to lower the image's saturation appropriately.

Stars

1   Create a new layer. With an appropriately sized brush, use white to sketch in the constellations. Make dots of varying sizes and arrange them in a desired configuration to determine the placement of stars.

2   Create a new layer, set its blending mode to Hard Light, and check Fill with Hard Light-neutral-color (50%) gray.

3   Render a lens flare on the new Hard Light layer (Filter: Render Lens Flare). (I prefer the 105mm prime or, better still, the lens flares found in Knoll's Lens Flare Pro.) You can make a selection to contain and direct the lens flare. A smaller selection will render a smaller lens flare. The flare will be rendered in the center of your selection unless you move it in its preview window. You may want to hide the selection outline (Command H) to better see the results as the selection outline can be visually distracting. Repeat this process for each star. Change filter settings as desired. For a great deal of flexibility, you can render the lens flares on separate layers.

4   Selectively reduce the intensity of specific stars to create a less uniform luminosity between stars. If stars are on separate layers reduce the layer's opacity. If stars are on the same layer add a layer mask and use varying shades of gray to reduce opacity selectively.

5   If you wish to incorporate color in select stars in your image, create a Hue/Saturation adjustment layer grouped to the Hard Light layer and shift hue as desired.

Path of the Sun iii, Elemental, 2000

XIII

FOCUS

I looked at the plane of rock, three feet away — the top of a cliff. I looked at the plane of water, a dozen feet below — and further into the depths. The image in my mind for Path of the Sun iii was all in sharp focus. But there was no way to bring it all in focus at one instant, even with my eyes. Stopping down wouldn't do the trick, even to f45. No swing, tilt, or shift would do the trick; both planes were roughly parallel. Consequently the technical solution lay not in shifting physical perspective (the composition would change) or equipment (from a normal lens to a tilt/shift lens or from hand-held to view camera) but in a mental shift in perspective. Again, two exposures did what one could not. One exposure was made for the plane of rock and another for the plane of water. I framed the image, focused far, exposed, focused near, exposed. Later the two images were registered, digitally. Out-of-focus planes were hidden to reveal in-focus planes. Depth of field was functionally extended.

Once again, the solution lay in thinking outside the established practices of my craft, but using it as a foundation from which to solve the problem. Tradition is not a prescription for action; it is instead a foundation upon which to build. It offers a useful set of guidelines. Those guidelines become liabilities if they limit, assets if they enable. Time and time again, I have found that I must reconsider my habitual practices in order to find an optimal solution. This solution lay outside a conventional formula, but the problem solved was quite typical. It can be challenging to shift your perspective; it's harder still to discover new ways of looking and fashion ways to record them. In the former, you can build upon the efforts of the past; in the latter, there are no precedents.

The process of making this image seemed appropriate. The image in my mind was a composite of many perspectives, involving the motion of my eyes. I tried to hold everything in sharp focus. It involved some effort. Looking at the final image is, in some sense, a relief. The visual challenge is finally resolved for the viewer. A great deal of the work of looking is done and held in place.

To my mind, while sharpness flattens an image visually, psychologically it adds depth. In an image that is sharply focused overall (as in this image), each element holds equal weight with regard to the element of focus. One kind of prioritization, lack of focus, a clue to depth, has been removed. Yet, conversely, when focus is removed, the viewer's efforts to penetrate to out-of-focus areas is thwarted. In these kinds of images we are constantly deflected away from soft areas to sharp ones. While the landscape that is partially out of focus will give the visual impression of depth, the landscape totally in focus will give the psychological experience of travelling through those spaces (albeit more easily, as the eye does not have to work as hard to do the travelling). In focused images, you can look to both near and faraway places and see them both in focus, thus the total psychological distance travelled is greater. Yet the visual impression is of reduced depth. The visual sensation can sometimes be at odds with the psychological effect.

This image is part of a series. For some time now I have been making multiple images of the same subject composed from different perspectives. In this image, I was pulled along by the reflection of the sun that moved with me as I moved through the image. The environment changed as I moved through it. The reflection changed position within it, and sometimes its shape shimmered in the wind. In this image the sun is positioned behind the floating log, but you can still see its halo. I often like to walk around, in, and through an image I have found. The process of making images for me is a journey, a path of discovery. I enjoy the physical and kinetic aspects of making images. The discovery of every composition involves a balletic dance between the observer and the observed.

It is at once less and more present in photography than in painting. In painting this process of discovery is often revealed in traces on a surface made by successive observations of the artist through gesture. Through a process of manually rendering an image, you understand the contours and space of things kinetically by reproducing or finding equivalents in motion for them. (This kind of understanding is one reason I like to make sketches of images, before or after they are complete.) In photography the image arrives instantly; fewer traces are left. But more frequently, the image is found by moving by or through an environment. Often the image itself is moved through, prior to or after exposure. Even if other images are not made along the way, the artist understands the spaces by moving in them or relative to them. Different and similar, in both cases, the body becomes a receptor. The sum total of the impressions yielded by all our senses is greater than their individual parts — it's sensory synergy. Often we conjure up ways to suggest these other missing dimensions in images — texture, temperature, sound, smell, and motion. In many ways this resembles the neurological condition of synesthesia. Synesthesia involves the crossing of sensory input from different senses, usually in diminished intensity, for instance hearing and tasting color or seeing images in response to sound. To one degree or another, we are all synesthesiatic. In the case of motion, no synesthesia is necessary. Vision itself is kinetic. We constantly move our eyes. We move through the world and are moved by it. Things grow more or less focused in the process.

"Experience is not what happens to man. It is what a man does with what happens to him."
— Aldous Huxley

As so little of our field of vision is sharp at one time, it's surprising we do not have a richer history of soft images. Or perhaps we do. Certainly there were the Impressionists, and it is appropriate that a dominant concern of the movement was to more closely approach the way the eye sees, not the way the mind is trained to think it sees. It is certainly no coincidence that this movement arose around the time of the invention of photography. And it is no coincidence that soon after, the Pictorialists favored soft focus in their photographs. They looked to the visual qualities of paintings to legitimize their work as art. In reaction, straight photography arose to legitimize photography as an art form in its own right by heightening the contrast between the painting and the photograph. Photography could portray a much greater level of detail than painting and so it should; an option became convention or "natura." Curiously, painting then also began to take its clues from photography. The rise of abstraction in subsequent modernist work was no mere coincidence. Later, focus and lack of focus became a preoccupation of the Photorealists. Their work employed both sharp focus overall and selective focus, with limited depth of field, favoring the ways the camera eye sees over the ways the human eye sees. Even in the fields of documentary photography, limited focus was revived as an important aesthetic as it was seen to be less controlled and thus more "authentic." Clearly focus or lack of focus is not an intrinsic quality of a medium since it is a property of seeing. While the two fields of photography and painting have been seen as separate, they have been influencing each other since the invention of photography and they continue to do so. When we look back on their development it is possible to take the view that they are both part of a larger history, which includes motion pictures, a history of the visual arts, a history of seeing.

While it is wise and useful to be mindful of history and current cultural concerns, it is also useful to get back to the visual basics. Focus or lack of focus affects us. To become aware of how, we can simply respond to it. A focused image has more information; an out-of-focus image has less. One allows for a maximum extraction of information, the other defies it. One favors a more analytic approach, the other favors a more emotional approach. One encourages a direct response, the other encourages continued interpretation. One feels more controlled, the other less controlled. One gives the feeling of being more in control, the other of being less in control. One presents a transparent atmosphere, the other a translucent atmosphere. One is clear, the other is murky. One is representational, the other tends towards abstraction. One is complex, the other is simple. One is textured, the other is smooth. One is sharp, the other is soft. One is busier, the other is calm. One is energetic, the other is quiet. (If we are speaking of motion blur, then this statement is reversed.) One is tightly packed and dense, the other is spread wide and diffuse. The list could go on — and should. Make your own list. There is a very personal dimension to visual responses which should not be overlooked. Our personal responses are our foundations for creativity. Very broad generalizations, such

1. Soft focus. The overlying layer in Normal mode.

as these, can be useful particularly if you are mindful of exceptions. Image content, shape, tone, color, and saturation can all modify these responses or even shift them in opposite directions, but these basic tendencies persist in a majority of images. As long as you are aware that there are no absolutes, it's useful to note tendencies.

You can control focus and use this basic visual element to shape and clarify a message. You can do so conventionally, digitally, or both. Knowing how it's done in both arenas opens up a world of possibilities.

SHARPEN

Digital sharpening can do wonders, but not miracles. While Photoshop can make images look sharper, there are limits to what it can do. No amount of Unsharp Mask will cure a substantial lack of focus or motion blur. (Again, digital technique is not a substitute for traditional technique but rather a marvelous extension of it.) But digital sharpening can be used to make relatively sharp images look sharper.

Sharpening an image in its entirety may subtly accentuate

virtual space. Overdo it and the sharpness of the image may become exaggerated and actually look flatter, even more abstract. In both cases spatial relationships are defined and controlled through focus.

Sharpening can even be used selectively. You can use the Sharpen tool. You can sharpen a selected area, even through a feathered selection for smoother transitions. Or, you can sharpen a duplicate image layer and add a layer mask to it to achieve a similar effect. The effects of the first two methods are fixed, while the last is flexible.

Selective sharpening can achieve at least three things: the attention of the eye can be driven to a particular area, the visual rhythm of an image can be accentuated or altered, or depth of field can be accentuated, globally or locally.

BLUR

While images can only be sharpened so much, there is virtually no limit to how much an image can be softened. Blur it. Gaussian Blur (which incorporates the mathematician Gauss' name as it uses his work as a basis for its function) blends the

204

2. Soft focus. The overlying layer in Lighten mode.

3. Soft focus. The overlying layer in Screen mode,
with adjustment to compensate for lightening.

values/hues of adjacent pixels. Radius controls the distance between pixels that will be averaged. Higher values in both create a greater blurring effect. Just as I recommend using Unsharp Mask rather than Sharpen or Sharpen More, I recommend using Gaussian Blur, not Blur or Blur More, because it provides a more precise level of control than a default setting. Just as with Unsharp Mask, there is no one setting that will work well for all images. Each image will have its own unique demands. File size is an important consideration. The intensity of the effect will need to be increased as file size increases. As the filter affects the pixel structure of an image, it makes sense that the more pixels a file contains the greater the intensity of the effect necessary to achieve a desired result. While it's necessary to see the effect on an entire image, remember to look at your document at 100% as well since other percentages do not represent the way an image will be output as accurately. Viewing a single document with two windows simultaneously is a great aid in determining the precise amount of blurring (or sharpening) necessary.

For very smooth transitions of varying intensity, try applying a filter through a selection made with a gradient mask. Very complex transitions can be created with complex gradient masks.

Photoshop has both Blur and Sharpen tools in the tool palette. While the settings on the filters allow you a maximum amount of control, the brushes allow you to apply a more limited control very selectively. As with any brush, varying opacities of an effect can then be glazed into an area with successive strokes of increasing or decreasing intensity, just as a painter would build up an effect by glazing an area of canvas to shape it. The smoothness of the transitions created depends upon the skill of the user. I often use the Blur and Sharpen tools to selectively modify a layer mask. This can be particularly useful for edge treatment.

Using different History states and the Histories brush can provide increased control. Again, as with any brush, varying opacities of a previous state can be applied in a highly selective manner.

One option allows maximum flexibility and control. Place a duplicate blurred layer above an unmodified layer, then use the layer's opacity setting to control the effect globally and a layer

4. The foreground out of focus.

mask to control the effect locally. Where the mask is black the blurred image will be unseen, where it is white it will be fully seen, while varying shades of gray will create opacity. By using the Paintbrush and/or Gradient tool on the layer mask, you can customize the placement and degree of an effect precisely. This achieves essentially the same effect as the previous methods but the layer mask can be modified any number of times, at any time, allowing you to undo, redo, and modify the effects infinitely and indefinitely with no loss in quality. This method allows the ultimate in control. Its drawback is that it generates a larger file. It's a small price to pay for precision and freedom.

There are many subtle uses for blur filters including reducing noise (sometimes in a specific channel rather than all channels, most often the Blue channel in RGB or the A and B channels in LAB), smoothing visual transitions (particularly in very evenly textured areas of an image), and creating blurred duplicate layers for retouching (reducing unwanted surface detail by using a layer mask to control the effect selectively). There are also methods of blurring that can be used for substantially altering an image, specifically its focus.

DEPTH OF FIELD

While there are many similarities between the camera eye and the human eye, there are also significant differences between the two. Primarily the camera eye can maintain a much greater area of focus and achieve a much greater depth of field than the human eye can at one time. Given time, the human eye can outperform the camera eye. Photographic vision is fixed, forever rooted in the past; by contrast, the human eye is changing, continually in the present. The camera eye creates enduring documents that can be considered at length while the human eye creates a visual sensation that quickly fades into memory.

Photographic images lack focus for the same reasons our eyes do. The plane of focus, film or fovea, must be at the proper distance from the hole that admits light, aperture or iris. As the hole grows smaller, the total distance encompassed increases.

The primary factor for controlling depth of field conventionally is the size of the lens aperture (or f-stop): the smaller the hole the greater the depth of field, the larger the more limited. The angle of the plane of capture (film or CCD) also plays

5. The background out of focus.

an important role, something larger format cameras are able to control better than smaller format cameras by changing the angle of the lens plane and the focal plane.

As depth of field is a matter of focus, or sharpness, there is less that you can do about increasing sharpness than there is about decreasing it. We can blur focused image information so that it will appear unfocused. When done skillfully, we can visually simulate the reduction of depth of field, and possibly the visual recession of space at the same time.

However, compositing can overcome many limitations. Make two exposures of a given scene, focus one near and one far, and composite the two, hiding out-of-focus information in the overlying layer with a layer mask, and as all areas of the image appear equally sharp, depth of field is functionally extended, perhaps beyond the range of existing capture devices.

OUT OF FOCUS

With two percent of our field of vision in sharp focus and ninety-eight percent out of focus, it's surprising how much we focus on focused images. Out-of-focus images are what we see most often. But they're not what captures our attention. Induced by sleep, turbulence, injury, illness, or intoxication, loss of focus connotes loss of control. Whether it's slipping into or emerging from oblivion, is it any wonder that out-of-focus images evoke connotations of altered states of consciousness? Out-of-focus images often seem to arise out of the subconscious or semiconsciousness.

The method for making out-of-focus images digitally has a Zen-like simplicity. Blur the image.

What's the advantage to doing it digitally? You can control the degree of blurring. And you can alter the effect at a later date should you wish to.

One note of caution. Digital blurring works differently than the blurring you will encounter with the camera eye. Certain effects of digital blurring are not the same as effects created with the camera eye. The interaction of lens and light causes certain artifacts due to flare, spill, and uneven buildup. The configuration of elements works in a certain way. Light flares out in cones in a three-dimensional space. Light successively builds up. With different elements at work, digital blurring works

6. Selective focus. Only the log is in focus.

7 Selective focus. Focus is reduced radially from the center of the log.

another way. Image information on a two-dimensional surface is averaged with its neighbors. Both dark and light values hold equal sway in the process. The results the two methods produce are sometimes similar and sometimes different. The primary difference I have seen is that the presence of light builds up in successive layers with the camera eye. Light is suffused into dark areas, sometimes causing transparent effects. A bright edge will spill into a dark area, but less frequently vice versa. The spread will be based on a cone of light. When blurred, images are moved up the cone of line from a point when focused to a widening circle as things grow less focused. Think of the shadows of planets that radiate out from the sun, a straight line drawn from its center through their center, fading as distance increases in a cone, wide at their maximum circumfrence, diminishing to a point far out in space, with an umbra (area of maximum darkness) and a penumbra (area of diminished darkness due to the spilling and splaying of light). Though the intensity of light diminishes as distance increases, the contours of shadows (the blocking of that light) contract rather than expand as distance increases. Digitally, the dark and light spread into each other equally. While outlines are softened, transparent artifacts are not created. By the same token, certain effects of the camera eye are not the same as the effects of the human eye. You can blur a photographic image more than you can blur your eyes. Our eyes cannot be blurred past a certain point. Past a certain point, our eyes create two overlapping blurred images. Slight halos at the blurred edges of things or flares may arise that are often not seen by mechanical eyes. For instance, stars captured with the camera eye are unusually crisp and do not contain the flares we see with the naked eye. A careful study of the phenomenon of lack of focus would aid anyone. In creating digital simulations it is useful to look at the ways the camera eye sees. It is as or more important to look at the way your eyes see the same things. Everything you find with eye, camera, or software can serve as a rich vocabulary for creating new images.

SOFT FOCUS

Soft-focus images involve a degree of transformation; that is, we rarely see the world as we see it in soft-focus images.

8. Selective soft focus
below the surface of the water.

9. Selective soft focus
above the surface of the water.

Often soft-focus images seem otherworldly. They conjure dreamlike feelings. They evoke reverie. In soft-focus images light spills and splays about diffusing into and extending, even thickening, the visual atmosphere. Heavy atmosphere or a translucent veil between us and the seen may create a similar diffusion of light. In some instances back lighting, where light spills around objects, has a similar visual effect. Still, the total effect of some soft-focus effects has no real-world equivalents. What we see is usually in focus or to some degree out of focus, unlike soft focus which is both at one time.

Traditionally, there is a variety of devices for creating soft-focus images. Most favor shooting through screens or filters placed in front of the lens at the time of capture. A variety of soft-focus filters come in assorted strengths and types. Once used, these effects are fixed.

Digitally, you can make an image shot with soft-focus filters appear convincingly sharper only by degrees. However, you can work the other way, making sharper images look softer, to greater degrees. Shoot it sharp. Make it soft-focus later. Combine an out-of-focus version of an image with an in-focus one.

It's never been easier. Duplicate an image layer. Blur the duplicate layer. Then turn down the opacity of the blurred layer. You might even find a compelling effect by changing the blending mode of the overlying layer. In particular, try Lighten and Screen.

There's never been more control. Effects and intensities come in an astonishing array of options. The ability to apply an effect with varying intensities throughout the image is unprecedented. (Add a layer mask with varying shades of gray.) You may try several variations before making a final decision. What's more, should you decide you would like to modify the effect, you can do so at any time — ten minutes, ten months, or ten years from now.

SELECTIVE FOCUS

Selective focus has been used to great effect as an expressive device in photographs. It controls the flow of the eye throughout an image (generally softer is faster and more fluid while sharper is slower and more rhythmic). It directs the eye to particular areas, the ones in focus. And, it is an indicator of spatial relationships.

As depth of field increases, the amount of focused image information increases and vice versa. Depth of field is a linearly proportional phenomenon. It falls off consistently on either side of the point of critical focus. Most commonly, focus is reduced as space progresses or recedes. Whether an image is out of focus far away and sharp close by, or vice versa, the transition between the two is proportional to the recession of space. When critical focus is placed between near and far, the middle-ground remains in focus, while nearer and farther objects both appear with diminishing focus, diminishing in proportion to their distance from the point of focus.

Again, the method for creating selective focus digitally is the essence of simplicity. As before, duplicate an image layer. Blur the duplicate layer. Set the amount with an eye towards the areas that want to be blurred most. That is, use the maximum intensity desired in one portion of the image on the entire duplicate layer. Then add a layer mask. Paint or fill areas of the mask with shades of gray to reduce the opacity of the blurred image, and then reveal the unblurred image below that image by degrees.

Some treatments will need very simple masks. Others will need very complicated ones. To decrease an image's depth of field after the image has been captured, you need to be able to make reasonably accurate predictions about the relative three-dimensional spatial relationships represented within the two-dimensional image. In spacious landscapes the recession of space is relatively linear and easy to determine. Usually areas higher on the picture plane are further away from the viewer than areas lower on the picture plane and/or areas grow increasingly far away as they grow further to the left or right on the picture plane. A linear gradient mask will often suffice. Remember, using Levels or Curves on the grayscale mask will allow you to shift the midpoint of the gradient after you create it. This way you can visually see the effect on the image as the mask is changed. In complicated environments such as forests, urban settings, or still lifes, the recession of space is rarely linear and so may be quite a bit more challenging to determine. Remember the basic principle: depth of field is reduced linearly and proportionally. Areas of the mask covering objects that are closer to the viewer will want to be proportionally lighter, while areas of the mask covering objects that are far away will want to be proportionally darker — or vice versa. The distance between the closest and farthest points will be represented by two tones, black and white, and shades of gray will darken or lighten between them in proportion to the recession of space. The masks used to achieve this effect are most often very soft, that is they look blurred themselves. If they are very complex, these kinds of masks will need to be painted by hand. Luckily the precision with which they must be rendered is far less important than it is with contrast masks.

While depth of field is an important consideration in soft-focus images, it need not be the primary one. As a rule, it holds true for a majority of situations, but there are always exceptions. You may want to break the rules for effect. When things are out of focus, texture is smoothed, edge is downplayed, shape and color/tone carry the composition. The tactile qualities or the visual flow of an image may be of primary importance. Or, one element may be left significantly sharper than others, driving our attention to it. You can use focus expressively, determining it arbitrarily but nonetheless intentionally, to shape the quality of attention a viewer gives to an image, to shape the quality of response an image elicits from a viewer.

Often paintings distill the information in an image to its essentials. In subduing detail, particularly surface detail, the focus of attention is more easily directed toward the foundations of an image. This simplification is not always achieved by lack of focus, it is sometimes achieved by an intentional omission of detail. In many photographs the vast wealth of

10. Out of focus.

information contained in them is secondary to the primary thrust of the image. It's icing on the cake. The wealth of detail photographs contain is sometimes more a matter of style than substance. Some photographs rely on the vast amount of detail they contain to communicate their essential messages. Others do not. Some are better served with less. Does a photograph's wealth of information serve its content or does it merely prove it is a photograph, perhaps a technically proficient one? Is sharp necessarily better? They're interesting questions. We're all different, so we'll naturally find different answers. (Similarly, different images may demand different answers.) But they're our answers, not the medium's. Convention need not rule our expression. We can modify the camera eye's response. Or we can modify the artifacts the camera eye produces for us. Either way, we control our images.

METHOD

Sharpen Selectively

1   Duplicate an image layer and sharpen it using Unsharp Mask.

2   Add a layer mask and selectively reduce the sharp layer's opacity.

Increase Depth of Field

1   Make two exposures, one sharp faraway and the other sharp nearby.

2   Composite the two and hide the soft areas of the overlying layer with a layer mask.

      Conversely, use the method below for selectively blurring an image.

Blur Selectively

1   Duplicate an image layer and blur it using Gaussian Blur.

2   Add a layer mask and selectively reduce the blurred layer's opacity.

Soft Focus

1   Duplicate an image layer and blur it using Gaussian Blur.

2   Add a layer mask and globally reduce the blurred layer's opacity.

3   Optionally, apply soft focus selectively by adding a layer mask.

4   Optionally, try different blending modes for the overlying layer.

Out of Focus

1   Blur the layer using Gaussian Blur.

Gaia i, The Sensual Land, 1999

XIV

MULTIPLE EXPOSURE

Into an abstract field of texture a smooth sculptural figure is interjected. At odds, the one counterbalances the other. At one, the two merge finding unity. Two worlds collide. The nature of both are clarified. A preexisting relationship is made visible.

Gaia. Mother earth. It's rare in mythology to have an earth father. Is this birth or death? Earth, from it we are born, to it we return. All races, all men, share a common "mother." We are only a small part of a much larger whole. In time, all return to the whole. For all our great deeds we cannot add one ounce to the whole.

The land encloses the figure. The figure encloses the land. Who's pregnant with whom? The earth with the woman? Or the woman with the earth? A portion of us is made of earth. A portion of the earth is made of us. One gives voice to the other.

Inside the land the figure is transparent, an apparition, a spirit. Inside the figure the land is transparent, an apparition, a spirit. The land and the figure are echoes of one another, within each other. Michaelangelo said of his sculptures he had only to reveal the figure that lay within the uncarved block of stone. With echoes of this in my mind, I find the reverse is true here too. We have only to find, inside the figure, the land that lies within. We have only to find the land within ourselves, ourselves within the land.

Ambiguity points to their inseparability. The two are one. In this image a metaphor is made literal. The union defies the rational but confirms the irrational. It simultaneously acknowledges and denies duality. It stops making sense to make sense.

Ambiguity points to a complexity of interaction. The answers found here are not simple. Things do not stop at the surface, rather they continue. Ambiguity does not always indicate a lack of resolution or intention. It can provide depth and continuance. It can do justice to incredible complexity. We are more than we know, more than a surface, more than a moment. Everything is.

Like the striking verbal conjunctions found in poetry, I find striking visual conjunctions whose meanings are not immediately apparent more compelling than those whose meanings are. In this image, the themes are all there, but they are found in suggestion more than in description. While the script is familiar, there's a great deal of room for the viewer to read into the image. It is open ended. It offers many possible conclusions. It's worthy of continued and sustained attention. It is not an equation with a fixed answer to be solved. It is full of variables. Its answer lies in successive iterations. As new solutions are discovered, a larger pattern emerges. I created it, or through me it was brought to light, but I do not fully understand it. It challenges me still. I know it will continue to do so for years to come. When I find an image like this, or when an image like this finds me, I realize I have found the seed of a new series. I know the theme is worthy of continued and sustained attention.

"Chance is always powerful. Let your hook be always cast in the pool; where you least expect it, there will be a fish."
— Ovid

Phantoms pass through sheets of light. A once solitary man becomes many. A stone floats weightlessly. A grain of sand rests, impossibly large. A woman discovers a new presence within her own body. Transubstantiation. Time disrupted. Gravity defied. Scale overturned. Interior and exterior comingle. The boundaries of the material world begin to dissolve. Object and object, object and environment, moment and moment, merge.

It's no wonder that images employing multiple exposures carry strong psychological overtones. They present a world that is at once our own and simultaneously not our own. Absurdity, chance, and random encounters play on our perceptions. Is this nonsense? Or has the inner connection between all things suddenly been made visible in the material world? Do miracles really happen? Is seeing believing? If not, then what is this? There must be an explanation. Our rational mind quiets us. We know the parlor tricks involved. But does this dismiss the images found as frivolous or irrelevant? Are we not still moved?

The Surrealists, along with a host of visionary artists that came before them, capitalized upon such questions. It's ironic that the camera eye, champion of representation and objectivity, is capable of creating fantastical realities beyond the imagining of even those so well versed in the imaginal world.

Traditionally, making multiple exposures presents many challenges and uncertainties. Few, if any, can truly envision the final result of making two or more exposures on one sheet of film. A general notion about the result can indeed be formed: compositional elements will merge with one another; the light will build up extra density throughout the image, speaking in a pronounced voice, and the dark will not, speaking in whispers, if at all. Precise alignment of combinations is difficult to arrange. It's possible to create a map of where the elements of previous exposures lie within the picture frame as a reference for where to make subsequent exposures. Want to change your mind after exposure? Too late. They're on the same sheet of film, inseparably locked. Add motion and the game becomes more complicated. In many instances you have to make a guess. No matter how well educated, along with that guess will come surprises. Only some will be welcome. While chance favors the prepared, chance nonetheless necessitates a dose of luck. Stack the deck. After all, if you win the game we all win.

Multiple exposure has been both enticing and frustrating for many. Our frustration diminishes in proportion to our tolerance for serendipity. Serendipity can be a powerful wellspring for creativity. Some like to celebrate it. Some don't. If you're one of the latter, rather than counsel waiting for a happy accident to occur, I recommend taking the accident out of the equation. If you're one of the former, I recommend postponing its arrival. Make the exposures separately and combine them later.

There's a simple reason why some photographers make multiple exposures in the darkroom rather than in the camera. It affords more flexibility and control. Rather than locking a set of relationships together at the moment of film (or CCD) exposure, a set of more fluid relationships are established during paper exposure. Subject, position, scale, tone, contrast, opacity,

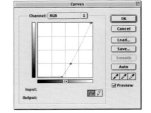

1. Opacity reduced.

2. Opacity reduced with increase in contrast.

all are relatively fluid. Unfortunately, if you want a second print after the balletic performance of the first, you generally have to do it again. Working digitally can take some of the pain out of the process and offer some new opportunities. It affords maximum flexibility and control.

It's a simple matter to make separate exposures. It's a simple matter to combine them digitally: drag one image layer into another. Repeat this as many times as you desire.

Want to change one element without affecting the rest? Highlight it and make the change, globally or locally. You can do this at any time, now or in the future.

Want to reposition one element? Highlight the layer it's on and use the Move tool. Link two or more layers if you want to move them simultaneously.

Want to rotate, resize, or distort one element? Transform it. (Edit: Free Transform). Again, link two or more layers if you want to transform them simultaneously.

Want to correct the image quality of either image independently of the other? Highlight the specific layer to be affected and add an adjustment layer grouped to it. The adjustment layer will appear offset with a dotted line above the layer it is grouped to. Hold the Option key and click on the line between them to group and ungroup a layer or adjustment layer.

Want to hide one area of an image but not another? Add a layer mask to that image layer and fill the area to be hidden with black. A paintbrush works well, but for large areas select an area and fill it with black, then refine the edge with a brush if necessary. If you use a brush only to fill a large area, you're more likely to miss small areas where brushstrokes don't overlap. It's a good idea to look at the layer mask after you've created it to make sure there are no missing gaps. Hold the Option key and click on it, to reveal or hide it. You can toggle back and forth with multiple clicks. Some like to see the image and the mask simultaneously, and this is useful for defining precise edges.

3. Variation in scale and position.   *4. Variation in scale and position.*   *5. Variation in scale and position.*

Hold the Option and Shift keys and click on the layer mask. Hold the Shift key and click on the layer mask icon to temporarily disable the layer mask. Layer masks can be refined infinitely.

In the same way, you can reduce an image element's opacity locally. While opacity can be reduced globally by lowering a layer's opacity setting (use this setting to determine a layer's highest opacity setting), layer masks can be used to reduce an image's opacity locally. It's all a matter of density. If a black brush hides an area of an image and a white brush reveals an area, a gray brush will create an opacity proportional to its darkness. Black or white paintbrushes can be used transparently. (Hit any number key and a brush's opacity will be reduced to the equivalent opacity (5 = 50%). The X key will reverse the foreground and background colors.) Use successive strokes of a lowered opacity brush to increase or decrease density. Smooth transitions can be created this way. Blur the layer mask for even smoother transitions. Gradients are wonderful for this. Use the Gradient tool or create them manually with a brush, or both. You can even do this within a selection.

Want to see many versions? Duplicate the layer to be effected in the separate versions, then make the change. Turn on the eye of the one you want to see and turn off the eye of the one you don't.

Want to see different versions side by side? Duplicate the file and open the duplicate with the original.

If you're working on large files you may consider creating low-resolution copies of the files for comparison. Any changes you make to adjustment layer settings can be used in the high-resolution final. Simply drag them from one document into another. Masks are resolution-dependent and so will have to be rescaled if they are brought from a low-resolution file to a high-resolution file. Hold the Shift key when you drag the layer to position the mask in the center of the screen and rescale the mask proportionally (Image: Transform: Scale while holding the Shift key). If you work this way, save precise edge work for the high-resolution version as masks will become soft when resampled.

Very often an image with lowered opacity won't have enough contrast when merged with a background. This is a simple matter to cure with Curves. If that's still not enough, duplicate the layer and turn the duplicate to Hard Light mode.

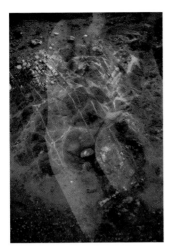

6. *Variation in opacity and position.*

7. *Variation in opacity and position.*

8. *Variation in opacity and position.*

A duplicate layer on Hard Light mode combined with a layer on Normal mode, both with increased contrast, will yield a different result than simply increasing contrast. Layers can have different blending modes. Though many of these modes favor a heavily manipulated look, even those not interested in employing this aesthetic may find experimentation with them rewarding.

When do you stop? When the image is done.

A few suggestions may be helpful. One, test many variations. Two, be careful not to overwork an image. Always be on the lookout for the point at which an image begins to lose its freshness. Three, be careful not to overdo it. I tend to strip down the elements needed for an image to a bare minimum, eliminating anything that is superfluous. Four, if you're really good (or lucky) any rule can be broken effectively.

In some cases, I find an image will evolve, not only in terms of the way it is printed (a currently accepted transformation over time) but also in terms of the way it is composed (a transformation some are still uneasy with). A digital image need not remain fixed, though it can be. One image can evolve over time. One image can become many.

METHOD

1   Combine two or more images. Click on and drag an image layer from one document into another. Repeat, if desired.

2   Reduce the Opacity slider of the overlying layers to reduce their opacity globally and reveal the underlying background layer.

3   Use a layer mask to further subdue or hide information by reducing opacity locally. Regardless of whether you fill broad selected areas or paint small sections by hand, as the layer mask darkens the image's opacity is reduced accordingly. The opacity of an image layer can be widely varied from section to section. Smooth blends provide smooth transitions in opacity. This can be achieved by using soft-edged brushes (which can be used at varying opacities) or by blurring the mask .

4   To accentuate an image element, increase its contrast by grouping an adjustment layer with an appropriate correction to it.

5   Further accentuation can be achieved by duplicating an image layer and turning its blending mode to Hard Light.

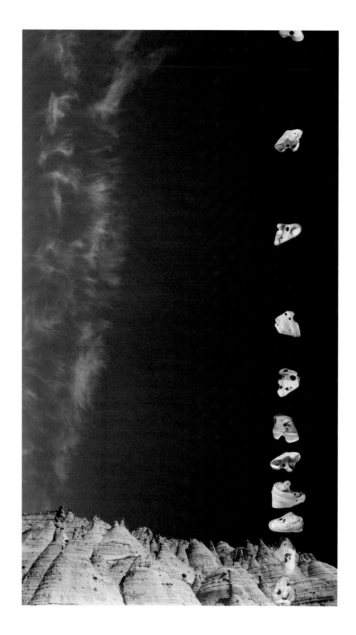

Wild Stones, Allies, 2000

XV

MULTIPLICITY

The challenge with Wild Stones was to pack as many angles of a single object into a single image and still have them look like separate objects. I'd done it many times by representing both the front and back of an object simultaneously. In other images, four sides of an object looked like four similar but distinctly different objects. To pull this off the objects need to be fairly nonuniform in shape. Spheres and ellipses are too regular; the contour of such objects from many angles is virtually the same. I knew I needed a complicated, highly irregular object for this image.

The form of the rock that my assistant brought me seemed organic. It was highly complex and irregular. Its contour as seen from multiple angles varied wildly. It even contained hollows and holes that when viewed at the proper angle could be seen through. At one angle, it reminded me of a Native American bear fetish. At other angles, it reminded me of internal organs, a heart and a liver. At another angle, it reminded me of African earth structures. At still another angle, it reminded me of a modern sculpture, perhaps a Henry Moore. At yet another angle, it reminded me of the shell for an unknown high-tech device. It was perfect.

Taking my cue from the stones, I searched my archives for an appropriate landscape to support them. I looked for a land with similar color and texture to imply a unity between it and the stone(s). Like the stones, the domes of Tent Rocks, New Mexico, are organic and seem curiously constructed. Every time I visit them I marvel at how highly structured they are. It's hard to think that someone did not make them or that they did not arise as the result of growth driven by a genetic code. The dichotomy between organic and constructed, an organ or architecture of earth, matched my associations with the stones.

I could have changed the scale, proportion, tone, or color of the rock to reinforce a sense of separateness. Instead, I limited myself to changing angle. I searched for a delicate balance between similarity and difference, pushing to see how far I could go without disrupting one or the other. Slight shifts in color between each stone arose due to the method of color correction I chose. I could have eliminated these variations, but the subtle rainbow of hues introduced accentuated each stone's individuality while creating a shimmering effect throughout the image.

I could have scattered the separate stones across the picture plane at random intervals, even choosing to hide them amid a similarly textured background, as I have in other compositions. I could have placed the separate stones in a rigidly spaced line, as I have in other compositions. But this time I chose to find a solution midway between the two. Here the stones compact as they descend and disperse as they rise vertically. Their placement implies a spreading or a settling motion, an expansion and a contraction, as well as a rotation. The rotation is erratic. If it were in smaller increments, if the adjacent aspects within the sequence more closely resembled one another, the impression of separateness would be undercut.

As I moved the long tall spine of rocks back and forth across the picture plane, they coalesced off center, flush right. I knew that the proportion of landscape necessary to fulfill the picture would be fairly small. That would leave a vast expanse of space in the upper left. The image would be composed of more space than figure and the center would be empty. All the action would be contained at the edges of the picture. I did not expect to echo the stone vertebrae with a line of clouds but the empty sky somehow did not fulfill the image. I found a spine of clouds that complemented both the separateness and unity of the stones and the curvilinear sway of the horizon. Stacatto rhythms punctuated each element, yet they all found a unity against a vast expanse of sky. Curiously the shape of emptiness, the negative space, between the cloud, horizon, and stones became stronger as a result. The invisible or the empty, has an equal presence with the visible or the full. The image found breath — inhalation and exhalation.

I often make multiple exposures, at times even multiple images, of an object or environment. As I move through or around it, my viewpoint changes and I make multiple exposures. I'm less interested in finding a single decisive moment within a larger span of time and more interested in seeing the entire experience as a decisive moment. So I make many documents of the transformations the appearance of something or somewhere undergoes as my experience of it evolves to encompass more and more of it. While we all use photographs to remember the way something was at a particular time, I also use a set of photographs to help me maintain a sense of the many aspects of something that arise through time. I see them not as separate but as parts of a whole. Multiplicity challenges me to take a longer view. Multiplicity challenges me to find the unity in what I had originally perceived as separate, but upon further consideration found to be whole.

ONE THING CAN BECOME MANY

"If the doors of perception were cleansed, everything would appear to man as it is, infinite."
— William Blake

Seeing is not always believing. What we know to be real does not always agree with what we see. At an early age we all learn to overcome the disparity between optical illusions and physical reality. We establish certain constancies very early in life. We know the parallel lines of a road seen converging towards the horizon don't grow closer physically. We know that objects moving along them don't grow smaller or larger, they grow closer or farther away from the viewer. We know that a white object, green under neon light, pink by firelight, remains white. We know we are seeing something that is "just an illusion" or not the way it looks. We understand how illusions are created. We learn to interpret the information our senses provide us. Optical illusions take us in. We make useful assumptions, ones that hold true for most situations. In rare instances those assumptions prove inaccurate and we become disoriented. This place of disorientation is a very interesting place to be. In these situations we are forced to look with a new perspective. Learning to momentarily disarm our habitual ways of seeing can be both refreshing and inspiring. My advice is to look and then look again. It's a tenuous game. And an interesting one. Optical illusions can be powerful allies when making images.

Consider shape constancy. Shape constancy confirms our knowledge that an object is the same even though it appears to be different from different angles. A figure turning in space, despite its wildly changing contour and surface characteristics, does not change — our perspective does.

If we do not know from personal experience what an ob-ject looks like from many angles, as is usually the case with still two-dimensional images, one object can appear to be many when several angles of a single object are presented simultaneously in a single image. This tendency is reinforced by the fact that we rarely see multiple aspects of objects within a single picture. When many images become one, one can become many.

The foundation of the technique is simple. Composite. Place multiple images of the same object seen from different angles on separate layers. The perceptual strategies are far more challenging and stimulating than the technical ones.

We habitually make the assumption that one picture represents one moment in time not many, which as a rule holds true, with exceptions. We know that this rule can be and has been successfully suspended. Consider multiplicity a partner to Futurism. In Futurist images, the separate images of an object are usually quite similar to one another. This repetition helps reinforce the notion of unity. When an object undergoes a significant transformation, from the beginning of a motion to the end of it, the separate stages recorded in between usually provide enough similarity from one aspect to the other that continuity is implied. Again, repetition, though more subtle, reinforces unity. Spread the separate aspects of motion apart, so that they do not overlap, and their contour is no longer one but multiple, and unity may be disrupted. Make the transitions very abrupt and unity may be further disrupted. You can further accentuate the illusion of difference by making alterations to tone, color, scale, proportion, or surface characteristics. Even subtle changes can dramatically reinforce the illusion of difference. When separateness is reinforced, motion is no longer implied.

Never forget light. If you photograph an object from many angles without rotating the object, but instead change only the perspective of the camera eye, the direction of light in the separate images will not be cast from a consistent angle relative to a single stationary viewer. The separate images will no longer share a single reality. Maintaining a consistent angle of light will allow the separate images to appear as if they share a single reality. There are at least two ways to do this. Change the angle of the object keeping the light source and viewpoint consistent. Or change the angle of the light source consistently and proportionally while changing perspective. Soft diffuse omnidirectional lighting is very forgiving and allows greater flexibility than harsh unidirectional light.

It is possible to make images of objects at opposing angles and later flip one image horizontally to create a consistent angle of light in both images. Take the example of an object that when seen from the side has a shadow that bisects it. Go one hundred and eighty degrees to the other side of the object and the shadow will still bisect it. Combine the two images and the shadows will indicate opposite angles of light. Flip one horizontally and the opposing angles will become the same. Cinematographers observe a rule: avoid cutting to an angle one-hundred-and-eighty degrees opposed to the viewpoint cut from. When this occurs, the visual disruption is often too great to support the sensation of continuity. If you want to create the illusion of difference, you can use this method for a positive end. When making exposures for multiplicity, try noting the proportion of shadow to the overall mass and find the opposing angle that has the same proportion. Break the rule

and disrupt continuity.

It is still possible to marry some images that are photographed under differing angles of light by creating appropriate shadows. Bear in mind that it is easier to create convincing shadows than create convincing highlights. As the complexity of the surfaces photographed increases, the difficulty of achieving this rises. Not surprisingly, these are the kinds of objects whose changing contours support the sensation of difference best. Attention to light before exposure is often more efficient. It may also be more revealing.

The illusions of similarity and difference can be called into question with simple objects that are nearly identical or very similar from many angles — several angles of a sphere for instance. The several angles of a relatively simple object often don't provide enough disparity to be read as separate within a single instant in time. Multiplicity may become multiplication.

A great deal of ambiguity exists in images. Ambiguity is a quality that can be made useful. Every object has many aspects. The one can become many. Being multiple is not a psychological disorder; it is a fact of life. We all play many roles in life. Cast the transformations of time aside for the moment; even within a single frozen instant, we are changeable and dynamic. We all have many voices within us. Reknowned psychologist Jean Shinoda Bolen explores the multiplicity of our very selves in her books *Gods in Every Man and Goddesses in Every Woman*. Perhaps there are "gods" in every thing. Everyone and everything has many aspects. We have only to awaken to the perceptual realities of our world to find the keys to an infinite realm of enchantment. Similarly, we have only to awaken to the statements we make about those perceptions, the stories we tell about our worlds, to find the keys to still other realms of enchantment.

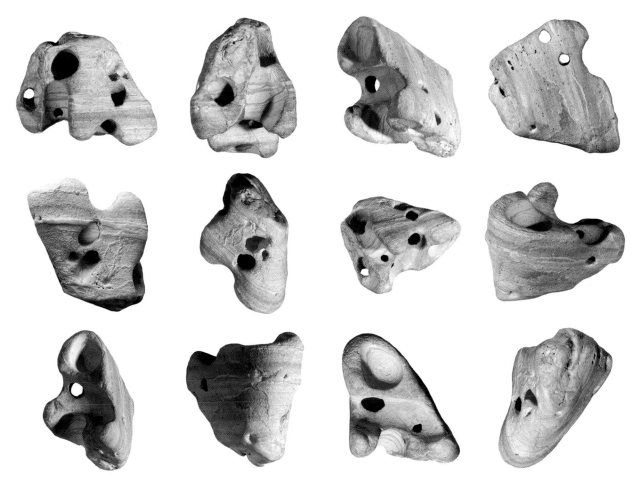

1. The original stone photographed from twelve different angles

METHOD

1   Composite varying images of the same object into a single file.

Maintain a consistent angle of light in the new image. (Flip and rotate if necessary.)

Create appropriate shadows as necessary, either on the object or the plane the shadow is cast upon.

Consider incorporating subtle variances (in color, tone, texture, scale, or proportion) to heighten the illusion of individuality between the separate components.

Surface details may be altered to enhance the illusion of difference. This works particularly well if repeated recognizable features are eliminated.

Emanation i, Elemental, 2000

XVI

FUTURISM

Emanation i presents a variant of the traditional Futurist image. While it employs transparency and successive overlapping images of a single object, it does so in an unconventional manner. The vast majority of Futurist images represent vertical or horizontal motion across the picture plane. Few Futurist images represent motion towards or away from the viewer. In those that do deal with the recession of space, or depth, an accompanying change of scale is represented along with a change in location.

As they are in motion, the contours of objects in many Futurist images change. The contour of a moving object changes only if its component parts move in addition to the location of the object or if rotation is introduced. As a stone is a whole piece, without limbs or appendages, its contour changes only if rotation is introduced. Here it is not.

In this image, the change the stone undergoes is less a change in position than it is a change in size. One of the factors that helps determine this is the anchoring of the bottom edge of the stone to a single point. The top edge changes position but the bottom does not. Part of the stone changes location while the other does not. If the position of any point in an object remains the same in successive representations, then the object is seen as moving around or relative to that point.

Another factor that helps reinforce that the type of motion in this image is more a change of scale than of location is the arrangement of the accompanying images and their transparencies. Here the larger, more transparent aspects are placed in back of the smaller, less transparent ones. If this arrangement were reversed, then the object would appear to recede in space, leaving ghostly residues behind its trajectory or further towards the viewer. Deep space would be created. Then the anchoring of the bottom of the stone to a single point might be read as coincidence due to a particular vantage point. But this is a less likely explanation. Coincidence creates an ambiguous tension in an image. When we read an image without sufficient information to guide us conclusively, we form hypotheses to determine the most likely explanation. When in doubt we defer to explanations that do not require coincidence, since by its very nature coincidence is unlikely, though not impossible. Sometimes coincidence is the very thing that thrills us. We struggle to disbelieve, but when a coincidence supports continued testing, we marvel at it. This can be undermined when too many coincidences occur simultaneously. One coincidence seems marvelous, two seem astounding, many seem impossible.

The repetition of the same figure makes it fairly certain that this is not a matter of multiplication. It is rather a matter of a change in state. The change of state is not just in location but also in duration or substance. In typical Futurist images objects in motion are, to one degree or another, transparent, but become less transparent where separate aspects drawn from separate moments overlap. In this image the entire contour of one aspect is contained in its next larger aspect, the separate aspects overlap entirely, and each aspect is successively more or less transparent. Again this reinforces the impression that the object's motion is not simply a matter of relocation but also a matter of expansion or contraction. While the stone in this image could be read either as expanding or contracting, it is most likely that we will defer to contraction because its smallest aspect is most opaque, while its largest aspect is most transparent. Transparency is a visual clue to impermanence, while opacity indicates durability. Within the vocabulary of Futurism increased opacity may simply indicate a larger duration of time in a single position.

What I did not expect was for this image to turn from day to night. A great many skies were tried, with varying amounts of information, stretched across many angles, in many shapes. In the end, simplicity seemed best. It allowed the focus of attention to remain on what was most mysterious, a stone in the process of transformation.

The relative uniformity of the light on the stone was at odds with the strong shadows contained in the foreground. I tested another image of the stone with a heavier shadow. It changed the geometry of the image entirely, unbalancing it. The strong dark line of the shadow competed with the light line in the stone. The stone became a semicircle rather than an oval. Besides an aesthetic balance, something else had been lost. In the night sky the stone seemed reminiscent of a moon or planetary body. Without the heavy shadow it seemed capable of either emitting its own or reflecting another's light. Somehow, the competing light sources needed to be married. So, rather than darken the stone, I lightened the ledge it rested upon. Two realities became one. Now the stone's emission of light was complete. It is not so dramatic that luminescence becomes the point of the picture usurping the motion of the stone; it is, instead, understated but present.

Right around the time I made this image I read about the strong sunspot activity that had been occuring and would occur throughout the year. The sun was radiating massive amounts of energy towards the earth. This actually compacted the earth's magnetosphere to half its normal size. The concentric ovals of the stone's outlines with a bright center seemed reminiscent of a diagram of a solar system. The stone's radiation of itself into the world, growing fainter and fainter, reminds me of a planetary body's magnetosphere or an organism's bioelectric field. The stone may be contracting, but it is also radiating both light and presence.

Five other images in this book (2, 15, 17, 19, and 25) present variants of Futurist modes of representation. Four (2, 15, 19, and 25), unlike this one, do so ambiguously. They present each aspect of a single object in an isolated fashion. Because the images of the object do not overlap and are not transparent, the individual images can be read either as separate objects or as a single object in motion. The connective tissue between each aspect has been removed and they are no longer as easily read as a single figure in motion (17 — Extension i). While the others involve a consistent rotation or twisting that can be deduced, the more dramatic, one (15 — Wild Stones) is particularly difficult to read as a single figure in motion because the transitions between each aspect are both dramatic and inconsistent.

Before making this image, I had been sketching an image of an ocean horizon that was echoed and continued by a line in a rock visually marking the waterline. In this image, the repetition of the single line at varying heights made this waterline fall. The motion of the line alone, separate from the whole stone, might actually be more typical of traditional Futurist motion.

"It is the artist who is truthful while the photograph is mendacious; for in reality time never stops cold.
… the horse has in him that leaving here, going there which is time; because the horse has a foot in each instant.
(Painting searches not for the outside of movement but for its secret ciphers.)
All flesh, even that of the world, radiates beyond itself."
— Auguste Rodin

Photographic images present discrete packets of time of varying durations. Some are short and some are long. Some are very long. Most are very short. However brief or long the duration of time, all photographs record the effects of time. How they represent those effects varies considerably.

Prior to the invention of photography, motion in still images relied on the suggestive powers of gesture and serial imagery. Gesture offers the suggestion of a motion's fulfillment implicitly. Serial imagery presents several moments discretely and contiguously with the repetition of recognizable figures or environments indicating continuity amid changing conditions. The conventions of streaking, blurring, transparency, or the overlapping of several images of a single object were rarely employed. The camera eye has brought to light latent visual vocabularies and at times even created new ones.

We see blurring, we see streaking, we see transparency, we see overlap, we see one object appear as many, we even see distortion in moving objects, but we don't always see these things the way the camera eye does. While the camera eye can indeed represent these visual aspects of motion the way we see them, it can also exaggerate them to such a degree that through the records it makes, we see the world in a new light. If the exposure is long enough the moving object disappears al-

together. Very short exposures slice time so finely they are able to represent a level of information we are unable to see with the naked eye. We simply can't capture information as quickly as the camera eye can. The shock of Eadweard Muybridge's photographic studies of motion was derived from the revelation of a new level of information not previously attainable with the naked eye. When running, horses do indeed pick all four feet off the ground for brief instants. The photographic document proved it. It was a very interesting point in history where man deferred truth to the documents he created over his direct observation which was comparatively limited. Muybridge's studies of motion through serial imagery also foreshadowed the coming of a new sensibility. While their preoccupation is the freezing of objects in motion for extended consideration in still images, the representation of motion within sequential but discrete frames align them closely with the sensibility of motion pictures. In one sense, they are another kind of "motion" picture.

Other notable photographic studies of motion are more closely aligned with the Futurist sensibility. Early in the 20th century, Futurism followed Cubism exploring images that represented multiple instants in time within a single picture frame. In both, successive representations of objects overlap each

1. *Horizontal motion.*

2. *Vertical motion.*

other within a single frame, signifying the passage of time. If the repetitions are tightly packed the result looks far from representational. Balla's adorable "Dog on a Leash" presents a flurry of canine parts. Duchamp's "Nude Descending a Staircase" depicts an energetic human cascade. Among others, the photographers Eakins, Marey, and later Edgerton all explored multiple recordings of moving objects within a single picture frame. (Ironically, in time, actually in *Life* magazine, Duchamp would himself descend a staircase multiplied in Elifson's famous photographic reprisal.) In these images the transformations of time work their strange magic on the material world. The laws of physics seem to come undone. An object cannot occupy two spaces at the same time. Two objects cannot occupy the same space at the same time. And yet, in these cases, they appear to. The catch phrase, at the same time, is our clue that these images represent not one time but many times. We quickly learn

to dismiss the possibility of impossibility as an optical illusion, learning instead to read the effect as a visual vocabulary used to represent motion. Sequential and Futurist images actually represent certain aspects of motion more clearly than motion pictures as they allow the separate stages of motion to be compared simultaneously. In considering them, a new depth of understanding of the effects of motion can be found.

The majority of Futurist images are concerned with horizontal or vertical motion. Much less frequently they treat motion as an indicator of depth. When they do, the separate images of a moving object change in scale as well as position. The artist then needs to give some indication that the object is to be read as growing closer or further away rather than expanding or shrinking. When contours overlap and occupy different areas of space, the repetition of an object tends to be read as progression or recession. When one contour is completely contained

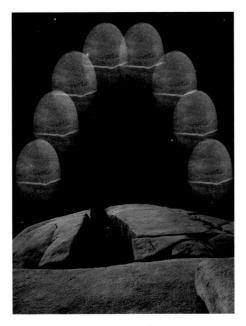

3. Curvilinear motion.

4. Recession/procession — using scale only.

within another, then the repetition tends to be read as expansion or contraction.

New levels of control of the various vocabularies involved in representing motion are available to you. You can control the light, the placement, the transparency, the degree of blurring and streaking, the level of distortion, scale, and the duration — after the moments of exposure. You need not rely on the camera eye alone to create and control such artifacts. You can even combine the separate artifacts of various methods into a single image. This might turn artifact into artifice, but a well-used conceit may yield a richer vocabulary and a more sophisticated technique capable of greater expression.

The premise of the technique is the essence of simplicity — composite. Shoot the elements you need separately and then combine them. Use this maxim as your guide: capture a maximum amount of information. If you make sharp undistort-

ed exposures without artifacts for the separate moments involved in the final composite, you will have a maximum degree of control. With digital technology, you can turn sequential imagery into Futurist imagery. What's more, you can precisely control the visual artifacts usually associated with such imagery. You can even eliminate them. You may also want to make recordings of the artifacts you intend to use, such as distortion, either for reference or for possible inclusion in the final image. A combination of conventional and digital imagery can work marvels. Think of the possibilities. If your intent is to be more expressive, rather than being faithful to a particular motion, you might even rechoreograph a motion, or choreograph a new one.

It has been said that the painter's intention is expression and the photographer's is objective representation. While the statement has some supportable general foundation, it is

5. Procession — using scale and opacity.

6. Recession — using scale and opacity.

overly broad. The qualities of objectivity and subjectivity are matters of intention. Neither quality is the sole province of one medium. The medium is not the message; the medium contains the message. Perhaps Futurism will offer new possibilities of expression for you in the near future.

Many have remarked that the sensibility of Futurism echoes the sensibility found in Hindu representations of divinity. This is appropriate for a philosophy that called into question the validity of the concept of an objective material world that limited existence to the logical by-product of linear time, seeing instead existence as a continuation amid transformations through cyclical time. Zen proposes there is only the here and now, but how long does now last? While we are here, we are constantly leaving, constantly going, constantly becoming.

Just how long is the "decisive moment"? How long is your decisive moment?

METHOD

1   Make an image of the environment without the object.

2   Make images of several instants of an object in motion. If possible make the exposures against a background that will make trapping the object easy, a blue or green screen for instance. You may want to use stroboscopic light to freeze aspects of a single motion. Alternately you might shoot different aspects of a repeated motion separately.

3   Scan and composite the separate images into a single one. Place each instant on a separate layer. Hide each one's background with a layer mask.

4   If desired, lower the opacity of each addition accordingly, leaving the background opaque.

To lower the opacity of an image selectively add a layer mask and create varying densities for nonuniform reductions, rather than reducing the layer's opacity for uniform reductions. A combination of both

7. Contraction/expansion — largest layer is most transparent.

8. Expansion/contraction — smallest layer is most transparent.

methods may be employed.

Interesting departures from the standard vocabulary may arise. Reduce the opacity nonuniformly but proportionally between separate aspects of a motion.

Alternately or additionally, modify the intensity of light consistently, making one end of the motion darker, lighter, or with more or less contrast. Objects on one end of the motion will seem more substantial than the others.

The number of separate image elements will affect the visual rhythm of an image substantially. Tightly packed images will seem more energetic, even faster. More spacious images will seem calmer, even slower.

You may want to incorporate some degree of motion blur. Make a copy of the appropriate layer. Blur it using the filter Motion Blur. Then reduce the opacity of the duplicate so that the original unblurred copy shows through.

Extension i, Elemental, 1999

XVII

THE EXTENDED MOMENT

I did not expect the challenge of Extension i to be as intriguing as it has become. I certainly did not expect the ways of seeing it represented to be as closely related to the ways of seeing I have been pursuing in other avenues.

Recontextualizing, placing objects in new environments or combining two separate environments into a new whole, seemed natural to me. Resynchronizing, resequencing events in time, was more challenging. When resequencing I was challenged to see an object or an environment not just for what it appeared to be but also for what it might soon appear to be.

Looking solely at the surfaces of things from a single point of view at a single time seems limited to me. I gaze at the azure sky above me knowing that unseen constellations pass behind it. I look at the reflections on the surface of the water knowing that an entirely different world lays below it. I look upon the surface of my own body never having seen the bones, the brain, the lungs, the heart, trusting they are there. Sometimes we need confirmation. Sometimes we need to look again. Sometimes we need to keep looking. I like to look at things from multiple perspectives. I also like to look at things many, many times.

Now. Between before and after. How long is now? I've learned to think of now as very fast. But I find it equally challenging, perhaps more, to think of now as very slow. Now could be a longer duration of time. Now could be a very long duration of time. It's a matter of perspective.

When the undulating distortions of my experiments with scanning moving objects first appeared, I was intrigued but I didn't know what to do with them. They were so unusual all I could think to do was present them as they were, without environments. These experiments offered many interesting insights. They were challenging enough to look at. It was difficult to find their logic. It was even more difficult to find their meaning. It took some time for this material to sink in. Rodin's statement that it is the photograph that is mendacious for it destroys the coming and going, the here and there of things, struck a chord within me. I had been fascinated with Hindu representations of continuity in time: Shiva had many heads; Kali had many arms; a man was an infant, an adult, and an old man in a single image. I was also particularly attracted to images found in West Coast Native American art; in them you could see both sides of an animal depicted simultaneously in a marvelous symmetry. Surely there must be ways of making images of things unseen from a single perspective, things seen from multiple perspectives, and their unity. I had not anticipated that this would be one way of doing so. Again, my curiosity functioned as a beacon for a solution I could not yet see. Even when it appeared, it took me some time to realize what had arrived.

This conjunction is particularly interesting to me. It is the first image of its kind that I created in which the environment plays an equal part in the drama of the object's passage. The stone twists in eleven one-hundred-and-eighty degree turns, expanding and contracting with varying rates of rotation. The seed of the motion stands at the beginning, but upside down.

I hadn't anticipated incorporating another convention of motion, transparency. As the composition took shape it suddenly seemed appropriate. As in much of my work, the image is full of ripples: the rippling undulations of the stone's transformation, the rippling bands of cloud above, the rippling surface of the water below, the rippling waves of light, even the shore is composed of waves of stone. Each set of ripples marks a different duration of time. There are many passages of time, both short and long, within this image. I find it ironic that the stick, which could be used as a sundial to fix the time of day, has fallen. The times of this image cannot be encompassed by a single object or the fixation of a single point of view. Two entities, the opaque stone and the stick, stand as solitary objects amid a field of change. But their durability is illusory. In point of fact, they will be the first things to pass to another place, another state, while the energetic undulations found in the environment will persist far longer. All are held still by the camera eye, but none are frozen in reality. All have long since passed into another state. Sky, water, stone, each from a different time, represent different passages of time, all at one time. Which angle, which moment in time will I choose to remember each event by? How long is the decisive moment?

As time has passed I find that working digitally has challenged me to become clearer about how the world looks and about how the images in my mind's eye look. I no longer take the information held within a photographic image for granted. I no longer assume that the images in my mind's eye, no matter how convincing, are as clear and static as I formerly thought they were or that they conform to the logic of the external world as often as I thought they did. There's a gap between what is observed (data) and what is seen (information). Seeing involves interpretation. I find it extremely stimulating to challenge myself to see more, to see more deeply, to see in new ways, to see how I see, to see how we see.

TRANSFORMATIONS OF TIME

"Everything moves, everything flows."
— *Heraclitus*

"All is procession; the
universe is a procession
with measured and beautiful motion."
— *Walt Whitman*

One object, one observer, one space, one instant — one reality, material and relatively static. That's the conventional way of thinking. It doesn't always work perfectly, so from time to time we make adjustments, compromises, exceptions. Add a second viewer at a significantly different vantage point. In comparing the impressions of multiple viewers, we often struggle to reconcile the differences with an abstraction we call reality, something that generally encompasses various viewpoints but describes none of them specifically. Add the effects of motion. The game becomes significantly more complex. Add the effects of larger passages of time. The abstraction and the ability of our minds to manipulate it to make reasonable predictions begins to fail far more frequently as the level of complexity rises. There's no substitute for direct observation. Still, as the amount of information increases, our ability to encompass it is taxed. Often there's too much information flowing by at one time to be directly observed, so we fit it into our abstraction, a useful convention for thinking and seeing.

We tend to think of the representations of space and time in Cubist and Futurist works as challenges to the supremacy of the camera eye and "its" rational objectivism. My understanding of the two movements was challenged by art historian Jamake

Highwater's statement in his book *The Primal Mind*, "For all the truly brilliant rebelliousness of Cubism and Futurism, and the refusal to accept the linear perspective of Giotto as absolute, the analytical and sequential dogma of the West was every bit as much in evidence in their alternatives to Giotto's painterly cosmos as it was in Giotto's own paintings. Cubism, after all, does not abandon the sequential conception of seeing; it only places more cameras around the same object." He later relates the story of a western explorer drawing in the West with a Sioux warrior present. The Sioux sees his rendition of a man on horseback and shakes his head saying, "Not good, men have two legs." The explorer explains to him that from that perspective you could only see one leg, the other was hidden by the horse, though still present. Still the warrior shakes his head insisting, "Men have two legs." It's a dramatic demonstration that different cultures have different ways of looking and seeing and expect different things from images, records of a process of looking. Think of the West Coast Native American renditions of animals which are highly symmetrical, the contours resembling the flattened skins of the things they portray. Seen from one perspective they actually contain more information than their Western counterparts. More importantly, what they aim to

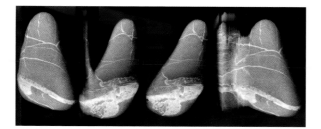

1. Two 180° rolls.

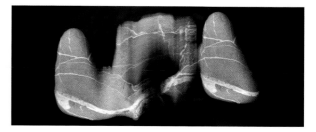

2. Two 180° rolls

record is entirely different. Rather than reproducing the way things look from a single perspective and a single moment in time, they seek to portray the spirit of the things they observe. To them, our more scientific documents might seem like an "aimless cartography." Thankfully, there is more than one way of looking. We have the ability to see in many different ways and appreciate many ways of seeing.

The metamorphoses of time and how to represent them in still images continues to haunt us. Gesture, sequential imagery, motion blur, and Futurism have all become a part of our traditions for representing time and motion. Clearly, you cannot separate time and space. In treating one, you must treat the other. With new technologies come new perspectives. New perspectives generate new questions. New questions yield new answers.

Scanners are new technologies. They were designed to reproduce images accurately. They function much like the camera eye, some even employ lenses. They were designed to be used in certain ways, but that does not mean they cannot be used in other ways. Take the flatbed scanner. It was designed to reproduce stationary flat originals. But does this mean it is incapable of making images of moving three-dimensional objects? A little experimentation will prove it is capable of other things.

Place an object on a flatbed scanner and, while the scan is being made, move the object.

There are several things to bear in mind when making scans. Typically the lighting of such images is frontal; it emanates from the bed of the scanner. You can modify the lighting on an object to some degree by incorporating secondary and tertiary light sources. Simply shine light on the object to be scanned from a source outside the scanner and adjust the exposure of the scan accordingly. If the background of the object is left open, it will become very dark fading to black. Typically a cover is placed over originals to prevent this falloff. With three-dimensional objects a flat cover no longer works well. You can create another cover that will accommodate three-dimensional objects, such as a box or a cloth. Doing so may interfere with external light sources. When scanning objects, you won't be able to see the face of the objects being recorded as they lay face down on the scanner.

If an object is moved during the scanning process, distortion occurs. Sliding an object will result in a distorted image with some similarities to motion blur. (Distortions of the human figure are particularly remarkable.) Twisting an object results in similar distortions, but the direction of the distortions is no longer linear. Rolling an object will result in an image that presents the front of an object at one point in the image and the back at another, and perhaps even both again at other points with a continuous stream of information joining all parts. If the object is perfectly synchronized with the rate of the travel of the CCD, then little distortion of the object's features will occur; however, the final image will possess an entirely new contour. In every case, the outline of the object will no longer

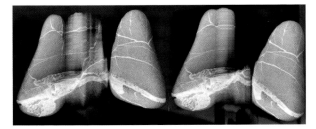

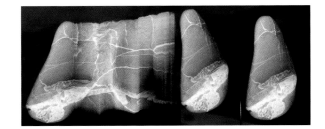

3. Two 180° rolls.   *4. One 360° roll and the stone.*

be representative of our traditional experiences of contour; it will be modified by the accompanying transformations of time. If the object is moved slower or faster than the CCD, the image of the object will appear compacted. If the object is moved too slow or too fast, it will disappear altogether. Some part of the object must be in line with the CCD to be recorded, otherwise, a recording of empty space is made. This process is guided by the flow of time. If things become out of sync they disappear. Changes in the direction of motion will also dramatically alter the final contour.

The scanner's resolution setting will control how fast the CCD moves. Low-resolution settings will cause the CCD to travel very fast. Higher resolution settings will cause the CCD's velocity to decrease. You may want to test the rate of travel in order to better predict your scanner's habits. Set the scanner's rate to allow you to move fluidly. Either that, or, with practice, you can learn to move fluidly at a rate optimal for scan quality. Be alert for sudden stops amid the scanning rate. Sudden changes in the rate of travel, either of the object scanned or the CCD, can cause artifacting — chiefly the introduction of lines caused by the pairing of noncontiguous areas of information. Some trial and error is inevitable. As in practicing musical scales, much practice comes before mastery. One consolation may be found: the unpredictable mistakes often generate fascinating results.

Uneven objects may be challenging to move across the flat surface of the scanner. Very even objects, such as a ball, are easy to balance. Uneven objects are much harder to balance as they move from point to point. If this is not corrected it may cause the path of the object to become erratic. The unusual paths objects make can be interesting in themselves. In working with objects you sense that each has a unique character.

Though all are limited, some scanners have greater depth of field than others. Only testing will determine this as manufacturers do not generally consider this an important criteria for a "flatbed" scanner.

Older three-pass scanners yield entirely different effects from newer single-pass scanners as the three channels they generate are likely to become out of phase with one another. The differences are most pronounced on highly reflective surfaces. In these cases a rainbow of red, green, and blue colors appears, much like the motion artifacts found with three-pass capture on many high-end digital cameras.

While I could offer a technical treatise on how best to roll a three-dimensional object across a flat plane in parallel with the passage of a CCD sensor, I prefer to offer another suggestion. Play. And in support of that thought I offer the following. "You have to know how to preserve that freshness and innocence a child has when it approaches things." (Henri Matisse) Experiment. Discovery awaits you.

Selective focus and motion blur are two examples of artifacts of technology that have been incorporated into our visual vocabulary. They now signify spatial relationships and

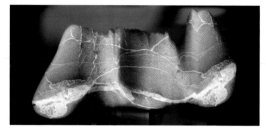

5. One 360° roll.

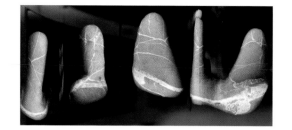

6. Two sides of the stone followed by a 180° roll.

motion respectively. Before the invention of photography, neither was used in the creation of images. The artifacts of this once new invention have since been adopted as standards of representation. From time to time, they have even been celebrated as things of beauty.

It may take some time for the new artifacts of the technologies we use to make images to become accepted. New artifacts are less readily embraced. They must present a useful way of seeing and also stand the test of time.

While selective focus, motion blur, and transparency all have the weight of history and familiarity, they also allude to the ways we habitually see and to the ways we look at photographs. The human eye has a limited depth of field and fast moving objects will blur somewhat. What's more, the vast majority of photographs are taken in a relatively short period of time. Ironically, these traditional artifacts may be pushed far beyond what we are accustomed to seeing with the naked eye and still be accepted.

The single biggest challenge for these new artifacts in gaining acceptance is the difficulty involved in grasping what they represent. They challenge us to consider an object from many points of view simultaneously, to hold its many aspects in our minds all at once, to expand our understanding of the passage of time, to grasp motion not by breaking it into its component parts but rather by seeing it as a continuous sweep of action. That is their power and their mystery.

Certainly it took some time for the streaming phantoms of moving objects to which we have become accustomed to become accepted. These new artifacts bear a great deal of similarity to previous artifacts. This may actually help speed their adoption. One might even think of combining both new and old artifacts to create an even more dynamic representation of motion.

When rolling objects, rather than twisting or sliding, this new vision bears similarities to panoramic photography. Three-hundred-and-sixty degree recordings of an environment are often disorienting as before and behind, left and right, are presented simultaneously within a single frame. In both cases the image encompasses a changing perspective. Motion is inferred, generally a turning of the viewer, but not necessarily described. There is a significant difference. One is the product of a moving point of view and a stationary object or environment; the other is the product of a moving point of view and a moving object.

Digital cameras are scanners and so there is no reason why this method might not be employed with them. In fact it has. Rather than moving the object, you can move the camera around the object. The difference is a matter of perspective. One looks outward (typically on an environment), while another looks inward (typically on an object).

There are links with Futurist vision here as well. In Futurist images, multiple aspects of a single object are seen simultaneously. The transformations of time are seen in images of the same object repeated side-by-side for comparison, generally overlapping, often with transparency. The difference here is that the image(s) of the objects recorded are seen as a continuity. One presents a succession of discrete instants simultaneously, while the other presents a single moment which is continuously unfolding.

All of these extensions of time are in effect still equivalents of what we see in motion pictures. Regardless of the artifacts generated, new or old, we are essentially representing something that is not there — motion. Still images do not move. They can only suggest movement.

What separates a gimmick from a device? It's a complicated question with many answers, some of them dependent on context, some of them dependent on an individual's treatment of the technique. Let me offer one answer, one among many possibilities. A gimmick imposes its style on an image without adding anything other than its novelty. A device is capable of suggesting other dimensions and meanings beyond itself. A gimmick might be compared to an affectation or an accent rather than as an addition to language or the introduction of new material into a vocabulary. One changes the way previously known things are said, the other enables new things to be said. One says old things in a new way, while the other says new things in a new way. In the visual arts a gimmick affects how things look while a device affects how things are seen.

Images are a recording of a way of looking. Here the ability to see front and back and their continuity simultaneously, without destroying the unity of each aspect with the other, is indeed an intriguing device. One sees many sides, many perspectives simultaneously and may compare them. Similarly the expansion and contraction of matter with varying rates of movement becomes another device for describing motion and the passage of time.

Here before us is a new representation of space and time. The moment is extended. There is motion within it. It may share some similarities with, but does not conform to, the standards of our previous vocabularies. Our vocabularies of representation prior to the invention of photography were updated by its introduction. Along with it came new artifacts and new vocabularies. Photography is evolving. The time is ripe to reconsider our conventions. This artifact is but one of many to consider.

METHOD

1   Prescan an object on a flatbed scanner to determine exposure.

2   Make a scan and move (roll, twist, slide) an object across the face of the scanner in sync with the CCD, as it travels across the scanning area.

Oriens, Elemental, 1999

XVIII

REORCHESTRATING LIGHT

Oriens represents a new line of inquiry for me. Take the most compelling passages of changing light throughout an extended duration of time and weave them into a single composition. I'd been looking for the right situation to use this technique for quite some time. When I returned from Death Valley a friend said, "Zabriskie Point? Again? Well, I'll bet you could photograph Zabriskie Point in a way that hasn't been done before." It was only then that I realized I had missed the shot(s) the first time. As I began the second journey, I realized there was a flaw in my plan. The "best" light in every area of the picture might not be as dramatic as I had thought. Every area of the image would demand equal attention. I nearly gave up hope, but I persisted. As usual something else worked out. While my intention was clear, the subject and the process informed me. I had to respond to the place and the images generated, not just what was in my head, to find the solution. As I looked at my transparencies it presented itself. The new solution even highlighted my feelings about the place more strongly than my original idea. I had been impressed by the way the light first struck the dagger-like peak after creeping across the valley floor. Its first appearance at each separate point throughout the landscape was a dramatic revelation, a crescendo in a magnificent performance. Rather than finding its epitome in a single moment, I found it in many. The result, different from my conception, but consistent with my intention, achieves a dramatic lighting effect never before seen at one time. Yet, a similar sequence of experience has been witnessed countless times.

The light on the foreground in this image is faithful to the transparencies that recorded it. The separate portions have not been modified substantially nor were they modified in an inconsistent manner. There has been no dodging and burning. Nothing has been added or altered. The light has simply been resynchronized. The background has been altered differently. To unify the composition the mountains have been made slightly darker and more yellow, a move akin to burning in the area.

The sky is an addition. The small sliver of sky contained in the original exposures cramped the composition. The vast sense of space found in the desert was missing. The sky had, in fact, been the first indicator of the presence of the coming light making a thousand transformations before its arrival. The sky that morning was not particularly noteworthy. I could have spent a lifetime waiting for the perfect sky. I chose instead to incorporate another sky that supported both the composition and the light. This sky I altered dramatically, both in tone and color. I did so to expressively highlight the drama of the light below, to support it and not detract from it. While the lower half of the image is a matter of resynchronization, the upper half is a matter of recontextualization.

Neither method, resynchronization or recontextualization, yields a classically objective document. But the results of their application may yield artifacts that are truer to our experience of events. In one respect they represent the events more faithfully — they encompass the passage of time.

COMPOSING AND CONDUCTING

"Three things are needed for beauty: wholeness, harmony, and radiance."
— *Thomas Aquinas*

Light is changeable. It changes constantly. It changes us. What marvelous transformations occur with every passing moment! Color shifts: warmer by dawn, cooler by midday, warmer by evening, cooler by night. Shadows grow: short and long, turning with the angle of the sun, twisting with the surfaces that carry them. Reflections splash sprays of light quilting surfaces in abstraction. A vast poetry is contained in light. As in music, every moment is a unique performance.

While many of us celebrate the wonders of natural light, and rightly so for it is truly divine, for the great majority of us there have been times when we have chosen to modify it. Traditionally we modify either the response of our materials to the existing light or we modify the existing light itself. We correct tone and color; we extend and contract development; we use different paper grades and developers; we dodge and burn; we use reflectors and fill flash. Sometimes we even go so far as to introduce artificial light sources to create new relationships of light. Still, many don't typically use multiple images to do so.

While compositing can achieve very different effects, effects previously unachievable with traditional materials and methods, it can also achieve very similar effects, even effects that could have been achieved with a single exposure given the right circumstances. While the practice of using multiple images to create a single image seems to challenge the nature of the photographic document created, at times undercutting its power for "objective" representation, certain kinds of photomontage can actually make a photographic document that is truer to the way we see.

Take two exposures of a single scene, one optimized for highlights and another optimized for shadows, and composite them into a single image. Certain limitations of the materials used are overcome but the nature of the artifact has not been substantially altered. Or, shoot two images, one sharp nearby and another sharp faraway, and composite them into a single image. Again, while depth of field has been extended beyond the capabilities of our equipment, the nature of the document has not changed. In both cases, what has been achieved is increased realism. Both use a nontraditional method to overcome the limitations of traditional materials and equipment, nothing more. While the method may not be traditional, the final result can be. What you do with compositing is what changes the nature of the photographic document not the act of compositing itself. The documentary nature of photographs depends less on the tools and techniques employed and more on their judicious application governed by the intention of their creators. So it follows that just as traditional photographs can be made to lie, nontraditional photographs can be made to tell the truth.

I think often of the luminous ballet many architectural photographers choreograph to get a perfect single recording of light, perhaps generated by a single exposure, perhaps by many. In a similar vein, you might orchestrate a magnificent dance of light (artificial or natural) that changes through time using multiple recordings to create a single image. Compositing allows us to change or extend spatial and/or temporal relationships.

This need not involve recontextualization, elimination, or distortion. It can be as simple as reorchestrating light. Imagine taking the most compelling passages of light, from a dawn, a day, a week, a month, or a year, and combining them into a single chorus of light.

The process is relatively simple. Shoot many variations of light within a single scene. Using a tripod and taking care not to move the camera/lens configuration will make registration easier. Scan each variation, if necessary. Composite the separate images. Each will become a separate layer in a single digital file. Take care to assure registration is carefully maintained. Choose the optimal information from each scene to create a final composite. Mask the information you wish to hide on each layer to make visible the final configuration. You may or may not choose to embellish the relationships you have captured. The separate exposures may or may not be corrected uniformly. If corrections are to be made uniformly, a single adjustment layer will suffice for all layers. If the corrections will differ between variations, separate adjustment layers may be grouped to individual layers making corrections layers-specific. If you want to go beyond burning and dodging, beyond what is achievable with reflectors or artificial lighting, to create a lighting situation that may be unachievable by any other method, try reorchestrating light.

Thinking in this new way is challenging. The task is much harder to conceive of than to execute. "Previsualizing" the final result can be

1. A separate sky.

2. Light on the far mountains.

3. Light on the near peak.

4. Light on the foreground.

extremely tasking. Nevertheless the practice can be highly rewarding. Often we tend to imagine moments in isolation. Perhaps in this respect traditional photographs do a better job of representing what we make of the world than they do of what's going on in the world. When seen from a different perspective, the photograph's propensity for freezing time, not to mention the accompanying effects of isolation, can be seen as a dramatic distortion. Rodin said, "It is the artist who is truthful, while the photograph is mendacious; for, in reality, time never stops cold." Obviously his statement must be placed in context; it represents only one of many possible perspectives, and so it is true to one degree, but it is by no means an absolute. There are other perspectives, ones that represent the presiding paradigm.

A shift in perspective can be highly illuminating. The single most challenging and rewarding shift in perspective that arises in this new practice of resynchronizing light lies in learning to expand our vision beyond a single moment to encompass many moments (past, present, and future) and to envision the relative relationships of each together. Making a successful image is as much a matter of knowing what to downplay as it is knowing what to accentuate. Only once the information has been prioritized will it make a meaningful statement. Make every area of an image equally luminous and you may achieve an unprecedented degree of homogeneity. Light blossoms in the presence of shadow. We see things in contrast to one another.

5. The sky added as seen through the mask.

6. The exposure for the far mountains as seen through the mask.

This is perhaps the reason that so often the final results of such a discipline can only truly be seen after its execution. We may have a general idea of the outcome, but the specifics are resolved as we engage in the process. Planning, preparation, and practice will only go so far. In the end, it is the surprises found in the final performance, born of the twin confluences of time and circumstance, that truly enliven it. Vision is truly a continuing voyage of discovery.

There are many ways of looking. And so there are many kinds of visual artifacts made. Typically photographs represent single moments in time. You might enjoy the prospect of creating photographs that represent many moments in time. You might enjoy looking and making images in new ways.

METHOD

1   Make multiple exposures of a single scene with variations of light.

2   Scan the separate exposures square and at equal resolutions. Registration is greatly facilitated if the separate images contain the same number of pixels and require no rotation.

3   Composite the separate images into a new single image. Open all the images simultaneously. Drag the background layers into a single master document. Hold the Shift key when dragging to keep the separate images registered.

4   Place the image that will show the greatest amount of information in the final composite at the bottom of the layer stack. Place the image that will show the least amount of information at the top of the layer stack. (Not a necessity, this step merely facilitates organization.)

5   Confirm the registration of the separate images. If you used a tripod and didn't move the camera, the edge of the frame, both top and bottom, provide excellent guides. Create a guide at the edge of

7. The exposure for the near peak as seen through the mask.

8. The exposure for the foreground highlights as seen through the mask.

the base image and move each successive layer flush with it if necessary. If the original exposures are not precisely aligned, you can use the edges of elements within the image to achieve registration. Slide mounts may vary, so you may want to scan unmounted film. Even then you must take care to scan at the same angle. If the separate images are scanned at the same angle but not square, I advise rotating all of them at once in the final composite after registration. (Link the layers and rotate them all in one move.) Otherwise, if rotating them separately, you must be extremely careful to rotate them equally when registering them. (Check the angle of rotation in the Info palette as you are rotating each.) If you are unsuccessful at maintaining registration at the scanning level, it can be difficult; rotating the scans in Photoshop will be necessary to assure precise registration. Registration can be checked by turning down the opacity of the top layer. If the two images are out of register, the image will look like it is suffering from double vision. As the two images get closer in register, the composite will look slightly out of focus. When precise registra-

tion is achieved the image will appear sharp. Critical focus is a matter of one or two pixels. You can activate the Move tool and use the arrow keys to nudge the images into alignment for precise registration. Don't forget to zoom in during this process. Check the image at multiple magnifications. One hundred percent is the most critical magnification.

Turning the blending mode of an overlying layer to Difference can help facilitate registration. The image will look terrible overlying but it will display lines at edges not registered. Move or rotate the overlying layer and they will disappear when precise registration is achieved.

6   Add layer masks to the separate layers to hide less desirable information. The bottom layer will need no mask.

7   Use adjustment layers to make corrections as necessary. A single adjustment layer at the top of the layer stack will suffice if all layers are to be corrected equally. Adjustment layers can be grouped to specific layers to modify image layers individually.

Enchambered, Allies, 1996

XIX

ILLUMINATION

I am often asked, "How long does an image take you to make?" Some take as little as an hour, some take years. In one sense every image has taken me the lifetime I've led in order to be realized. Enchambered is one of those images that evolved over quite some time. Unlike others that came in a lightning flash, unlike others that slipped through my fingers at every turn until completion, this one arrived in the first few moments largely realized but took years to finally resolve.

As soon as I saw it I liked the environment. A cliff became a cave. A flat wall suddenly presented an enclosed space. Its stained and chiseled surfaces presented marvelous calligraphy and carving. The environment was firmly established. The stage was set. It needed an actor.

Light became a powerful factor. Light from above became a light from within. An external light became an internal light. The light defied easy description. It came from below, but more importantly it came from within the central enclosure. Its source begged to be made visible. I tried several objects as possible sources of light. None seemed quite right. I settled on a tiny pale fox tooth that looked like a crown. It almost glowed. It could have been the source of light but something was still lacking. I added light. It was good. I lived with the image for quite some time before realizing the object was not needed. The image had become too loaded. It would be better if the actor were stripped down to the light alone. I removed the tooth. I added a new light. And it was better. The true inhabitant of the space was more clearly revealed. It was less descriptive but far more suggestive. The mystery of the image blosssomed. It came alive.

It was all a matter of space. Placing the light was critical. First, a custom shape from two separate lens flares was created. Second, size was determined. Initially too small, then too large, it found its resting place when its circumference touched the chamber's walls on four sides. It reminded me of the idea of squaring the circle. Third, the light was held back selectively from the walls. When the flare flooded all four directions — above, below, to the left, and to the right — it hovered in front of all the elements, veiling them. When the flare was contained to the dark space between the walls it fell behind, no longer the primary source of illumination. When the flare was withheld from the walls below, it sat above them. When the effect was diminished, but not withheld from the outer walls and left to bloom within the inner walls, it fell to rest within the center of the chamber. It found its place.

I had no idea the image would ultimately take me in a new direction. Though some incorporate drawn elements, I am cautious about creating digitally generated images or including rendered objects in my images, which are photographically based. Photographic information is far richer than anything I have seen generated. Still, these flares can be beautiful. Several times I've been tempted to create images with flares alone. So much for formula. Inspiration is anything but predictable.

"I sense light as the giver of all presences, and material as spent Light.
What is made by Light casts a shadow, and the shadow belongs to Light."
—Louis Kahn

"Material lives by Light … You're spent Light, the mountains are spent Light,
the trees are spent Light, the atmosphere is spent Light. All material is spent Light."
—Louis Kahn

Light is a presence. Light can be an actor in a larger drama. Every actor alters its environment. The actor can be created.

Light can be ground. Often we think of light as an intrinsic part of the environment. It pervades and suffuses space. Light and its absence render form, volume, and space. It even defines an invisible but felt ground, time. Light is dawn and twilight, dawn and twilight are light. Light can be an environment.

Light can be figure. Rather than being omnipresent, light may be contained, localized, illuminating or becoming an object of attention. Rays of light descend from the heavens, fires flicker in harvest fields, fireflies weave dizzying dances at dusk, stars shimmer in night's inky cloak, the moon blossoms from beneath the horizon. Light can be an entity.

I use very few filters — Unsharp Mask, Gaussian Blur, Maximize, Minimize, Noise, and Lens Flare are my standbys. Unlike many other filters, I've found Lens Flare can be very convincing. I use it for creating spectral highlights, stars, flares, and halos. There are several types of lens flares. The lens flare filters found in Photoshop's filters offer three settings: 50–300mm zoom, 35mm prime, and 105mm prime. The brightness/size of each is variable. Depending on where the flare is rendered in the image, an accompanying set of artifacts will be created to sim-

ulate the effects found with a traditional lens. The effects of a flare can be positioned and contained by rendering it inside a selection. Each lens flare filter has a different set of accompanying artifacts. Both the 50–300mm zoom and 35mm prime flares create pink circles around the central star. One difference between them is that the star is more concentrated with more pronounced points with the 35mm prime and more diffuse with the 50–300mm zoom. Each has a different set of accompanying artifacts. The 105mm prime is the one I use most often as it produces the smallest pink ring, seen only at higher settings. This simple white light seems most naturalistic. Consequently I have the most use for it.

Noteworthy is another software package, compatible with Photoshop, Knoll's Lens Flare Pro. Created by Industrial Light and Magic supervisor John Knoll, the software creates the most convincing lens flares I've seen to date. With dozens of presets, each with up to a dozen individual characteristics that can be customized separately, it offers far more control.

Flares must be rendered on an image layer. They cannot be rendered on a transparent layer. Would that it could but it cannot. When the flare is rendered, it changes the background substantially and permanently. There is a way around this however.

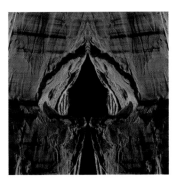

1. The environment.

2. The lens flare.

Duplicate the layer to be affected by the flare and render the effect on the duplicate layer. With the effect on a separate layer, changes can be made at any time in the future or the original image can be restored. What's more, the opacity of the layer can be used to further modify the intensity of the effect. Furthermore a layer mask can be added to remove additional artifacts that may be unwanted. It is not necessary to duplicate the entire layer; only the area affected by the effect need be copied. To save file space, delete unaffected areas of the duplicate layer. Alternately, copy the image area to be affected and paste it, duplicating only a small portion of the underlying layer; then the lens flare can be rendered on this small portion only.

There's an elegant way to do an end run around this tedious and somewhat limiting process. First create a new layer, specify a blending mode of Hard Light, and fill with Hard-Light-neutral color (50% gray) upon creation. With this background value in Hard Light blending mode, no change is made to the underlying layers. If it were darker or lighter a change would be made. That's where the lens flare comes in. Render the lens flare on this Hard Light layer, which has a uniform image that remains invisible due to its blending mode rather than transparency on which a flare cannot be rendered, and the flare will appear but

the background will not. Unlike the previous method, with this method you can reposition or rescale the lens flare at any time. On rare occasions this method has caused shifts in color or tone, so it is helpful to know the other way as a backup, but in most cases it is superior.

Lens flares can be used to create stars as well as specular highlights. When creating constellations I work fast and free, first making decisions in placement and size before I spend time rendering them. I create a new layer and sketch the relative positions of the stars with a white paint brush. Once placed, I then render the lens flares on another layer. You can move a duplicate of a rendered flare by simply selecting it and holding the Option and Command keys to drag a duplicate to any desired position. The duplicate can be resized as needed. This won't work if the halos of two flares intersect; then you must render a new flare. Be careful as flares have very long smooth transitions that can seem almost invisible but are nonetheless significant. Move another flare into this kind of area and you may produce unwanted lines. To be safe simply render a new flare in the appropriate position. You can always render separate flares on separate layers. This allows you to change them independently of one another. Again to

3. The environment and lens flare.

4. The layer mask used to contain the effects of the lens flare.

save file size, delete unaffected areas of the Hard Light layer.

As stars have varying intensities you will likely want to have some stars appear more intense than others. Add a layer mask and use a black paint brush set on a low opacity to reduce the intensity of particular stars. The layer mask can also be used to hide unwanted artifacts.

Stars also vary in color. You may want to shift the color of specific flares. Create an adjustment layer linked to the Hard Light or flare layer. Hue/Saturation works well, but avoid the Lightness slider as darkening or lightening the 50% gray will produce a change in underlying layers. Curves also works well, but for the same reason make sure you place a point on the curve to anchor the midpoint and don't move it. Substantial changes can be made as long as the midpoint (50% gray) is not changed. A flare can even be inverted or solarized without changing lower layers if the value of the 50% gray is preserved.

You can also create halos using lens flares. Position the lens flare over the object or area to be affected and then add a layer mask and mask out the area that should be unaffected, typically within the outline of the object. Depending on the effect desired, the lens flare may affect the area to a lesser degree within the outline. In this case lighten the layer mask to let an

appropriate percentage of the flare through.

Introduce an object into a new environment and you will want to make sure the quality of light on it is consistent with the light in the environment. It should appear that the light in the environment affects the object. Introduce a light into an environment and you will want to make sure that it appears to affect the environment. Introducing light into an image should alter more than just the area where the light appears. Were the light there in the original scene it would create highlights and shadows, even alter color and contrast, in surrounding areas. If your intention is realism, when you introduce new light into an image you will need to think of all the ways in which that new light will affect it. You may want to mask the effects of the light you introduce digitally from shadowed areas. You may even want to create new shadows. What you do will depend largely on the content of the image. The existing light within some images may simply be at odds with the introduced light to such a degree that a reconciliation is impossible.

It's very hard to create light. Light is even harder to create than shadow. While an enormous amount of liberty can be taken with photographic information and the quality of light can be dramatically modified, nothing can fully duplicate the

5. The effect of the mask on the image.

6. The lens flare reduced in opacity.

presence of light. This would seem to be of great importance in a "light drawing." Consequently, you may want to photograph a scene with more light than needed in the final image, rather than less. Soft even lighting is particularly malleable. It is easily made darker or lighter, its contrast can be increased or decreased, and shadows can be convincingly added. By comparison, it is very difficult to remove shadows convincingly.

The introduction of a new light into a previous recording of light is indeed a compelling challenge. It's one well worth meeting. Even failure to do so can be inspiring. It fosters greater appreciation of the miracle we are surrounded by every day.

METHOD

1   Create a new layer with a mode of Hard Light and a background color of 50% gray (Layer: New: Layer. Select a Mode of Hard Light and check Fill with Hard-Light-neutral color (50% gray)).

2   Render the lens flare (Filter: Render: Lens Flare) or equivalent lighting effect on the new Hard Light layer. You may want to make a selection before rendering the flare to pinpoint its location or to constrain its effect.

3   Reposition the lens flare as desired. Move the entire layer or select the area of the flare and move the information within the selection rather than the whole layer.

4   Reduce the opacity of the layer with the flare to modify the intensity of the effect.

5   Add a layer mask to hide the effect of the flare where it is not desired.

6   Add an adjusment layer grouped with the Hard Light layer to modify the flare's color or contrast.

To reduce file size, delete any part of the flare layer that is not displaying the effect of the flare.

Procession ii, Elemental, 2000

X X

S H A D O W S

Stones, clouds, shadows; in shape they are all echoes of each other. The clouds will pass, the dunes will drift, even the stones will pass. All seem to be in motion. Like the clouds growing progressively smaller, the shadows growing progressively softer and lighter are caught in the act of shifting and disappearing. Nothing in this image seems fixed or eternal, even stone.

Stone, cloud, shadow — in volume they are equal. While we might take them for granted, directing our attention to other actors in the image out of habit, the shadows are equal players in this drama. The shadows of the stones alter the rhythm and the visual flow of the entire image.

In Procession ii, shadows articulate the volumes of separate forms and bind them together. Shadows reveal the ripples that shimmer atop the undulating swells of a larger wave of sand. Shadows announce the forms of monoliths, standing out all the more clearly against an azure sky for their darkness. Shadows anchor the stones in space relative to the planes below them; without the shadows their positions would otherwise be ambiguous, their presence questionable. The shadows marry elements within this image and describe their relative relationships.

The shadows also indicate motion. While the stones appear separate, they are in fact one. Disparities in their contours belie this fact. An illusion of separateness and difference is reinforced by the ways that light and shadow articulate particulars of the three-dimensional forms unique to the differing angles. That the light is seen from a consistent angle in each instance helps reinforce the illusion. Once their unity is discovered, the consistency of light helps reinforce an appearance of motion. The stone rotates between the various points marking its ascent. The stone moves in two ways, rising and twisting. Just as the sun rises and turns, so does the stone.

To confirm that the separate stones are one stone, we need additional information. There is not enough information contained within the image to reach a conclusion that leads to certainty. It's challenging, and I think important, to be able to read an image in more than one way. Shifting our perspective can provide both confirmation and illumination. In doing so we take less for granted. There may be times when we grow wiser in uncertainty.

I'm fascinated by images where shadows display what would be an otherwise unseen character of the things photographed. I'm fascinated by photographs where shadows comingle, uniting what would otherwise be seen as separate. I'm fascinated by images with shadows whose sources remain off camera. In looking at this image and focusing so much on the shadows, it occurs to me that, as in a great many images, perhaps even a majority, the source of light is not included, but rather implied. We make assumptions about what is invisible based on the visible residues we find. Often we look habitually. Simply looking can be illuminating.

"The shadows are full of play. What resourcefulness in their relationship with each other."
— *Edgar Degas*

"Light of the moon
moves west, flowers' shadows
creep eastward."
— *Yosa Buson*

We tend to focus on what is fully revealed in the light, but what lies obscured in the dark can be equally important. In rare cases, this is more important. Sometimes the darkness itself is most important. Shadows can be the life of an image.

Shadows accentuate volume. In Edward Weston's "Oceano," 1936, the sensually undulating ripples of shadows on sand dunes articulate both the grand gestures and the nuances of their forms.

Shadows can be marvelous graphic devices. In Andre Kertez's "The Fork," 1928, the intersection of the shadows of a plate and fork unite to create a single compelling graphic shape. The negative spaces created are equally interesting.

Shadows create magnificent patterns and visual rhythms. In Ruth Bernhard's "Lifesavers," 1930, a forest of lifesavers dance unexpected arabesques of shadow and light weaving a rhythmic visual tapestry. Because of the dramatic side light, those wide with visible holes have thin solid shadows while those in thin solid profiles have wide shadows with holes. Form and space dance.

Shadows are marvelous framing devices that direct our attention to important areas of an image in dynamic ways. In Harry Callahan's "Bob Fine," 1952, a tiny figure stands in a sliver of light contained in a largely black image.

Shadows can fill an image with the evocative poetry of darkness. In Matt Mahurin's "Texas Prison," a doberman pincher paces barely seen below the looming presence of a prison wall. What is suggested can be more powerful than what is fully seen.

Shadows may be the primary recording of some photographs. Adam Fuss's "Invocation," 1992 , a photogram of a baby in water, is a record of blocked rather than reflected light.

Shadows tell us of the hidden communion that exists between all things. In Kurt Markus's "Marla with Leaf on Chest," 1990, the shadow of a leaf and vine cast on a woman's breast allows the two to touch without touching.

Shadow's natural distortions may take on mythic proportions. In one Manuel Alvarez Bravo photograph an old man shuffles down a dark alley pursued by his own monstrously enormous shadow.

Shadows may reveal the presence of off-screen actors in a visual drama, either about to make an entrance or recently departed, perhaps even performing the main action but yet unseen. In Minor White's "Vicinity of Dansville, New York," 1955, the presence of a windmill on a rundown farm is seen and felt only through its shadow, which would otherwise be invisible.

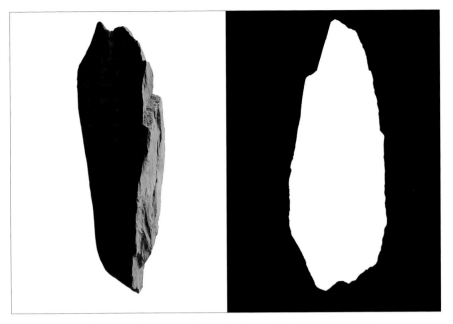

1. The contours of the stones contained in this image can be used to create convincing shadows. However, for maximum accuracy the contour as seen from a vantage where the stones are totally backlit or fully lit are used — as seen here. As this stone was photographed from varying angles, alternate exposures contain the most accurate outline for individual shadows.

Its passing may foreshadow another's.

Shadows that have been relocated or dislocated can be compelling. In Francis Ford Coppola's *Dracula,* the shadow of Dracula is capable of independent action. Dracula's lit surface belies a darker hidden truth revealed in his shadow, the id made visible.

Shadow substitution is pregnant with possibilities. Jerry Uelsmann's "Yosemite," 1995, a tree has the shadow of a running man, echoing Daphne. Transformation is implied.

There are always at least three actors in a play of shadows: the light source, the object that blocks the light, and the plane the shadow is cast upon. Shadows shift as the angles between the light source, the object, and the plane shift; reposition any one element and the shadows will change. Shadows transform as the surfaces they are cast upon ebb and flow. Shadows grow more and less intense as the intensity of light is increased or decreased, as the light grows more concentrated or diffuse, as the distance between the object and the light source increases, as the distance between the object and the plane decreases or increases. Edges soften as the distance between the object and the plane increases or the light source becomes increasingly diffuse and multidirectional. Shadows grow paler as secondary light sources enter them, including reflections, whether in defined shapes or broad areas. Shadows change color as the color of the plane changes. Shadows may be altered significantly by the reflective nature of the surface of the plane: on lighter or shinier surfaces ambient or reflected color shows through in shadows, at times creating a marked contrast between the colors of what's in shadow and what's not. A shadow appears to hold the same shape as the object casting it only if

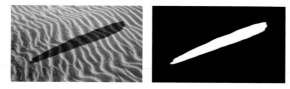

2. The shadow created with a transparent black fill.

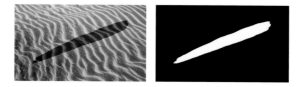

3. The shadow created with a Curves adjustment layer.

4. The mask distorted to conform to the surface the shadow is cast upon.

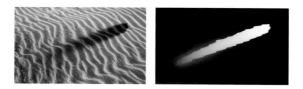

5. The mask blurred through a gradient mask.

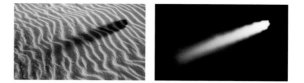

6. The mask blurred with the Blur tool and then
blurred through a gradient mask.

our viewpoint is placed in line with the angle of the light source and the shadow is cast on a flat plane, relatively close to the object, perpendicular to the angle of light — for instance, an object before a wall lit from the front. Silhouettes, figures entirely in shadow, are created when objects are placed directly between the light source and the viewer. Light source, object, plane — change the qualities or positions of one or more of these three and the shadow transforms. Radical shifts in the variables produce radical transformations.

Shadows are not just black. They often contain subtle amounts of color — blue, purple, green, brown, orange, even red. Some shadows are highly saturated with color. (Monet's haystack series transcribes marvelous transformations of light and shadow.) This is true in the natural world. It is doubly true of man-made environments, which often contain multidirectional, variable intensity colored light — and shadows.

If there is only one light source, and no reflected light, shadows will not build in intensity. The cross section of two or more shadows will not appear darker than the shadows alone. If, however, there are multiple light sources, it is possible to have multiple shadows that build up additional density at their intersections, just as light builds up when two rays of light intersect. In the presence of multiple light sources of varying color, a game of light and shadows arises akin to three-dimensional chess in complexity. The variables increase and the level of complexity rises. One can still, mindful of the ground rules, make accurate predictions about the final results — it just takes a little bit longer.

The contour of many shadows can be created from the outline of the object that casts it. This works particularly well if the shadow is cast on a flat plane directly behind the object. Simply select the object. Or, select the ground it is on and invert the selection. The outline created can now be used as the foundation of a shadow. Many simply fill the outline on a sepa-

rate layer, turn the layer's opacity down, and have done with it.

A perfect sphere will likely cast similar shadows from many angles as it has the same shape from all angles. Few objects are so consistent; most contain a great variety of shapes when seen from different angles. If the angle of light is not frontal or the plane it is cast upon is not perpendicular to the light source, the shadow cast may undergo significant transformations. You can alter the shape of a shadow placed on its own layer quite dramatically in Photoshop, enough to solve most problems. You can scale it, skew it, apply perspective to it, or distort it. None of these will allow curvilinear distortions. For these you can use the Smudge tool. This is a highly effective way to reshape the contour of a shadow. If you use it, take care not to let the edges become overly soft. Edges (whether fill or mask) that become too soft can once again become hard-edged by sharpening them or increasing their contrast or even retracing them with a hard-edged brush. At high resolutions the brush can be quite slow. There's no harm in working at a lower resolution and resampling a shadow that is an outline or a flat fill. The Liquify feature offers some of Photoshop's most advanced distortion capabilities. If you could see the effects of the distortion overlaid on the other layers, while making the distortion, this would be the right tool for the job. However, the best you can do is view the distorted layer in the Liquify preview window next to the undistorted image window. While seeing both side by side provides some guide, without more accurate reference the precise amount and kind of distortion needed is difficult to determine. With a little guesswork, persistence, and some luck it can be done, but expect to be frustrated by the time you finish.

Even this level of sophistication won't adequately solve the problem for highly irregular objects or objects that contain significant portions of open space. Imagine a simple hoop. Seen from the side it appears as a straight line. Light it from the

7. The shadow for an object close to the plane it is cast upon is harder and denser.

8. As the object grows further away from the plane the shadow is cast upon, the shadow grows softer and more diffuse. Here it also grows further away from the object.

side and the shadow that appears is a hollow ellipse. The selection of the contour of the straight line is a pitiful foundation for the elliptical shadow. Another strategy is clearly called for. You may want to make exposures of an object from multiple angles using the appropriate one to create the foundation of an outline for a future shadow. If you don't have such an exposure from the original scene, it is possible to recreate it by setting up a similar one. As a last resort you can draw the outline of the shadow, creating it from scratch. While it can often be the most laborious method, there are many times when there is no substitute for it. This is especially true when shadows are being projected on very complicated surfaces. It may be that in some instances, complex surfaces would distort a shadow so significantly that you would be better off drawing the shadow rather than creating it from the outline of the object. Paths can help you here as Bézier curves are excellent drafting tools. In such

situations, using like or similar reference material will help guide you in your efforts.

Once the contour of a shadow has been established, density and color may be addressed. Start by creating a new layer and filling the selection of the contour with black. Place the shadow layer below the object layer, reposition it, and reduce its opacity.

While many favor creating shadows by filling a selection on a new layer with black and then reducing its opacity, two problems arise with this method: detail may be unnaturally obscured and the shadow remains relatively colorless. You can use a shadow created this way as the basis for one more convincing.

First, create a selection from the shadow's contour. Click on it with the Magic Wand. Then hide it by unchecking the eye on the shadow layer. Next, with the selection still active, create a Curves adjustment layer and darken the area inside

9. As distance is increased, these tendencies increase.

10. Shadows both near and far.

the outline appropriately. The selection will automatically become an adjustment layer layer mask. Saturation will increase, meaning the shadow will have significant color, the color of the surface the shadow is cast upon. Depending on the strength of the correction, the saturation may be too great. To cure this, reload the selection outline. If you have the Curves adjustment layer highlighted, you can go to the Channels palette and load its layer mask as a selection. Then, create a Hue/Saturation adjustment layer to lower the saturation of the shadow. Should you decide to modify the color of the shadow, say to incorporate reflected color, you can do so with the initial Curves correction. Select only one channel in the Curves to adjust the color balance. Alternately, the Hue slider of the Hue/Saturation adjustment layer may be used. When shadows are created on very light objects, there may be insufficient information to "burn in" a shadow without lowering the white point. This adds

density without information just as a flat fill would, but doing so may be necessary nonetheless. As light grounds are more reflective than dark grounds, a shift in color may be particularly appropriate. A compelling case can be made for burning and dodging in LAB color mode as it minimizes both increases in saturation and color shifts. You can convert a file to LAB or simply change the blending mode of an adjustment layer to Luminosity.

Once a convincing contour and density for the shadow has been created, its softness may be addressed. Use Gaussian Blur to soften the edges of the shadow. Blur the layer mask appropriately. Every image will be different so use your best judgement and create a convincing effect. It is quite likely that the shadow will need to be harder where the object is closer to the plane and softer where it is further away. If the transition is linear, as in a flat plane receding at any angle, you can apply Gaussian Blur through a Gradient Mask. Create a new channel.

It will be black. Make the image simultaneously visible by clicking on the eye of the background. Next, use the Gradient tool with black-and-white foreground and background colors to make a smooth transition from the beginning of the shadow to the end of it. Getting the angle right is important, so drag the line of the Gradient tool down the center of the shadow, bisecting it. Make the gradient dark where the object is close to the plane and light where the shadow is furthest from the object. Load the new gradient channel as a selection. Click on the shadow layer to reactivate it. (Affect either the filled image layer or the adjustment layer layer mask, depending on which method you choose.) Applying Gaussian Blur through the resulting selection will affect the shadow most where the gradient alpha channel is lightest and least where it is darkest. A smooth transition from hard to soft will be created. You can modify a shadow manually in much the same way with the Blur tool. While it's difficult to achieve such a flawless transition manually and can be tedious, this method can enable greater control and flexibility for customizing the softness of a shadow. On high-resolution images, blurring through a gradient may leave unnaturally hard lines in portions of the blurred areas. If you encounter this, undo the blur and use the Blur tool to soften those areas substantially by hand before reapplying the blur. This will eliminate these kinds of artifacts.

You may want to blur a duplicate shadow layer or adjustment layer layer mask and keep the hard-edged shadow, hidden of course, as a safety net or to alter the effect later.

Nothing can escape its own shadow. Shadows are a critical anchor point in photomontage. Without the correct shadow, an object won't appear to be a part of its environment. Instead object and environment will appear to share separate realities.

Like reflections, many of the shadows we see created digitally are unconvincing. They give us answers that are far too simple. They are too dense, too pale, too hard or too soft, too uniformly hard or soft, bereft of color or detail, or they confirm an obvious contour but fail to reveal the complexity of a three-dimensional object. They seem indifferent to the natural poetry contained in any play of light. They merely represent a failure of attention. There is a simple cure — attention. There is no substitute for careful observation. The more you observe them, the wiser you will become in the ways of shadows. Become a hunter of shadows. They are poetry made visible.

Photographers may be at an advantage. Not habituated to constructing images from memory, they may more easily avoid the hubristic assumption that they know exactly how the world looks and so take the time to look more closely at the world as a basis for their creations. Painters who do this are at an even greater advantage, as the time spent in similar observations represents a wealth of experience to draw from. The wisest observers are those who are always ready to be surprised by a new discovery.

Many shadows are decidedly peculiar and unexpected. The mercurial world of shadows is too often taken for granted or only dimly noted. It has been the subject of too little scrutiny. As it is unfamiliar terrain to the conscious minds of many, great liberties can be taken with shadows. My advice is to take these liberties for effect, not just to get by. This is perhaps one of those territories where because of a viewer's lack of attention, he or she may find simple answers, even inaccurately simple answers, more convincing than the highly complex and unpredictable answers found in nature. Whereas before the advent of digital imaging the viewer might give the photographic image more authority, and thus accept the strange and unusual answers found therein, it may be that today a viewer is less likely to do so, filled with a prudent caution about making such assumptions, and so call into question the validity of many strange but found realities. Rather than issuing condemnations that might limit the enormous potential found within these new freedoms of expression, this should instead be a clarion call for us all to look a little more closely — and to keep looking.

The realm of shadows is a gateway to enchantment. Shadows have long been a theater where magic makes a regular appearance. Children play at least two kinds of tag: in one the body is touched, in the other the shadow is chased. By evening candlelit hands conjure forth birds and wolves. The Balinese have a highly evolved puppet theater (Wayang Kulit) where fables are reenacted. The puppets are paper flat and go unseen as audiences watch instead their shadows projected on screens. In many ways they are precursors to the enchanting silver screens of cinema and television.

METHOD

1   Create a convincing shadow outline. Whenever possible get the image to do the work for you. In this case, create the outline by selecting the object. Alternately, draw a selection with the Lasso tool. The Quick Mask mode is particularly helpful here.

2   With the selection active, create a Curves adjustment layer and darken the area appropriately.

3   Offset the shadow appropriately. Use the Move tool on the new adjustment layer. Use the angle of light in the image as your guide.

4   You may find that you will need to distort the shadow. Using Distort (Edit: Transform: Distort), bend it back in perspective to conform it to the plane it is cast upon.

5   You may also find that it may need further distortion if the plane is very complex. Use the Smudge tool to distort it appropriately. Be careful to blur the edges of the mask minimally. If the outline becomes too blurred, you can use the filters Maximize or Minimize or Unsharp Mask to sharpen the edge. Increasing the contrast of the mask also helps.

6   Alternately you could use a displacement map (a Grayscale copy of the image) and the filter Displace to create distortion. (See XXV. Reflection.)

7   You may find as well that you want the edge of the selection to be soft. Use Gaussian Blur on the adjustment layer to soften the edge of the shadow.

8   Many shadows have both hard and soft areas, harder closer to the object and softer further away from it. To blur a shadow selectively first create a new alpha channel, then use the Gradient tool placing white where the shadow is to be blurred most and black where it is not to be blurred. If you make both the image and the alpha channel visible simultaneously, you will have a visual guide as to where to create the gradient and what angle to use in its creation. The gradient will create a smooth transition between the dark (0%) and light (100%). Load this new alpha channel as a selection and use the selection to blur the shadow adjustment layer layer mask. If hard lines persist within blurred areas, undo the blur, then blur those areas with the Blur tool, before reapplying Gaussian Blur.

At each stage you can duplicate the adjustment layer about to be affected. Turn the original off, and affect the duplicate. That way if you don't like the result, you can readily go back to the previous version at any time, now or in the future.

I recommend the following exercise. Take an object with a complicated three-dimensional structure (a whisk, an open pair of scissors, a flower with stem and leaves, etc.) into the light so that it projects a shadow on a flat plane. Note the difference between the shape of the contour of the object and the shape of the shadow. Push and pull the object closer and further away from the plane the shadow is cast upon. Twist, turn, and rotate the object. Observe the changes that take place in the character of the shadow while making comparisons to the changes that occur in the contour of the object. Change the angle of the plane the shadow is cast upon or move it to new surfaces. Watch the shadow metamorphose as it passes from simple to more complicated surfaces. Repeat the procedure with an object that is translucent or transparent (a half-filled bottle of water for instance). Now reflection becomes a part of the play of light and shadow.

Causeway, Elemental, 1994

XXI

RECONTEXTUALIZATION

Up is down and down is up in Causeway. Turn the background upside down and the image might not seem unusual. It's a simple little twist, but it produces a dramatic effect. There's wish fulfillment here. A walk in the clouds awaits. And, there's anxiety. A deluge hovers overhead. The fate of the moment is uncertain. The destination is unseen. And yet, it's quite beautiful.

All the elements are beautiful. One thing is particularly special — the light on the causeway. It would be extraordinarily difficult, if not impossible, to duplicate it digitally. Digital renderings don't yet have the richness of photographs. I wonder if they ever will. The causeway was particularly beautiful that morning, but the elements around it were not as extraordinary at that time. It was having its moment; they had had theirs or would have theirs later. I could wait a lifetime until they were simultaneously equally radiant. Or I could make exposures of them at separate times and combine the best moments into a new whole. That would be resynchronization. This was recomposition. Call it photomontage, call it photocomposition, call it post-visualization, call it what you will, the image is composed after exposure rather than before. The photograph does not document a previously existing moment in time, rather it creates one from many sources. It presents a totally new reality. To those who paint, little is novel about this method. The musician and the writer alike understand how many ways a blank page can be filled.

I find I make photographs differently now. I constantly shoot objects separate from environments. Often the essence of an image is found in its figure/ground relationships. These can be found. Or created. In shooting this way I find I need to keep many things in mind. First I need to be very clear about my intentions. A sketch or a note in the field does wonders. Still there are times I operate on instinct. I have faith it will lead me where I need to go, a place my conscious mind might not have learned to recognized. At these times, I shoot as I normally would and I shoot a little extra; I bracket composition. I find if I don't crop in the field, I may forget the picture later. But if I crop too tightly, I leave too little room to maneuver in the future should the process of creating the image continue at a later date. With several exposures in hand, I empower myself to make those choices rather than having my working methods determine them for me.

Often I find myself having to overcome my previous photographic training about how to make photographs. The traditional methods may limit my options at a later date. Operating with them, I might pass up a photograph with distracting details (which could later be removed saving an otherwise interesting picture) or crop them out (even though in so doing I crop out a great set of relationships with them). I find this maxim serves me best: shoot for maximum information. Once I've captured that information I can edit it at will, but if I don't have it to start with I've got to start all over. Without the traditional foundation I would not be able to capture premium information and I would have missed out on the perceptual modes it encourages, which can be very useful. Traditional photography brings with it a set of questions which yield very interesting answers. If I cast it aside I would have missed them. Again, digital technique is not a substitute for traditional technique; it's a wonderful extension of it. I have not abandoned my conventional roots. I've simply placed them in a context that is meaningful to me. I still make conventional photographs when they present themselves. They can be wonderful indeed. Often found images contain more surprises than preconceived images — but not always. The real question is: at what part of the process is the image found, before or after exposure? The limits of my perception are stretched every time I engage in a disciplined exercise of looking at the world around me. I am confronted with the many ways it works. Similarly, the limits of my perception are challenged every time I look at a blank page. I am confronted with the many ways I work.

CONTEXT IS KEY

"Without context, the code is incomplete since it encompasses only part of the message."
— *Edward T. Hall*

In recent history, we tend to think of irrationality as the province of the Surrealists, adept at the art of surprise, sometimes with the by-product of humor, and the Dadaists, whose weapon was shock. While officially Surrealism might have been a short-lived movement, its sensibility is still with us today. Never was a movement so quickly or thoroughly co-opted. It is, arguably, a resurfacing of a visionary sensibility that has been with us since before the dawn of culture. As the rate of change accelerates and the world seems to grow smaller, life seems to grow ever more "surreal."

Jerry Uelsmann's work could be seen as a precursor to a new digital aesthetic, a continuation of Surrealism, or a continuation of a sensibility that has long been with us and continually resurfaces throughout many historical eras. He is neither the only nor the first photographer to employ this aesthetic, though he is certainly the most popular. He has charted this territory extensively.

Such work, drawn from within rather than from without, confronts us with our desire to believe and our desire to suspend our disbelief. We all have an imaginal world and confirmation of its "reality" can be thrilling. In Western Culture the subjective world is usually the underdog. We don't quite know what to do with it, so we learn to forget it. We wake up by day to "reality" and slip back into another by night.

The "surreal" aesthetic has enjoyed a resurgence with the popularization of digital imaging, so much so that a few assume that a digital image, by its very nature, looks "surreal". The reality is we have been looking at digital images far longer than we generally assume; for the past few decades images in print, video, and television have been digitized, relatively few of them "surreal." Contrary to popular opinion, digital need not mean "surreal." The same can be said for the device of recontextualization.

A rose may indeed be a rose. But a rose can mean many things. A rose in a spring garden (reawakening), a rose in winter (impending doom or magical presence), a rose in the city (reassertion of the organic), a rose in the desert (the triumph of life), a rose in trash (love rejected), a single rose (solitary romantic love), a rose among roses (overflowing love), a single white rose amid many red roses (a pure unique love). A rose may be unchanging, but in a changing environment its significance changes.

Context is everything. Context is so important we sometimes participate in an underlying assumption that it should not be changed photographically. If object and environment can never be truly separated, then perhaps they never should be. After all, in certain contexts, representation of a new context may be misrepresentation. But this need not be so.

Photojournalists have an ethical responsibility to present images that represent what they witnessed as they witnessed it. Photographers working commercially, not unaware of these concerns, feel these pressures less frequently; quite often they may be asked to represent something not as they see it but as someone would like to see it. Recontextualization may be permissible or even appropriate in one discipline and not in

1. Environment.

2. Environment.

another. It's a matter of intention. A spectrum of possibilities exists between these two poles.

The rules also depend on context, the context the image will be placed in. We (both artist and audience) learn the rules of the game and so we know how to read an image. When we change the rules of the game, we change the nature of the images we make. The two are inseparable.

You could certainly come up with exceptions to the rules. In certain instances a manipulated image might be able to represent the truth or even the facts better than an unmanipulated one. But making this judgment would require a very complicated process of reassessment, both on the part of the creator and the viewer. Rather than invent a new language, in general, it is better to work within the bounds of an existing one. It's certainly more efficient.

We need not play by the old rules simply because they exist. We can play another game. It's our choice. We need only to be conscious of the connotations, what the choices we make bring to the image. Our images will change in kind. It's a choice. We must clearly announce our choices if our message is to be understood correctly.

As Dr. Richard D. Zakia said, "What people experience depends upon external and internal factors — what they are looking at and what they are looking for." The creation of an image is the creation of a new reality. Ultimately, images are statements. Intent determines method which determines kind. This is true not only of creation but also of interpretation.

Relocation is the essence of montage and collage. Compelling new relationships may be created. They may be subtle or dramatic.

Recontextualization relies as much on substitution as addition. Addition is combination: a new object is added to an environment or vice versa. Substitution is replacement: one element is added in such a way that another is subtracted. Substitution occurs with any addition: space is taken up by the replacer substituting what was in its place; i.e., many kinds of elimination are really substitutions. They substitute information that blends in with the ground for information that does not. Elimination in its purest form leaves a void or a smaller image.

In any combination, Gestalt principles apply. The effect of the total visual field is determined by many qualities of relationship: figure and ground (object/environment or lack of) delineate identity; closure (open/closed or lack of) creates visual elements seen as figures (even new optical figures such as a closed negative space); continuity (together/separate or lack of) causes visual elements that require few interruptions to be

3. Object.

4. Recontexualization.

grouped; proximity (near/far or lack of) provides association and disassociation; similarity (like/different or lack of) supports echoes of agreement and disagreement. The result may be synergistic where the entire conjunction creates something above and beyond the sum of its parts. Change demands attention. In general our visual systems tend to minimize stress and maximize stability. We capitalize on these tendencies (by amplifying, and/or reducing them) in successful image creation.

The art of recontextualization lies first in finding resonant combinations and second in establishing sensitively articulated visual relationships between them.

If context is key, we should be mindful of it in our new creations. It's all about relationship. One of the wonderful things about conventional photographs is that the relationships between object and environment or object and object usually look consistent and shared. Their relationship creates a shared reality. Relationship within an image confirms that context is genuine. Insensitivity to relationships within an image will permeate an image with that same quality. Sometimes the relationships we find in the world are strikingly complex or unexpected. We need no shock of the new; the world is new enough. With the camera eye we often see the world anew —not as we think it is but as we find it to be. Like any good fiction writer, if we are

to create credible new "truths," we must become keen observers of the world and its workings. When we use this as our guide and our compass, we align ourselves with a greater reality. Let the elements of photomontage be your guide, but above all look to the world around you.

With recontextualized images there is the expected and the unexpected. Both offer new views but markedly different kinds. In the first, the new sum did not exist before, but the combination and its execution leaves the viewer no clue that it did not. Despite the many possible transfigurations of media, technique, or vision, the source clearly remains. It is "illusionistic," that is, it seems "real." Though it is fiction, it nonetheless confirms our "reality." In the second, it is quite obvious, either through execution or through content, that we are looking at an event that would be "impossible." We know it is an illusion. We know this from prior experience. Its fiction questions our "reality." Both throw us back upon our assumptions about reality and ask us to ask a very useful and interesting question: How do we know what we know? The degree to which we don't take things for granted is the degree to which things become interesting.

When we suspend our disbelief, the mind's rational objections are put aside. In the realm of the irrational, where the ordinary boundaries of time and space can be but aren't necessarily

5. Recontextualization. The simplicity of this environment makes this in essence decontextualization.

disrupted, our emotions are our compasses. We have little else to guide us in our quest for understanding.

Which well do we draw from? We operate on a variety of levels simultaneously: the personal and the cultural; the timely and the timeless; the known and the unknown (to name just a few). If each pair represents the poles of a spectrum, then the respective lines generated between them may intersect at any point. They interpenetrate one another continually. Each realm can be tapped. Then the task is to find a compelling relation-

ship between one, or more, of the others.

Clearly the known tends to be less interesting than the unknown. As we are always on the lookout for something new, the cliché and the conventional, whose powers lie in ease of recognition, quickly grow stale. Turning the conventional on its head can be stimulating, but the true test of an image's resonance is usually found over time and found in the things you can least explain. While it is certain that the absurd can generate intensity, greater resonance can be found in relationships

6. Recontextualization.
Gravity is defied. Day is turned to night.

that seemed unlikely before but once viewed seemed inexplicably appropriate. The less we know the more we project. Mystery is tantalizing. It is beyond formula. This is visual poetry. It's a call to association. There is no right. There is no wrong. But still, some poems are better than others. To become a better poet, study the best poems.

Next time you see a beautiful object or event in an environment that does not support it well, you don't have to pass it by. You could recontextualize it.

METHOD

1   Shoot an object.

2   Shoot an environment.

3   Composite the two. Drag the background layer of one into the other.

4   Hide the original background of the object with a layer mask.

5   Position as desired.

6   Make corrections to color and perspective to unite the two.

7   Optionally, repeat with multiple objects.

Avra, Allies, 1996

XXII

SKIES

A small number of images in this book do not contain a sky. While the skies in some of the images have been left as they were found, the majority of them have been chosen specifically for that image. Similarly in a majority of images the sky holds equal importance with the land or the sea. In a few of the images the sky is more important; it is the subject of the image. That's true of this image.

Avra is one of those magical images that practically made itself. It took me completely by surprise. It resolved itself very quickly and remains one of my freshest images to date. It was a breakthrough. I had no intention of making it. It found me. I was sorting through images on a light table one day, looking for a replacement sky for another image, and I moved a small mirror from one side of it to the other. Out of the corner of my eye I saw something happening as I moved it. I moved the mirror back across the light table and found this image. Time and time again I find that being alive to the process, being sensitive to what unfolds as you engage the activity of creation, allows you to find unexpected riches. Ironically, I find that these "departures" are actually returns. At first these unplanned moves seem to be moves away from a vision or a personal direction, but uncannily I find that they actually bring us closer to a way of seeing that's our own. It has nothing to do with accidents revealing something novel, something new that's new for the sake of being new. It has everything to do with allowing our unconscious reserves, our hidden resources, to well up and present themselves. Controlled abandon allows us to delve deeper into ourselves, into areas that have gone unseen, unrecognized, or unacknowledged.

Prior to this image my use of symmetry defined broad planes, spaces, or environments. After this image I also began using symmetry to define objects, mass, or figures. This image hovers in between the two poles. The strong contrast between the cloud and the sky defines a definite shape while at the same time the sky and cloud form a unified space. The configuration can be read as both very deep and dimensional or as flat and planar.

The sky was so dramatic, it needed no competition. A simple seascape offered the best support. It echoed the color. Even the highlights at the far horizon mirrored the luminous form dissolving into vapor and mist. And it provided a deep recession in space making the configuration in the sky seem larger.

It is nearly impossible to read the image as just a cloud. I've had many discussions with people about what they see in this image. An angel, a high priestess, a phoenix, a sea monster, an x-ray, a harp; I love collecting all the stories and I've learned to see them all in this image. One of my favorites came from a four-year-old boy who exclaimed, "It's a giant sneeze!" In his words I hear a humorous echo of a primary force at work in the image. Avra is Sanskrit for breath.

It has become automatic now. Whenever I go outside, I look up.

A few years prior to making this image I met another artist who was painting angels abstractly. I appreciated her subject matter. And I appreciated the abstractness of her approach as it stripped the subject of its iconography down to its essence increasing its universal appeal. But I felt I had to be called to approach such a subject.Out of respect I did not feel I could dare to presume so much. I see the fulfillment of that wish in this image, which has since become a series unto itself — Heaven's Breath. What impressed me is that when I did find my way to this material spontaneously, the results were more my own than I could have conceived of had I proceeded earlier. Earlier I would have approached the challenge more directly, relying on preexisting iconography. Later the solution that arose spontaneously contained a deeply felt connection to the natural world, a connection I place great value on. Are these images of angels? I appreciate the association but I would not want to pin one association on them. To me clouds and smoke are visible signs of breath. I see these images as spiritual presences revealed.

That many people see many different things in these images, yet they also share a similar emotional response to them, is fascinating and reaffirming to me. A basic chord is struck but the final interpretation is left to the viewer. This encourages a lively dialog between the viewer and the work, and between the work's many viewers, of which I am one. It allows the life of the image to continue on, to continue moving and growing long after it coalesces. This image continues to evolve for me.

"You must not blame me if I talk to the sky."
— *Henry David Thoreau*

"The sky is the daily bread of the eyes."
— *Ralph Waldo Emerson*

Never mind Steiglitz's equivalents; they're all sky. LeGray found wonderful possibilities for expression in his photocompositions. Constable made a life's study of the sky. He felt that very often it was the sky that determined the mood of a landscape. Cumulus, cirrus, stratus — each contains a unique beauty.

Photographer Bruce Barnbaum wrote of chasing a quetzal shaped cloud, which hovered past a South American pyramid. His group rushed to establish the right relationship between the ground and the sky, from their singular vantage points, before the magical conjunction evaporated. Multiple vantage points can achieve something similar. One might even recreate what had been seen but missed. One can also achieve something very different, a relationship that had never been witnessed or a relationship that had never existed.

Some suggest that skies can be created digitally. Simple skies can be filled with blue. But, transitions are found in almost every sky (one of the things that makes retouching skies a matter of some delicacy). Transitions within skies can be created with the gradient tool blending a darker blue with a lighter blue. But, these transitions are rarely purely linear in nature. Gradients can be created radially, a large radius will better approximate transitions in skies, particularly as the view grows closer to the sun. But, digital skies often have banding. Work in a color space with a higher bit depth. But, digital skies seem artificially smooth; like distilled water they seem too pure. Add noise — this will also cure some banding problems and the resulting "grain" in the sky will more closely match the grain in the ground unifying the two. But, skies usually have clouds. Some filters can approximate cloudy formations and clouds can be painted with some skill. Still, I've never seen a digitally created sky that truly fooled the most discriminating eye. Moreover, there are some heavenly occurrences it would never occur to us to portray. I still prefer to photograph a sky, rather than create it digitally. The resulting images are fully informed by a rich language of subtlety and complexity beyond my imagining.

While I find the patterns of the heavens offer me more than I could have imagined, on occasion I will create new conjunctions — painting with photographs if you will. If you create new conjunctions you will want to manage transitions carefully. Maintaining their impossible smoothness and consistency is challenging. Big soft brushes work well. Be careful, as lower opacities can produce areas that are overly smooth. The introduction of noise may be able to compensate for this effect. Progressions in tone and color should be consistent with the lighting in the foreground below. Almost any portion of a sky can be moved to another position, but remember the effects of a thicker atmosphere at the horizon. Controlling it will control a great deal of the atmosphere of the image. At high altitudes or

1.   2.   3.

in very dry climates there is less shift in color and tone; at sea level or in very wet climates there is more. You can simulate this accumulation, lightening and shifting color through gradient masks. It's harder to remove it. You can also control the softness of the horizon line by blurring it or by placing the sky on a new layer and using a soft-edged layer mask to composite it.

There's a decision we must all make for ourselves. Should the grain or noise structure of a sky match the structure of the ground? The fundamentals of photomontage suggest so. We are used to seeing this arrangement and reading it as real. If we accept this answer, when compositing differing formats or film speeds, e.g. a sky shot with a larger format or with a lower ISO film (this applies to filmless capture as well), theoretically we should add a little extra noise to unite the two. It would be nice if we could work it the other way, making things less noisy, but, unfortunately, we are generally left working with the lowest common denominator. Yet I'd suggest there is another way to approach this problem. Skies usually seem smoother than the textured grounds below them. In certain instances it might seem truer to our experience to have the sky smoother than the ground. How much smoother is a matter of some interpretation. If we accept this answer we may add less noise in composites, perhaps none, we may even decide to blur a sky, slightly, in images that are not composites. It is interesting to look closely at the way we perceive skies. Upon careful examination, we will notice noise is introduced by our own visual apparatus. Tiny flotsam and jetsam moves within the fluid on the surface of our eyes, there are imperfections on the surface or our lenses, there is even noise introduced at the back of our retina. One could make the case that a little noise in the image more closely approximates the way we see. On the other hand, that noise is usually changing, rarely fixed, and even with very smooth images, our eyes will continue to introduce their natural noise. Why add noise to noise, unless you feel the noise is aesthetically compelling? I've never heard a definitive answer to this argument. The questions are very interesting though. With them in mind I find I look more closely at the world and at the way I see it.

4.   5.   6.

Because of their expressive possibilities, my largest image file is labeled "skies." Only meteorologists are able to tell if a sky belongs in Australia or Tibet. Often, even they can't. Anyone is able to respond to differences in color and shape. We would all do well to learn the languages of the heavens in order to correlate the events above us with the effects they produce below and within us.

If you are willing to create a dislocation in either time or space or both, new visual conjunctions can be found almost anywhere. Sometimes, they alone can make, or break, a picture. One simply has to look up and imagine the possibilities.

I remember my father relating an amusing story. Someone was teasing Ansel Adams, who had dramatic skies in the majority of his photographs, "What have you got in that bag of yours, a cloud stick next to your light meter?" Even now I can hear the sound of my young voice whispering when I heard that story, "Wow! I wish I had one of those!" Now I do.

METHOD

1   Pick a sky. Pick a foreground. Composite the two. Click and drag the background layer of the foreground into the sky document. Hold the Shift key while doing this if you would like the new layer to be centered in the destination document.

2   Use the Move tool to reposition it as desired.

3   Add a layer mask (Layer: Add a Layer Mask: Reveal All) and mask out any unwanted elements in the foreground. Sky will be revealed. Broad areas can simply be selected with the Marquee or Lasso tools and filled with black. Care should be taken at the boundary lines between ground and sky. In cases where there is a significant amount of contrast between the ground and the sky this is a perfect scenario to use a contrast mask to get the image to make the selection for you and eliminate a lot of tedious selection and masking.

4   Optionally, blur the boundary of the layer mask to soften the transition between the background and the sky.

5   Use adjustment layers with localized gradient masks to control the hue, saturation, and brightness of the sky along the horizon.

Triple Goddess, Allies, 1996

XXIII

EDGE

Edge was critical throughout the entire process of composing Triple Goddess. First there was contour. What shape would the stone finally take? The original had been buried in sand. The stone was far too large to dig out, so I cut away the background that threatened to envelop it. This made certain determinations of shape. It may even have been the shape the sand made out of the stone that first attracted me to it. Had I seen the entire stone I might not have been so drawn to it. To date I have no idea what the full stone looks like, as I was only able to see a portion of it. Yet the line the sand created still needed refining. In my first attempts the bottom of the stone remained full and heavy. Later, I cut it more angularly, which lent it a new motion, but more importantly it altered its character. As I searched for the final shape, I was reminded of shapes I had seen in Brancusi's sculptures. I had to fight my tendency to cut a clean precise line, opting instead to let the wobble of my hand with a brush give the final appearance of the stone a very subtle rough hewn look. The resulting line was personal not clinical. I feel a physical or kinetic understanding of things is achieved through drawing, which imparts a different sense of knowing to the image. Then the issue of how hard or soft the line should be arose. I cut the mask hard first and blurred it later to determine this precisely. To turn the space, I softened the dark side slightly more, forcing it to recede, and the light side slightly less, forcing it to rise forward. Volume was increased. Again, the effect is subtle, but present. Through a process of searching for shape, which is defined by an outline or edge, the character of the stone was clarified. Who was the sculptor of this stone — the rock itself, the forces of nature, the sand, or I? Undoubtedly, the final effect was generated from the confluence of all of the energies involved. In one sense the work is collaborative.

The horizon line needed similar attention, too hard an edge and the landscape would look cut out, too soft an edge and the atmosphere that enveloped it would seem too thick to hold the level of contrast and detail found there. Without the right balance, the land and the stone would not breathe the same air.

Several edges were made invisible, the seams at each of the points of symmetry.

There are four more edges at work here, ones we take for granted so often that they are nearly invisible. The edges of the picture frame contain the forces of the interactions within the image, setting the stage for the drama, giving a definite shape to the entire composition.

There are other edges at work here. The edges of the clouds, air flowing energetically in contrast to the stability of the earth, seemed to want to touch the edge of the stone in a specific way. I split the sky and filled the resulting gap to pull a feathered breath from behind the monolith and suggest a caress.

"Good fences make good neighbors."
— *Robert Frost*

In a material world the line between one thing and another, this and that, I and thou, can be found in an outline. The outline is one of the first things children, or beginning draftsmen of any age, learn to draw. Rarely do they begin by defining fields of tone like Seurat or texture like Van Gogh. This "primitive" sensibility can contain a great deal of raw energy, as in the petroglyphs and cave paintings of many primal cultures. Greek and Egyptian artists brought their exquisitely refined sensibilities to the line. Oriental ink drawing and calligraphy found a way to marry both raw power and refinement in their celebrations of line. Many modernists, Keith Haring and Franz Kline, for instance, could not escape the power of the line.

The character of line can shape an image entirely. Try describing as many different kinds of line qualities as you can: rectilinear, curvilinear, zig-zag, curlique, rigid, oscillating, trembling, rough, clean… you could go on and on. My point? A line is not just a line. It's vocabulary.

There's something fundamental about the line. It is a foundation of structure, or at least our understanding of structure. Prefigured by Renaissance artists, as seen in many of Leonardo Da Vinci's drawings, the framework for three-dimensional rendering is line drawing projected conceptually beyond the two-dimensional plane. A set of intersecting lines is used to represent not just contour but also volume. Edge is a basic fundamental of the visual language that helps representational images hold together. Line quality must be carefully controlled to ensure that all the elements in an image appear to share the same reality.

There are at least two kinds of lines: matter too thin to be experienced as a definite mass, including markings, man-made or otherwise; or the optical end of a solid mass, the juncture between one mass and another or between a mass and an area of space. The former is a thing in and of itself, the line as object. The latter is an optical phenomenon. It's the latter I'm primarily concerned with here. Line, when it is not the figure itself, helps separate figure from ground or object from environment. It demarcates beginning and end, perhaps not always the true end of something, but certainly the end of our ability to perceive it. Oddly, like a rainbow or the horizon (both lines), lines seem to be virtual images. They are not fixed in space. They move as we move.

Do lines exist in nature? Picasso claimed so. Monet said no. The debate did not originate in the last century; it has been with us far longer. Lines are mercurial in nature, they change based on the context in which they are seen. If contrast is weak, then lines are weak. If contrast is strong, then lines are strong. When two distinctly different tones/colors abut each other, an intensification occurs at their shared edge making the dark side appear darker and the light side lighter — the Mach effect. The stronger the difference, the stronger the line. Op artists capitalize on this. Part of what we see in their brightly colored canvases is not painted. The flashing white lines and colored afterimages are not painted; they are purely optical phenomena. It may be that lines are optical illusions, that they have no physically measurable characteristics. Nonetheless we experience them. Phenomenologically, or experientially, they exist.

As in a majority of representational images, in photographic images line is often determined by subject matter, less often by individual style or expression. Outlines, or contours, take their shape and character from the objects they define as seen from a certain vantage point. Outlines are defined by at least two other defining characteristics — some are dark, some are light, some are hard, some are soft. In a few instances, lines may be colored. Generally outlines are fairly sharp, though lighting conditions and atmosphere may modify them. Outside influences will modify lines, such as atmospheric buildup, as with heat waves or images seen on far off horizons. As fog, smoke, or haze builds up, outlines grow increasingly diffuse and even begin to disappear. The same happens as light grows very dim. In extremely bright lighting conditions a similar phenomenon occurs, particularly in the case of strong back lighting. Light and shadow produce lines: the outline of one object is cast upon another. While light (absent of the effects of extreme gravitational forces) travels in straight lines, it also spills around objects, softening their edges. All lines are not created equally.

Far too often, in digital images we see edges that are too sharp or too soft. There are at least three factors we might look to when this happens. One, the image has been composited from multiple sources and the selection outline or mask used to isolate the newfound intruder is too hard or too soft. Two, the selection outline or mask for a local correction is too hard or too soft. Three, the amount or kind of Unsharp Mask applied when sharpening has accentuated edge quality creating halos and sharp lines. Edge is not solely the concern of compositors. No intruder is necessary to dispel credibility; old fashioned heavy handedness will do the trick just as well.

Digitally, edges are created with selections and masks. When making complicated outlines, favor letting the image do as much of the work as possible. Always keep in mind the fig-ure/ground and positive/negative relationships within an image. Try the Magic Wand or selecting by color range. It may be simpler to select unpatterned ground and quickly inverse it than to select a patterned object on it. Check the outlines generated this way carefully. Often too jagged, they will likely need a little extra attention. A single channel with contrast in the appropriate area of an image may provide the basis for an excellent mask/selection. The alpha channel created by duplicating it may be modified substantially. Accentuate the contrast in the important areas. Fill or paint other areas of the alpha channel with white or black appropriately. Remember, you can copy information from any channel and paste it into any other, including an alpha channel. A combination of the most useful portions of several channels may make a superior mask.

Use a combination of the Lasso and Marquee tools, or a quick mask and brush, if you can't get these other selection techniques to do the work as quickly or precisely. Naturally, the quality of the edge of the brush used will determine the quality of the edge of the mask.

The Pen tool is best for geometric selections. Remember a path can become a selection and vice versa. And, a selection can become an alpha channel or layer mask and vice versa. It's all fluid, one can become another. Very often a combination of selection methods will yield the best results.

Selections or alpha channels and masks can be expanded, contracted, softened, sharpened, distorted and distressed. Selections can be feathered to soften edges. Alpha channels or masks can be blurred to soften edges. To soften the edges of the mask, use Gaussian Blur for an overall effect or the Blur tool for a local effect. This accomplishes the same thing as feathering a selection. I blur the mask rather than feather the selection because I can see the results of a given value before applying it rather than guess and then guess again. Selections can be grown or contracted. Filtering alpha channels or masks with

1. Overly soft masks can create halos if they allow the original background to be seen.

2. Overly soft masks can create soft, transparent edges if they cut into the object.

Maximize or Minimize accomplishes the same thing. To obtain an effect at a setting lower than the minimum value, apply the minimum value, then fade it back to reduce the intensity. Again, with a mask, you can see the effect as you modify it; with a selection, some guesswork is involved. When stored as masks, edges are infinitely modifiable. Their flexibility is tremendous. Still, I start many masks with a simple selection, which is then refined. No one selection strategy will work for all situations. Quite often a combination of methods will yield the most efficient and/or best results.

A concern for edge is not the sole province of compositors. Edge is affected by the kinds of corrections you make; the more extreme the correction, the more carefully you have to treat edges. For instance, dramatically darken a sky behind a light object and if the edge is not handled carefully, artifacts will appear. If the mask cuts into the object, the correction will create a dark line. If the mask spills into the sky, the sky around the object will remain light, creating a halo. Too hard a line will look artificially sharp. Too soft a line may appear similar to lack of focus. An optimal mask will leave neither of these residues.

When compositing I favor making rough selections to copy soon to be imported material, selecting more than I need, and then creating a tight layer mask in the composite to hide the additional unwanted information. You could create a tight selection to start with and then use it to copy the subject into the new environment with no additional information, but you would lose some control over edge quality. If a composited element has already been tightly selected with a soft or hard edge and then imported, it is very difficult to modify the quality of that edge without cutting into it. With a little extra material at your disposal, the edge can be blended into the new background in a variety of ways. This also provides greater opportunity to modify the results at a future date, increasing flexibility.

One technique for curing edge spill in composites is to sample the color of the ground with the Eyedropper and run a paint brush around the edge. This may produce a result that is too uniform. If you do not wish to shift tone but only color, you can turn the mode of the brush to Color Only. If you choose to employ either method, take care to sample the ground color often enough to create a convincing transition, as the color

3. A very hard-edged mask will make unnaturally hard transitions. Objects may look like they have been pasted onto the image rather than existing within it.

4. An optimal mask is neither too hard-edged nor too soft-edged. For subtle effects, the sharpness of edges can be both hard and soft.

may vary markedly from point to point. You can accomplish the same thing by using the Rubber Stamp tool on either Normal or Color Only mode. This way color will be continually updated as the brush is moved across surrounding areas. Just make sure to resample as the angle of the edge changes significantly. This is tedious work. Making a good edge to start with will eliminate a majority of cases where these techniques will be needed; still, they can be useful on occasion.

Draftsmen accentuate the thick and thin qualities of line to stress specific areas, turning volume or creating shape with line or edge quality. Thick lines rise forward; thin ones recede. Sharp lines rise forward; soft ones recede. You can use this optical effect when trapping objects, leaving the mask harder for rising edges and softer for receding edges. This will create a subtle accentuation of volume, adding depth to your images.

All lines need not be created equally. When they are not, the likelihood that they will be compelling lines is increased.

What's in an outline? Everything. Edge is all important.

METHOD

1   Use any selection strategy (Magic Wand, Select By Color Range, Lasso, Marquee, Path, Quick Mask, contrast mask) to create a mask.

2   On a layer mask or adjustment layer layer mask, fill the selection outline (or its inverse) with black.

3   Refine the edge of the mask as needed.

Use the Smudge tool, the Distort effect, or Distort filters to change the shape of the mask.

Use a black brush or white brush to change the outline.

Soft-edged brushes can be used to create smooth transitions. Blurring a hard-edged mask will create uniform transitions. Brushes can be used to customize nonuniform transitions.

Use the filters Maximize or Minimize to expand or contract edges.

Use Gaussian Blur or Unsharp Mask to make edges soft or hard.

Use the Blur or Sharpen tools to soften or harden edges selectively.

For edges with gray tones, use Curves to accentuate contrast, making transitions more abrupt, or to shift the placement of the midpoint value, just as you would to affect a gradient mask.

Path i, Elemental, 1999

XXIV

ELIMINATION

Almost every move made in Path i involved elimination. Whether it happens before or after exposure, cropping is really the only form of elimination that does not replace information. As the placement of the image frame is the single most important factor in the creation of an image, every image involves elimination to one degree or another. Almost all of my images are hyperconscious of the border. The border defines the image. I use it to control the visual flow in an image. I'm drawn to images that suggest the spaces that exist beyond them. Limits can be used to create or destroy, to include and exclude. The frame is a creation and a destruction, an inclusion and an exclusion, a continuance and a cessation.

Every act of elimination within the picture frame involves the introduction of new information. If this were not true, the act of elimination would leave a hole through rather than in the image. In Path i, mountains at the horizon were eliminated or replaced by sky. This had been my intention all along. Without the mountains the recession of space is allowed to continue indefinitely. The horizon line is a border within borders. Borders set the stage. The horizon line marks the limits of our perception; a vast space beyond it remains unseen but is implied. It marks the point at which one thing is visually eliminated and another revealed. The flat plane of the blue sky is a similar boundary. We know an even vaster space exists behind the sky.

The clouds echo unseen starry constellations. A few clouds were eliminated at the edge of the horizon. Their presence impeded the visual progression stopping the eye at the horizon and the border of the image and calling unecessary attention to the limits of the image. Without them the vast spaces beyond the borders of and within the image were more readily implied.

The cracks in the earth were eliminated. This was the root of the image. The elimination of the cracks does far more than enhance latent qualities, it creates a new entity, an entity that is defined by its emptiness. The utility of the path is its emptiness. If it were full we could not walk in it. By virtue of absence we are drawn to empty space. But something must remain for it to become empty. If all the cracks were eliminated there would be no path.

Ironically the elimination of the cracks makes it debatable whether this strategy for creating this image rests solely on elimination. As the cracks are empty spaces they needed to be filled in order to be removed. Has matter been added or space eliminated? The filling of one space (the cracks) creates another space (the path). Has a three-dimensional physical space been eliminated and a two-dimensional conceptual space been created?

What is left unseen in this image is greater than what is seen. One senses that the portion of the path that is revealed is small in comparison to what is not revealed beyond the picture frame and beyond the horizon. It is inferred that all the surfaces extend beyond the border of the image indefinitely and that behind what we see of them there is a great deal more space, even very different realities than the ones revealed by the surfaces. The image is a meditation on kinds of space, their uses, and our ability to perceive and relate to them.

"Less is more."
— *Mies Van der Rohe*

"More is less."
— *Ad Reinhardt*

We edit. Our work is better for it. Writers edit. Dante's *Divine Comedy* was not written in a sixtieth of a second. Sculptors edit. When asked about his technique Michaelangelo stated that the figure lay waiting inside the uncarved block of stone; he had only to chip away that which was not the figure. Musicians edit. Salieri marveled at Mozart's music, "Not one note is misplaced." Think of all the notes that were left out, or removed, from the first draft.

Preserve the essential; eliminate the unessential.

To edit or not to edit is not the question. It is, rather, how to edit. Though their practices may or may not differ, editing is just as important for photographers as for other artists — perhaps more so.

The most important form of elimination occurs when the border of an image is fixed on a scene at a specific time eliminating everything else around, before, and after it. The elimination of less important or distracting information creates greater clarity of focus within an image. Information within single images is frequently edited after capture. Some crop further. Some augment the characteristics of an image, darkening or lightening. Alteration is a form of addition if the changes stand out as a new picture element, but it is a form of elimination if the changes make an existing picture element less visible. Spotting and etching are standard practices for removing unwanted information introduced by the physical process, minor forms of retouching. Less frequently, but not infrequently, images are retouched. Information in specific areas is "removed." So as not to leave an intrusive hole in the image, existing information is replaced with less intrusive information, usually information that blends with its surroundings. As groups of separate images amass, bodies of work are compiled and edited. The elimination of weak images lets strong ones shine brighter. It seems all statements, and images are visual statements, start and end with inclusion and exclusion, addition and elimination.

Painters learn to practice the art of elimination early on, not just with the frame of the picture but also through omission. Many times they simply don't record undesirable information. If they discover they have done so, they erase it or replace it. Scraping down, rubbing out, and painting over are essential techniques. Painters edit; they reorchestrate relationships found in the world or found on the canvas. Their statements become more meaningful as a result. Whether they do so before or after they make the first draft of an image does not determine either the skill of the artist or the merit of the image. (As Ananda Coomaraswamy said, "If a painter had to plan out every brushmark before he made his first he would not paint at all.") Sometimes visible traces of this process are left in the final work. In one Degas painting the traces of the moved arm of a dancer complement her swaying rhythm, their presence implies motion and makes the final choice even more telling. The inclusion of such residues allows the viewer greater entrance into the dialog of process.

Photographers go to great lengths to subdue information within an image — soft focus, selective focus, dodging, burning, etc. They may even go so far as to physically remove the offending elements from the scene before the exposure is made. Less frequently they do it afterwards. To retouch or not to retouch? That is the question. Some think you shouldn't do it, for a variety of reasons. To some it signifies compensation for deficient skill or technical practice. For others it signifies unethical practice. The reality is we've been retouching photographs since their invention. Some even pay large sums to see that it is done well, a certain sign that it has value to them. Think of all the wrinkles that have been eliminated and the waists and chins that have been reduced. Still the debate continues. The debate is most useful when we discuss images not in terms of "is it still photography?" but rather "what kind of photography is it?". The last question helps viewers evaluate an image's message and draw their own conclusions while the first merely attempts to cast doubt on the obvious before its inevitable reconfirmation. It is after all the practices of the photographer, not the media and their processes, that determine the nature of the photographs created and thus what kind of messages they send. Usually, but not always, people want to know if an image has been retouched. This is reasonable. It's part of defining the rules of the game. You have to communicate to viewers what the rules of the game are, otherwise they are liable to make incorrect assumptions and may feel misled. Standard practices are useful in so far as they set standards of expectation. Deviate and you must alert your audience that you are doing so or confusion will result. That's part of the process we're going through culturally today. Our practices are changing and in the process some of our time-honored constructs about photography and its practices are being reexamined. As we often take too much for granted, this is very healthy. Everyone wants to know the rules of the game before they play. But most know there's more than one game to play photographically, not just one. Individuals will be served best by choosing the practices that suit their intentions in an informed and conscientious manner, not by blindly following convention. We make choices. Well chosen, we make very interesting statements.

Today there are new ways of crafting images. The new methods may or may not lead to new messages. These new freedoms have a twofold benefit. They allow for new possibilities in expression. And, they ask us to reconsider our traditions, sometimes offering the possibility of expansion, sometimes reconfirming their value, sometimes both.

It's entirely possible to practice the art of elimination digitally with the same intentions as the conventional photographer. If the tool changes, but the intention remains the same, the essential nature of the document created does not change. It is also possible to practice new forms of elimination and create new kinds of images. There are many kinds of photography, not one. It's not the tool that creates the difference, it's the practice which is determined by intent.

Conventional photography, a discipline that proposes a set of acceptable practices with somewhat flexible parameters, offers us useful conventions — useful for certain purposes. It creates a positive bias about what photography is and can do. When some insist that this is the only valid way, they foster the creation of a stigma against other ways turning positive bias into negative prejudice.

If you choose to limit the number of solutions possible, it is a personal choice. Make it intentionally. The establishment of a discipline, though it limits a practice to certain kinds of activity, is not without merit. It's quite the opposite if the reasons for

1. The base image.

2. Clouds and cracks eliminated.

its establishment are clearly understood and thoroughly thought through. As with any set of rules, it helps to know when to make exceptions. And it helps to know the possibilities. Knowledge is power. Use it wisely.

There are many ways to simplify an image through elimination. The standard way is "cloning" or using the Rubber Stamp tool to redistribute duplicate information within an image. Duplicating information by copying and pasting may also work well, particularly when dealing with larger pieces of information. The addition of a layer mask greatly facilitates seamless blending of the "new" information. Both methods operate on the same principle. Adjacent or like information is used to replace damaged or distracting information. All that is required is that the replacement information blend in naturally. If like information does not exist within a single image, information from another source may serve well as a new replacement, provided

it blends into the surrounding area. One can easily copy or clone information from one document into another. Texture, which includes sharpness and grain, and angle of light are particularly important as tone, color and saturation may all be substantially modified after insertion. In an ideal situation, if you know you are going to retouch the image at the time of exposure, you may find a second exposure made of surrounding information not included in the primary image's frame a wonderful resource for retouching. Barring that, you could draw on other existing image stock or find a suitable subject for a new exposure to make any necessary repairs.

Digital retouching is extraordinarily powerful, flexible, and easy in comparison to its traditional counterparts. One advantage of digital retouching is that repairs can be done and undone flexibly. Various solutions can be tried and compared before making a final commitment. Another advantage

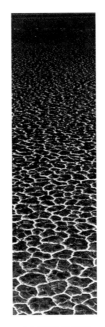

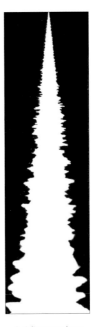

3. The path lightened.

*4. Layer mask used
for figure 2.*

*5. Adjustment layer
layer mask used for
figure 3.*

is that the surface of the final image is not disturbed since the replacement information is made of the same "material" as the replaced information. The retouching is truly two-dimensional.

The ability to access previous states in the History palette is very useful in retouching. One can undo previous states or restore information selectively from a previous state. As retouching often involves many separate strokes, each of which is recorded as a single state in the History palette, increasing the number of history states recorded and enabling nonlinear editing is very useful for this kind of work.

Keeping substitute information on layers separate from the background maintains maximum flexibility. You may find cloning from one layer onto another not quite as fluid as cloning directly onto the background, but the future flexibility it offers generally makes this desirable. Checking the Rubber Stamp tool's Use All Layers option makes this easier. Information placed on separate layers can be changed or removed indefinitely, even years after an image's creation. It's generally not necessary to follow this policy with the removal of minor imperfections such as dust, scratches, and hair. If you are certain you want to remove small elements permanently, you will do well to contain your work to a single layer. Larger areas involving multiple strokes, where the outcome is uncertain, benefit from the added flexibility of having the changes placed on a separate layer which can be changed, moved, or removed at will at any time in the future. This is one of the benefits of duplicating information by copying and pasting. You simply use a layer mask created with a soft-edged brush to smoothly blend the edges of the new information in with information surrounding it. The downside is that the method may not be as intuitive.

For challenging retouching, the mode of either the brush used or the layer created may be modified to contain its effects.

The two most frequently used blending modes are Lighten and Darken. Lighten allows the replacement information to be visible only if it is on top of an area that is darker than it. Use it for removing dark areas, such as dust spots. Conversely, Darken allows replacement information to be visible only if it is on top of an area that is lighter than it. Use it for removing light areas, such as scratches.

The opacity of a brush or layer is often used to increase the success of a retouching job. After all, the transition of a soft-edged brush is based on transparency or reduced opacity. Most retouching relies on it heavily. It's a quality that can be overdone. While a lower opacity may make transitions smoother, it may make some areas too smooth. Practice everything in moderation. When cloning at lower opacity take care that the technique does not adversely affect sharpness. The introduction of small amounts of noise will give texture to areas that become overly smooth.

Regardless of which method you use, take care that the repetition of the same information does not become a signal for order where there should be chaos. It is rare to see the same configuration repeated more than once. This happens most frequently in man-made environments or with man-made objects. It happens far less frequently in nature. Repeated information sets up a pattern and pattern demands attention. Most retouching does not want to demand attention. It would prefer to be invisible and so favors random or "all over" patterns with little discernible order. Cloning by sampling from multiple points or vectors helps randomize information. Make many clicks, not one. You may want to use this method to randomize larger blocks of information that have been copied and pasted. It only takes a little work to set up a new order within the replacement information, making it look unique.

In extreme cases busy or distracting information can be replaced wholesale. Replace or block an area entirely with a new element, either simpler information or information that establishes a more desirable harmony within the image. This is a minor form of image combination. Things generally exist along a spectrum of possibilities between two or more poles. As we get closer to the borderline, our language becomes less precise and requires clarification. All "elimination" through retouching involves the addition of replacement information rather than the complete removal of information, as in cropping. While one thing is eliminated, another is introduced to replace it. It's a bit more complex than saying the introduction of ground is elimination while the introduction of figure is addition. I'd make the following clarification. If the replacement information is a similar substitute, that is it blends in with the original image information in such a way that it merely modifies but does not substantially transform an image, then we are dealing with retouching, be it minor or extensive. If, on the other hand, the replacement information establishes a qualitatively new relationship that goes above and beyond modification to transformation of the original image, then we are dealing with montage, image combination that involves the creation of new content.

Every image is an individual. It will require its own set of solutions. Every artist is an individual. He or she will require his or her own set of solutions.

Our predisposition to focusing on what is included rather than what is excluded may lead us to relate to image creation as a matter of inclusion and addition. Yet, exclusion and subtraction are equally important and can be powerful tools for shaping an image's content. While we may be focused on making an image of the things before us, the success of any composition depends as much upon what is excluded as what is included. The perceptual shift you make in learning to notice what's not there, the negative space, the "empty" space, is truly rewarding. It's a concept other cultures seem more comfortable with. Think of the magnificent use of negative space as seen in much Asian art. Though "invisible", negative space is far from passive.

Elimination can be your path to simplicity. Simplicity concentrates attention on what remains. Simplicity offers room to breathe. Simplicity is truly divine.

While reducing the quantity of information concentrates attention on essential forms, space itself can be an essential form. At times, elimination may actually introduce rather than remove. Some South American tribes identify constellations by the arrangement of the spaces in between stars rather than the arrangement of the stars themselves. Empty space can become a presence. Is a bowl useful because of its material casing or the space contained within it? Think of the cave or the canyon. Environmental sculptor Michael Hizer explored the power of shaping space not by placing objects within an existing field but by carving out new spaces. Figure/ground, object/space, ultimately, you can't have one without the other. Emptiness is an entity as much as the material(s) surrounding it.

Knowing what to leave out is just as important as knowing what to include. The guiding principle of elimination is that less important information is suppressed accenting more important information. The affects of an image can be intensified and clarified in this way. More signal, less noise. Less can indeed be more. Thinking of elimination is often a key to successful image creation. How many times have we passed a good picture by because it had a minor flaw or it was too busy? Mindful of elimination we might shoot an imperfect image and then perfect it later. Mindful of elimination we might create an entirely new composition from an existing one.

METHOD

1 Using the Rubber Stamp tool, clone away damaged or distracting information.

Check Use All Layers and clone onto a new layer separate from the image for maximum flexibility. Sample from many points to randomize information. Avoid repetition of obvious features as they will set up a discernible and distracting frequency. Small modifications in texture go a long way towards randomizing information. Pay particularly close attention to transitions. Cloning at a lower opacity may make transitions smoother. When cloning at lower opacity, take care that the technique does not adversely affect sharpness. At times the introduction of small amounts of noise (through the filter Add Noise) will give texture to areas that become overly smooth. You can add noise to a separate layer set to Hard Light filled with 50% gray. This allows you to resize the "grain" if it doesn't match the original grain size and it can be changed indefinitely without altering the original image.

Replace larger image areas by copying, pasting, and positioning appropriate information over areas to be replaced. Similar information may be drawn from the same image or from a separate image. Replacement information may be modified in hue, saturation, or brightness to enhance unity. Use a layer mask to smooth transitions between the new information and information surrounding it. Larger brushes create smoother gradients. For smoother transitions consider painting with successive strokes of lower opacity or the edge of the brush rather than single strokes of the center of the brush. For the smoothest transitions, combine successive strokes at a low opacity to create a gradient. Transitions can be smoothed further by blurring a mask. If the transition is uniform, the gradient tool may be used to create smooth transitions. Any gradient can be localized by first creating a selection and then applying a gradient inside the selection. A gradient may serve as a fine base from which to begin further refinement, either with brush or smudge tools or by affecting its brightness

Trust your eye. If you convince yourself, others will be convinced.

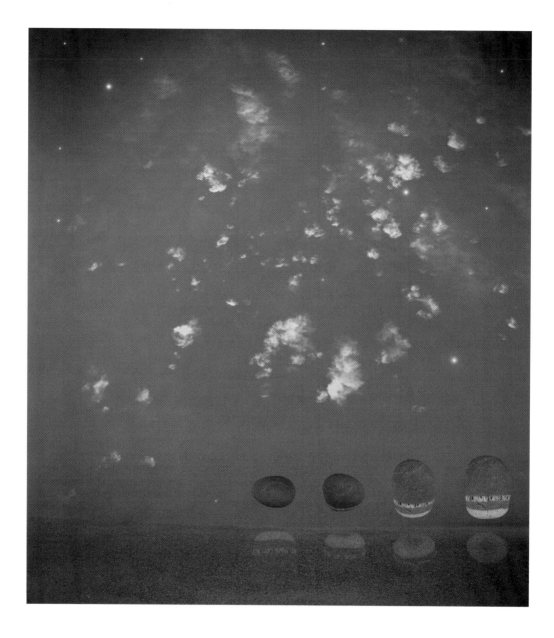

Reflections iv, Elemental, 1999

X X V

R E F L E C T I O N

I have many fond memories of gliding on still waters, parting the world doubled, glimpsing the world below, floating in the world above. Piercing the surface of the water, looking above and below it, is one of my favorite things to do. It is a tangible horizon line. It places limits on perception, defining space. It both separates and unites two worlds. It creates the illusion that one world is two. It is likely that it was these experiences that planted a fascination for symmetry within me.

Reflections iv started as a simple exercise in transparency and angle of reflection. The final solution eluded me several times. Unexpectedly a whole new subset of images arose. The first few were rich in color and form. Between the abstract shapes drawn from the world above the surface and the world below the surface, the resulting union was complex enough that there was little room left for the addition of a stone floating above the surface. The images were best treated minimally. With additions, the compositions became too packed, busy to the point of distraction.

The sky in this image is certainly energetic. The dappled clumps of cotton rhythmically echo the repeating shapes of the stones in a soft syncopated staccato. But, the volume is subdued. The color is unified and contained; there is variance but not variety. And the contrast is smoothly modulated with enough contrast to be luminous, but not enough to be harsh. It would be quite difficult, though not impossible, to balance a great variety of color, tone, and shape without overwhelming the ideas contained in the variety of reflections. The picture is clearer and more direct as a result of establishing clear priorities.

My preparatory sketches favored a central placement of a single stone. Once a fitting combination of sky and water coalesced, the composition needed to be redrawn completely. Time and time again I find I must make adjustments between my initial conceptions and their final renditions. I submit myself and my ideas to the process. Both are tested. And both are made stronger as a result. While the essential elements of the concept are maintained, the final composition must take into account the presence of the particulars found within the source material. I listen to the image.

This is, no doubt, why my sketches are made as simple broad strokes delineating only the essentials. They leave room for fluidity in the final rendition. They maintain the capacity to grow and evolve. Often the final image will make a dramatic departure in composition. When this happens, I will frequently sketch an image after it has arrived, rather than before. I find that in stripping things down to the barest essentials and in rendering the image manually, I often understand the image better, both abstractly and kinesthetically. For this reason, sometimes I even make sketches of finished images.

There was a great deal of flexibility in choosing the source material for the reflection of the sky. Any angle would have sufficed. Nonetheless, variances in the angle chosen would shape the angle and depth or recession. As the image reflected displayed a greater amount of information towards the horizon, the image receded more deeply; as it displayed less, the image became flatter and more frontal. Intrigued by the possibility of an image that could be read as both flat, because of the abstract

291

nature of the subject, and deep, because of the recession of space within it, I chose an image with substantial information towards the horizon. Yet, still there remained a great deal of spatial ambiguity which provided considerable leeway in the choice of reflections for the stone.

To confirm my selection of images for the reflections of stones, I staged a replica of the situation. I took a mirror, placed it in front of me at an angle I felt approximated the angle of the reflecting surface, and turned the stone I had selected above it. I had misjudged the necessary angle by some degrees. I needed to make a new selection of images for the stones' reflections. Luckily, I had made exposures of the stone at varying angles. I simply rotated the stone before the lens, by roughly forty five degrees at a time, making complete rotations, both left to right and top to bottom. If I had not done so, I would have had to make new exposures. I chose four stones, and I did not realize until I tested the image that with the chosen angles of rotation I only needed exposures from top to bottom since the other side remained hidden. Five stones or one more rotation and it, too, would have begun to appear.

It wasn't until I sat back and considered the image that I realized just how important motion was in it. Certainly the stone appeared to move. But even when the hovering stone(s) were fixed, if the reflecting plane moved so did the reflections. One slight turn and the whole image changed. The plane of reflection and the angle of rotation displayed a nearly infinite number of possibilities.

In order to see significant detail below the reflecting surface, the reflection of the sky had been made transparent along the newly placed shoreline, and so the reflections of the stones needed to be similarly transparent. The reflected image faded from opaque at the top to nearly transparent at the bottom.

This image hovers delicately between abstraction and representation. The image would be substantially different had I chosen to simulate distortion of the surface's plane. It would have tended even more towards abstraction. The reflections would have shifted wildly. Then only the surface beneath and the stones above would be literally rendered and comparatively stable. Then the mysterious ambiguity between the reflected and the reflection would be dispelled. Here the plane of reflection is perfectly still. Without disturbance the image is serene.

"In every pool one moon. One moon in every pool."
— Anonymous

We live in a shimmering world surrounded by light. Light rises and falls, drifts and wanders, cascades and sparkles. However dim, each moment is preceded and followed by a wave of light. If shadows are one trace left by this phenomenon, then reflections are another. I often think of reflections as the light counterparts of shadows. Both are ephemeral reminders that our floating world is not permanent or fixed, rather it is constantly changing, transforming from one moment to the next.

Reflections transform and are transformed. They shift and slide easily presenting phantasms and apparitions that drift by, sometime startlingly clear in glassy surfaces, sometimes so diffuse as to be almost invisible. They change the appearances of the things they caress. They transform our world with their presence. They show us our world transformed. They show us other worlds and possibilities hidden within our own. They show us dimensions hidden within us, our other selves. If we take notice of the poetry of reflections, we discover another world of possibilities within our own.

As with shadows, reflections bind things together. Their presence implies a unity, a shared coexistence. They are anchors and confirmations of solidarity. They may seem less omnipresent than shadows, but they, too, inevitably envelop us.

At first glance, shiny surfaces may seem like the sole province of reflections. In reality light is constantly being reflected. Few surfaces, if any, do not reflect light and few will not support reflections. If light is reflected from a soft surface or onto a soft surface, the light becomes diffuse. It does not disap-

pear. When diffuse, its effect is considerably more subtle, but nevertheless significant. Just as distant shadows grow soft and thin, so too do reflections. Both are prone to dissolving into veils of light and darkness.

There are two sides to every reflection: the image of the object reflecting the light and the image of the object receiving the light. One or the other may be completely dominant, or a hybrid image may occur. In an area of reflection you may find portions where all three cases are true: there may be parts of a reflected image that can't be seen through; there may be parts of a reflected image that are nearly invisible; and there may be parts of a reflected image that are transparent to varying degrees. If the reflecting surface is transparent, images behind it may be seen. One image may make another invisible or several worlds may merge visually becoming one.

The world seen through the looking glass can be different than our own; it can be reversed, upside down, skewed, distorted, darker, cooler, or transparent. At times the reflective surface may distort our world beyond recognition. On other occasions we may catch a glimpse of another world lingering on the other side of the thin glassy mirror to our own. The question then becomes, how do we modify existing image information so that it convincingly resembles its possible reflection?

Creating certain reflections is the essence of simplicity. For reflections on smooth, flat, totally reflective planes, you need only copy image information and composite it in the appropriate position. This is true of any surface that functions as a mirror.

1. Only if the plane of reflectance is along the line of sight will the reflected image be the same as the image of the object. All reflections will be flipped.

It's true of a completely still body of water where the waterline is at eye level. Copy the image above the proposed waterline, paste, flip vertically, and reposition. A subtle shift in tone, usually darker, and color, usually cooler, may provide the finishing touches. Watch the seam between the two areas. It is rarely a perfectly straight line. It may need softening. There are times when it may be more convincing to eliminate small repetitive artifacts that are distracting to the eye.

Add a single factor and the task quickly becomes more challenging. Shift the angle of view so that the waterline is no longer at eye level. As reflections are only perfectly symmetrical from one point of view, when the intersection of the two planes, cast and reflected, are at eye level, if the viewer's eye level is above this intersection, a frequent occurrence, the perspective of the reflected image will shift. It will in fact look like the image of the objects reflecting the light seen from a slightly lower vantage point. There is no way to truly recreate this shift in perspective with digital manipulation without resorting to three-dimensional rendering, something that has yet to compare to true photographic quality in my estimation. You can, however, simulate it with traditional methods. If the situation allows and you know at the time of capture that you would like to create a convincing reflection, or you can go back to the scene to make similar additional exposures of your subject, take two shots: one at desired eye level and a second at a slightly lower vantage point. Use the second shot, from the lower vantage point, to create a reflection when the viewer's eye level is higher than the intersection of the two planes. The angle you will need will be the inverse of the angle between the viewpoint and the plane of reflection. (If the angle between the viewpoint and the plane of reflection is 45° in the first exposure, the angle in the second exposure will need to be -45°.)

We may shift our viewpoint, but one thing does not shift — the angle the reflection is cast towards us. Unlike shadows, reflections always come directly towards us if the plane of reflection does. Both effects have a single cause: light travels in straight lines. In the case of shadows the light travels past the edges of the contour blocking it, maintaining its linear trajectory toward the surface it strikes, or in the case of a shadow the surface it doesn't strike. There is only one shadow to be seen from many angles. In the case of reflections, we only see the ones that are reflected directly towards us, again in straight lines, but there are many others that we could see from another vantage point. Heisenberg's uncertainty principle might give

2. A variation of the angle of reflectance yields different reflections.

3. In this variation the reflections show the undersides of the objects, which would otherwise remain hidden.

us cause to pause, when we say that in all probability many other reflections exist, perhaps an infinite number; we simply don't perceive them until we shift our perspective.

Making images of a subject from multiple perspectives can be useful in other situations. The image we see of ourselves in mirrors is not the image we see in pictures, or the image that others see of us since it is reversed. Similarly, the image we see of others in reflected surfaces is not the same as the one we see of them; it may reveal a hidden face. What is seen frontally may be reflected in profile and vice versa. To create a convincing reflection we must often have a second exposure made from an appropriate angle. In situations where there are multiple reflective surfaces, you may need more than two variations.

Size and placement, tone and color are all easy and straightforward to deal with. Image transparency is similarly straightforward. Universal reductions in transparency may be achieved by turning down the reflection layer's opacity. Selective reductions in transparency may be achieved with the addition of a layer mask. The content of such layer masks can be staggeringly sophisticated, but the concept is the essence of simplicity — greater density increases transparency and vice versa. Whether you use a luminance mask as a foundation, add

a gradient mask, or paint a mask by hand, a mask is ultimately nothing more than a grayscale image used to reduce a correction or effect. In this case, the mask is used to selectively control an image's transparency.

As with shadows, when dealing with reflections, complicated surfaces cause quantum leaps in the complexity. Here the reflected image begins to make great transformations. When it comes to reshaping image content for reflections, the capabilities of Photoshop vary. Linear transformations are quite easy to achieve. It is a simple matter to flip, skew, stretch, push or pull an image. (All the appropriate tools may be found under Edit: Transform.) As with any distortion, when the image is enlarged new pixel information must be invented by upsampling. As downsampling yields higher quality information than upsampling, for the highest quality, favor making things smaller rather than larger. At times this may mean making your original scan larger than your expected final image size. Nonlinear transformations are much more challenging. For everything but the simplest and crudest transformations, the Smudge tool is inadequate. It's slow, cumbersome, and seriously degrades image quality. With the Liquify feature (Image: Liquify) you can do a great deal more: it is entirely possible to convincingly distort a

4. No distortion in the surface.

5. Surface distorted uniformly with large ripples.

surface and simulate reflections. However, as the complexity of the distortion rises, the challenge grows exponentially.

In many cases, the use of a displacement map may be helpful. Displacement maps use the luminance values of a mask to distort an image. A luminance mask based on another rippled surface offers another solution.

Some surfaces distort images to the point where they are reduced to pattern and texture. The surface of liquids, for instance, do not conform to an underlying shape and are changeable, so almost any distortion with the appropriate texture will do. Several distort filters within Photoshop create convincing effects for planes that are perpendicular to the viewer (Ripple, Ocean Ripple, Wave, Glass). The more a plane recedes, the less convincing these effects are. This is because the effects are uniform. One must create a texture gradient to convincingly portray the recession of space. In essence the texture becomes more compact as virtual space recedes. The deeper the space, the tighter the texture. If only you could apply a filter through a gradient mask to achieve such an effect, but all these attempts reduce the intensity of the filter rather than provide

variable settings for it. It is possible to filter a plane that is perpendicular to the viewer and then correct its perspective to create the appearance of a plane in recession. This reduces the usable image area. It is also possible to selectively filter successive slices of an image, the number of divisions necessary will depend on the image, with gradually increasing filter settings and later blend the separate slices with gradient layer masks. You can determine the various proportions needed by creating a grid on a separate layer and then distorting it with Perspective until it appears to lay on the plane within the image.

Wouldn't it be nice if you could take a distorted surface from the real world and use it as the basis of this effect? You can. The Displace filter and its accompanying displacement maps can be used to create textures, but they can also be used to conform one image to the surface of another. While Photoshop provides a set of displacement maps (found in the Plugins folder), it's likely that you will want to create your own.

The Displace filter requires two files: the image you wish to affect and the displacement map. There are two kinds of displacement maps: single channel and two-channel displacement

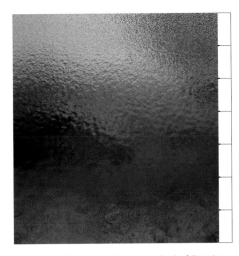

6. Surface with successively increasing levels of distortion spliced together in equal steps.

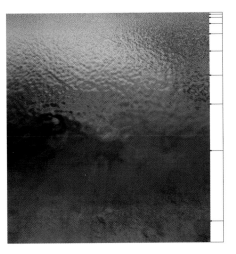

7. Surface with successively increasing levels of distortion spliced together in exponentially decreasing steps.

maps. In both, tone controls the degree and direction of displacement. The lighter or darker the value, the greater the displacement. Middle gray produces no displacement.

In a single-channel displacement map, white (255/255/255) displaces image information up and to the left, while black (0/0/0) displaces image information down and to the right. Both do so at maximum intensities. As tonal values within the displacement map grow closer to middle gray (128/128/128), the effect is diminished. You can change the directions of the displacement by using negative numbers in the Displacement dialog box when applying the filter.

In two-channel displacement maps, the values in the Red and Green channels of an RGB file are used to create displacement. The Blue channel is ignored. Consequently these displacement maps often look oddly colored. The tones in the Red channel displace an image one way, while the tones in the Green channel displace an image the other way. With one-channel displacement maps you can displace an image in two directions, while with two-channel displacement maps you can displace an image in four directions. White displaces up and

left, magenta displaces down and left, blue displaces down and right, cyan displaces up and right. Middle gray produces no displacement.

A displacement map may be created by hand or from an existing image. To create a single-channel displacement map from an existing image, convert it to Grayscale. To create a two-channel displacement map from an existing image, fill the Blue channel with white. To create an even more dynamic effect with a two-channel displacement map, you may want to offset the channels or shift them out of register with one another. You can use the Move tool to offset the two channels by hand (use the arrow keys for more predictable shifts), or you can use the filter Offset. Offsetting each channel in opposite diagonal directions is usually most effective. How much you will need to offset the channels in a given displacement map will be dependent on subject matter and the resolution of the image. As an aside, it does help, but is not necessary to have the displacement map be of equal proportion and resolution as the image displaced. Larger displacement maps will simply be centered on the image displaced, while smaller displacement maps may be tiled.

8. The image distorted using a displacement map.

9. The image used to create a displacement map.

Some images will contain a wealth of unwanted texture. Take, for example, a displacement map created from a speckled stone, half in shadow. The dark and light speckles of the stone will displace the image along with the dark and light values of the highlights and shadows. You can easily subdue this kind of texture by blurring the displacement map. Then only the larger tonal values will be used to displace the image.

To use a displacement map apply the filter Displace (Filter: Distort: Displace). Specify horizontal and vertical displacement values, and finally select the desired displacement map to be used as the basis of the displacement.

Until there's a better way to preview the effects of the displacement values along with the map, this method remains no small matter of trial and error. Two factors are equally important: the numerical values used in the Displacement filter and the tonal values found in the displacement map. If you find a displacement map needs to be adjusted tonally, you can make any kind of correction to it before you use it. Lighten it, darken it, dodge it, burn it, increase or decrease its contrast, paint on it to localize an effect, as you please. The calculation is intensive

and so can take time. You may want to save time by testing the effects on low resolution copies of the image to determine optimal settings and contrast levels before proceeding to a high resolution displacement. Quite often the low resolution displacement map can be resized for use with the high resolution image, but if this subdues significant detail, you may want to make corrections to it with adjustment layers that can be transferred to its high-resolution counterpart.

To make the effects of some displacements even more convincing, you may want to go even further than this. Once the overlying image has been distorted, place it on top of the image used as the basis for the displacement map and experiment with the layer's blending mode. To control the specific effects of the way an overlying layer blends with an underlying layer, you have several options: reduce the layer's opacity globally; add a layer mask to reduce a layer's opacity locally; use the sliders found in Blending Options; or change the layer's blending mode. I find simply turning the overlying layer's blending mode to Hard Light and reducing its opacity often works well. The addition of a Curves adjustment layer grouped to the

10. The displacement map.

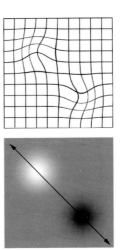

11. In a one-channel displacement map, white distorts up and to the left, while black displaces down and to the right. 50% gray does not displace.

overlying layer may help compensate for shifts in contrast or color that occur as a result of the change in blending mode. Alternately, you might try using two layers, each containing the same displaced image, but set the first to Multiply with a lower opacity and set the second to Overlay with a higher opacity. Every image (and every combination of images) will be different, so here again some experimentation is necessary.

I also find that accentuating the brightness of highlights and the darkness of shadows (and sometimes, their respective colors) can add a subtle touch that makes a big difference. Two Curves adjustment layers are necessary for this, each with a luminance mask. The luminance masks need to be made from the underlying image only, so turn off the overlying layer (uncheck the Eye icon) and highlight the underlying layer. First, make a selection from the channel that contains the greatest amount of contrast. (Drag the channel to the Load channel as selection icon in the Channels palette.) Turn the overlying layer back on. Then, with the selection active, create a Curves adjusment layer and make an appropriate correction with it to lighten the highlights and accentuate their color subtly. Second,

make a selection from the channel that contains the greatest amount of contrast again and inverse it (Selection: Inverse). Then, create another Curves adjustment layer and an appropriate correction with it to darken the shadows and accentuate their color subtly. These adjustment layers can be placed at the top of the layer stack to affect all layers or they can be grouped to specific layers to restrict their effects. You can further modify the effects of each luminance mask by lightening, darkening, increasing or decreasing its contrast by applying Curves directly to the mask (Image: Adjust: Curves).

While there are limits to how much an image can be reshaped, you may be surprised just how much an image can be and just how useful this technique is.

There are times when a distorted surface will pick up reflected colors from outside the picture frame or below the plane of reflection. No amount of digital distortion will be able to simulate this effect. The best you can do is introduce it before distortion and this takes the game of reflection into a whole new level of complexity.

Many digital attempts at creating reflections in planes that

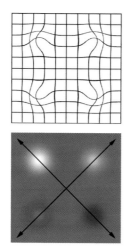

12. In a two-channel displacement map, white displaces up
and to the left, cyan displaces up and to the right, blue
displaces down and to the right, magenta displaces down and
to the left. 50% gray does not displace.

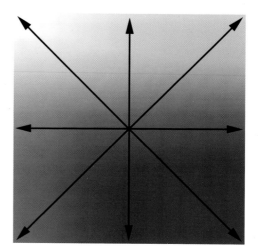

13. A map of the direction of displacement based on color in a
two-channel displacement map. Note as well as diagonal
displacement, vertical and horizontal displacement can be
achieved with the proper hue.

are not flat, those that bend and curve, undulate, ripple, or take abrupt turns in angle, are overly simple. They often fail to accurately simulate the distortion that occurs. Even the seemingly flat planes of water, glass, and metal can distort images more dramatically than you would expect. Bearing in mind that an image is two-dimensional and that many reflections take new shapes based on the three-dimensional surfaces they fall upon, you can easily see how complicated it becomes for software to extrapolate the effects found in a three-dimensional world from a two-dimensional one. It might be possible to easily and affordably take note of or even map three-dimensional characteristics within an image at the moment of capture in the near future. Until then we'll need wetware instead of software to make accurate predictions about reflections. It is possible to make highly accurate predictions about reflections and it is possible to bring those predictions to light. After all, painters have been doing it for centuries. Though the tools might have changed, those same strategies apply. As always, there's no substitute for direct observation.

Like the world of shadows, the world of reflections can seem wildly chaotic and unpredictable. It too is often taken for granted. Here again we may run the risk of accepting simpler or more familiar answers than the stranger realities that surround us. They are stranger realities only because we do not take note of them. You might give the saying, "A stranger is a friend you just haven't met yet", a little more reflection. Attention makes the unfamiliar familiar. Again my advice is to look. Look often. Look closely. And keep looking.

Apart from containing reflections, many images are reflections. Their visual poetry is found in the reflected image, not the object that is reflected. We can use the power of reflection to create new images, new visual poetries. Should we choose to create new relationships, we would do well to look first at the richness and complexity of the world, using it as our compass and our guide when charting new territories.

METHOD

REFLECTIONS

For simple reflections where the viewer's vantage point is equidistant between the reflected and the reflection, only one image is needed.

1   Copy an image (Layer: New: Layer via copy), creating a new layer.

2   Flip the new layer vertically (Edit: Transform: Flip Vertical).

3   Reposition it using the Move tool.

4   Hide any unwanted elements using a layer mask (Layer: Add a Layer Mask: Reveal All). Remember, the layer mask can be unlinked and moved separately from the layer.

5   Use a Curves adjustment layer grouped with the reflection layer to shift hue (typically cooler) and tone (typically darker).

For reflections where the viewer's vantage is not equidistant between the reflected and the reflection, a second image is required. Make the second exposure by changing your angle of view appropriately. Composite it with the first exposure. Change perspective, tone, and hue as necessary.

RIPPLES

To simulate rippled surfaces use an appropriate distort filter. I used Glass for the above effect.

For surfaces that are completely perpendicular to the viewer, simply apply the filter at the appropriate setting.

If the surface needs to be distorted in one area but not another, duplicate the reflected image layer, apply the filter to the duplicate layer, and add a layer mask to hide the effect in the appropriate areas. Use the Gradient tool to create long, smoothly blended transitions.

If a surface needs to be distorted to varying degrees, as in a receeding plane, duplicate the reflected image layer a number of times, as little as two times or as many as ten. Apply the filter to each layer at increasingly intense settings. Use layer masks to reveal the layers below in successive slices. Start with a straight hard-edged mask and then blur it to create a smooth blend between it and the layer below

it. A short gradient mask will have the same effect. Plot an appropriate recession of horizontal lines, given the perspective of the image, then use those decreasing heights as guides to place layer masks. Blur the edge of the layer mask to create smooth transitions.

DISPLACE USING A DISPLACEMENT MAP

Or, try using a displacement map to distort a surface.

Select an image of an appropriately distorted surface. Use it as the basis for a displacement map. Best results are achieved when the displacement map is the same proportion and resolution as the image displaced, but it can be larger or tiled.

To create a single-channel displacement map, convert the image to Grayscale. To create a two-channel displacement map, fill the Blue channel with white.

Apply the filter Displace, specifying both horizontal and vertical displacement values and the proper displacement map as its basis.

If texture within the image is creating unwanted distortion, subdue it by using Gaussian Blur on the displacement map file.

If the distortion created is not great enough, use higher settings for vertical and horizontal displacement, offset the two channels diagonally equally but in opposite directions using the filter Offset, or increase the contrast (globally or locally) of the displacement map.

Trial and error is a necessity with this technique. As displacing images is processor intensive, consider making initial tests on low-resolution copies of the image to be displaced.

Optionally, after the image has been displaced, try various Blend Modes for overlying layers (try Hard Light first). A reduction in Opacity may also be necessary.

Finally, try adding Curves adjustment layers with luminance masks grouped to the overlying distorted image, one for the highlights and one for the shadows, to make highlights brighter and shadows darker. As well as lightening and darkening, you may also want to accentuate or shift the colors of the highlights and shadows to increase the impression of volume.

Budh, Allies, 1996

XXVI

SYMMETRY

I knew instantly that something new had happened when I saw Budh appear on the screen. A discrete outline had been introduced to symmetry. Previously the symmetries I had been creating were unbounded. They defined planes of space. These defined sculptural objects. I had always seen faces and figures within the symmetries I created. The outline had now intensified the effect.

I didn't know it then, but it was the beginning of a whole new series. I knew it after it began happening repeatedly. The process had led me to a new point of departure. The work was a surprise. I hadn't planned doing it. It came to me. I had planned to do another body of work, but this one seized me and asked me to stay with it while it was fresh. I listened. I have a feeling that if I had ignored that voice I would not have been able to return to it later, certainly not with the same intensity or understanding.

Repeatedly, the associations most offered with this image are that the figure looks like a buddha. I would not want to limit associations to one interpretation, but I do like that one. The working title for the piece was Unseen Watcher. In the end it named itself. Budh is the root of the word buddha. It means awake.

Budh sat there looking back at me. I could not look at the object as a mere lump of clay. It had a definite presence. The landscape it was drawn from had a presence too. Somehow, the two felt compatible.

While many of my images have qualities similar to environmental sculpture, these images create sculptural forms made from the environment.

One day, as I made apologies to a friend for needing to get off the phone quickly and chase a cloud that was drifting across the yard, Michael More kindly informed me, "It was considered a legitimate pastime in Samuel Johnson's day to watch clouds." Who hasn't spent a hot summer afternoon looking for things in the shapes of clouds? A train of thought starts moving towards an unknown destination. As the clouds shift, one thing transforms into another. Nothing is fixed. Sometimes it all evaporates. If you're not fully present to the moment, you'll miss it. I still like to do this. It's meditative.

We project meaning onto the world in order to give it an identifiable shape. Think of the things we see in the patterns of the stars above us: dogs, bears, serpents, swans, and all manner of heroic figures. Think also of the stories that go with them. If this is a "primitive" way of thinking, it is a very vital one. The great wells of folklore and mythology have their roots in this primal way of relating to the world. Beyond the confines of psychotherapy, we should relegitimize it, not as fact, but as a vital, much needed fiction.

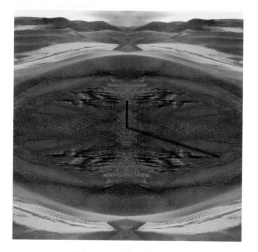

1. Symmetry defines the space.

"Simplicity of shape, especially symmetry, predisposes an area to function as figure."
— *Rudolf Arnheim*

Symmetry can be found throughout the organic and the inorganic worlds, the natural and the artificial worlds. It is often a visual clue that a higher level of order is present. Architectural settings and man-made objects typically favor symmetry heavily, so much so that very often we think of symmetry as something created, even unnatural. For quite some time Western Culture has been heavily influenced by Platonic notions involving the purity of the ideal world and the imperfection of material reality. Those who subscribe to these notions more easily fall sway to the notion that creating symmetry, a pure order, in the material world perfects it. (I would not make this claim.) Culturally we've constructed a number of polarities which we use to navigate the world. One of them is natural versus man-made. We might think of it instead as natural and constructed.

Other animals are also architects. They too build structures, they too shape the world. It may very well be natural for life to create new structures. While the world of nature favors complexity, a more intricate and implicate order, it is full of symmetry. We need only look to ourselves. We, along with countless other life forms, are bilaterally symmetrical — a dividing line can be drawn vertically to demarcate two equal halves. Moreover, animal architecture, the structures animals create in nature, quite often favor symmetry. Nature embraces symmetry. Perhaps its symmetry is more nuanced than the symmetry created by man. In many cases the symmetry is not exact. Think of the two halves of a face; they are never exactly the same. Cover one side of a face, then the other and compare the very different expressions each carries. Try creating a whole face from one half; the

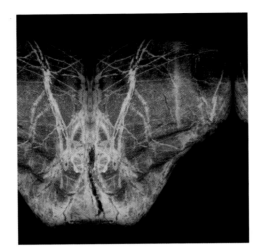

2. Symmetry defines the object.

result is unusual, sometimes unnerving. Nature usually throws in a twist. Man's symmetry is generally simple and balanced while nature's is generally complex and unbalanced.

I've found symmetrical patterns created along a vertical line, rather than a horizontal line, are more engaging to the viewer. I would hazard a guess that this is because this type of pattern is similar to the bilateral symmetry we find in so many life forms. Still, there are other kinds of symmetry; one is radial, for instance.

It's instinct to recognize pattern. Along with this instinct and our own anthropocentrism comes a tendency towards animism and anthropomorphism. In reading abstract patterns in nature, a rocky cliff for instance, the interpretations that arise most often are faces and figures. A subtle shift in the dividing line created can alter the character of the pattern dramatically.

Some people love symmetry; others disdain it. I have yet to identify a common denominator in each group. It might be found in their emotional reactions to it, which are in part culturally constructed. If you were to list qualities that symmetry evokes, many of the following words would appear — simple, formal, abstract, created, balanced, static.

Repetitive symmetry, particularly when one area of an image is repeated more than once, can become decorative. In such images the rhythm of the repetition becomes the foundation of the image. As this tendency increases, the image becomes more and more clearly constructed, departing further away from the "natural" into the realm of abstraction.

One day, during a workshop, we were discussing the basic elements of photomontage, the clues that tell us how an image hangs together and whether an image has been manipulated. Mike wanted to add symmetry to the list. I take his point and include it under the category of repetition.

3. Bilateral symmetry around one axis of rotation.

4. The same axis compressed.

5. Further compression.

Symmetry is found in very specific circumstances. When it appears in contexts where we ordinarily don't see it, we are likely to assume that an image has been altered.

Symmetry has very personal meanings for me, and it is a very important aspect of much of my work. Symmetry is something that came to me. I had no idea what fascinated me about it, but I found the results thrilling. I was particularly interested in symmetries created from the complex patterns in nature. I was curious about the tensions created between Euclidean geometry and fractal geometry, both being different levels of order abstracted from nature. Both are at once "natural" and "created." Once symmetry was introduced another level of order appeared. Initially I was interested in creating fields of pattern to define space (in the series Elemental and its subset Mandala). As things progressed I also became interested in a symmetry that created discrete objects within space (in the series Allies). Throughout I was enchanted by the notion of making visible the spirit of nature. The challenge of confronting the limits of our perception and making the invisible visible intrigues me. It seemed appropriate to make vessels for its description drawn

from the surroundings in which it was sensed. I struggled to describe the results; the phrase fictive evocations of the spirit of the land arose. Later I learned that in 1857 a man named Justinius Kerner published a series of inkblot drawings. He felt that the process brought him in closer contact with the spirit world. Since 1921, Kerner's invention has been applied in psychotherapy in a slightly altered form commonly known as the Rorschach test. I referred to the patterns I had found/created as Rorschachs. I have heard psychologists are often more interested in the strategies patients use to solve the problem of interpretation than they are in the products that arise during the course of that interpretation. I'm interested in both. I enjoy discussing what people see in these images. I intend for them not only to reveal but to be interpreted as well, since every viewer brings his or her own unique experience and I hope to leave room for and encourage that dimension. I feel a work of art takes on a life of its own and what it generates continues on in the viewer in a very personal way.

I'm certainly not the first person to use symmetry and I'm sure I won't be the last. Should you choose to use it as a visual

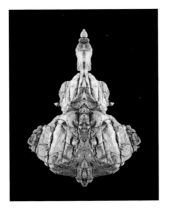  

6. Bilateral symmetry around another axis of rotation.

7. The same axis compressed.

8. Further compression.

device, you might first want to explore what it means for you. Your work will no doubt be richer for it.

The technique I use to create symmetry in my images is the essence of simplicity. Select an area. Copy it. Paste it. Flip it. Reposition it. Fix the seam. It's so simple I really didn't consider writing a chapter on it until I found that time and time again my students and many of the people who viewed my work kept asking the same question, "How did you do that?" Again, the technique is less important that what you bring to it.

METHOD

1   Using the rectangular Marquee tool, select an area, copy, and paste it, creating a new layer. (Layer: New: Layer via Copy)

2   Flip the new layer, either horizontally or vertically (Edit: Transform: Flip Horizontal).

3   Reposition it using the Move tool or the arrows on the keypad.

If you are flipping an entire image, you will need to expand your canvas size before following the above steps.

Care should be taken to align the seam between the two sides. Even when perfectly aligned, distracting artifacts can appear at the seam. You may want to clone away these artifacts.

You may want to copy more information than needed onto the overlying layer. Then use a layer mask, created with the rectangular Marquee tool, to hide information selectively. Unlink the layer mask from the image so that it will move independently of the image. Finally, slide one in relationship to the other to determine the desired relationships in the image.

If I am working to find a midpoint for symmetry quickly, I often use a small mirror with my original (film, print, or monitor).

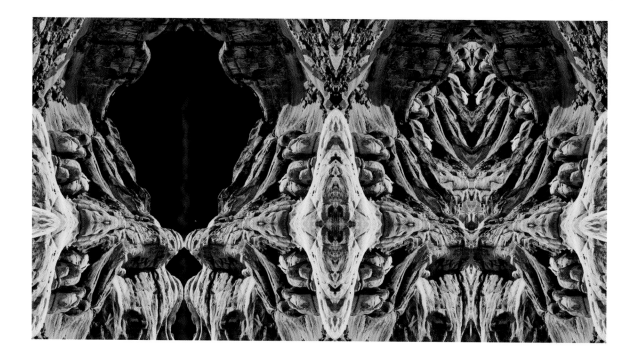

Grotto of Madness, Allies, 1996

XXVII

TESSELLATION

Grotto of Madness evolved organically. With each pass, it kept unfolding. Normally I use a mirror to quickly determine where to place the seam of symmetry. This time, the angles kept changing. There were too many combinations to hold in my mind at one time. I found myself trying successive combinations on the computer. It could hold them all in memory simultaneously. I could return to each combination individually, compare them together, shift to another, or go back to the first. The image kept coming and going. One variation unfolded after the other. There seemed to be no limit to the number of combinations that were possible.

The process reminded me of fractal geometry, where equations are solved by successive iteration. The value generated by the first solution is placed back into the same equation, generating a new solution. The process is repeated endlessly. Over time patterns emerge. New orders are discovered.

Successive symmetries coalesced kaleidoscopically. While subtle shifts in the dividing line usually produce marked transformations in the character of the patterns created, in this instance the transformations were dramatic. There was no one clear choice. When one symmetry is created, a single decision is made and a single possibility is revealed. Here many decisions and many possibilities cohabit the same space. The flow of both space and time are disrupted.

The originally open composition kept closing in on itself. This seemed to be a primary decision, whether to create an open or a closed space. "Why not both?" I thought. As with simultaneous contrast in color, side-by-side one would play against the other, synergistically reinforcing each other. Exit was first allowed and second denied.

I was building a space. It was clearly architectural. It was vaulted and soaring. It had the quality of a cathedral. It was dizzying in complexity and perspective. Are we looking out past carved niches through arched windows or are we looking up at a mosaic ceiling into the empyrean? It had no ground. How deep, how wide was the space? It felt like it could continue forever. One could imagine the echoes and the winds that rushed through the space. It was like an organ. It was visual music with a mathematical substructure.

It was organic. The soft pink sandstone already had the quality of flesh. Portions looked like slices of a biological specimen. It was richly varied with clearly articulated structures. It had folds, crevices, protuberances, openings and closings, masses enclosing inner spaces. It had a thousand skins, like an onion, a thousand eyes, like a potato, a thousand arms and legs, like a millipede. It was no longer mere dirt. It moved energetically. It multiplied. Its breath was made visible in the sky.

Who knew what lay hidden within the original landscape? Can you find the original landscape? It's there.

Who knows what lies hidden in this new landscape? I continually see new things.

1. The cell image.

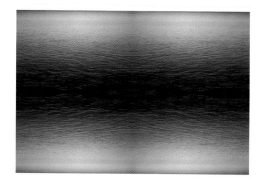

2. Quadrilateral tessellation.

"Repetition and multiplication — two simple words. However, the whole world of the senses would collapse into chaos without these two concepts."
— M. C. Escher

The word tessellation comes from the Latin word *tessera* meaning cube, referring to the small pieces of material used to make a mosaic. When a repeated geometric shape covers a plane entirely, it tessellates it. Owing to Western Culture's obsession with the grid, a checkerboard is the most often repeated, most easily found example of tessellation. Triangles, squares, and hexagons are the only regular (having sides of equal length) polygons that can fill a plane without gaps — "regular" tessellation. "Semiregular" tessellation, where multiple polygons are arranged around a central point, every point surrounded by an identical arrangement, offers eleven possible combinations. Regular and semiregular tessellations are also called "Archimedean," "homogenous," or "classical." Any nonequilateral triangle or quadrilateral will tessellate a plane. Certain irregular pentagons will too.

M. C. Escher is perhaps the most celebrated Western artist

to employ this technique. He was tremendously influenced by mosaic patterns found in Islamic art, specifically in the Alhambra. Noting that in these situations the negative and positive shapes shared common contour lines, one line defined both the inside and the outside of the object, object and environment, so much so that it was no longer possible to distinguish the one from the other, he said, "On either side of it, a figure takes shape simultaneously. But, as the human mind can't be busy with two things at the same moment, there must be a quick and continuous jumping from one side to the other. The desire to overcome this fascinating difficulty is perhaps the very reason for my continuing activity in this field."

Escher created tessellations from very complex shapes by using a simpler underlying geometric foundation and consistently distorting one or more sides. If more than one side was distorted they were usually opposing sides.

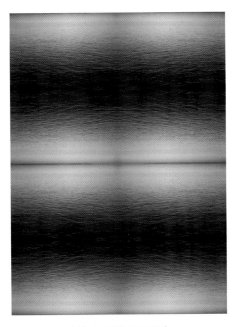

3. The tessellation repeated.

*4. The top portion of the image is
undistorted while the bottom is distorted.*

Tessellations are usually designed by hand; they are less frequently created photographically. The often simpler surfaces of manually rendered information lends a grounding simplicity to an already complicated structure. Add richly detailed photographic information to tessellated complexity and the quantity of information provided takes a dizzying quantum leap.

Tessellated images have a tendency to move away from representation towards abstraction. Tessellation heaps artifice upon artifice. Repetitive symmetry can become decorative. It is very hard to control. The image has a tendency to become completely constructed. Design or pattern dominates the image. It becomes harder to sense the hand of an individual artist at work. The work is so formally driven, so conceptual in nature, that it is often the sophistication of thought brought to the creation that separates one pattern from another. If not carefully managed, tessellation subverts individuality, both of

the artist and the basic material used.

It is nearly impossible to make such an image appear natural. Such images are clearly created, not found. What's more, even when created from photographic information, they depart from representation. Perhaps in certain architectural situations or in the presence of multiple reflective surfaces, this tendency could be convincingly suspended.

Rhythm is extremely important. This is particularly true of any image that uses repetition. The rhythm of the repetition becomes a foundation of the image.

Simple symmetry evokes many words — formal, abstract, created, balanced, static, simple. Tessellation evokes others — formal, abstract, created, balanced, kaleidoscopic, disorienting, complex, dynamic, rhythmic. Symmetry and tessellation share certain common qualities and yet remain quite distinct in other respects.

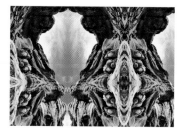

5. The cell.

6. Bilateral symmetry.

7. Quadrilateral symmetry.

8. Further iteration.

With symmetry, the eye easily fixates on the midpoint; in tessellation the eye finds no easy resting place. While symmetry increases our tendencies toward animistic and anthropocentric interpretations, tessellation subverts this tendency, overwhelming it with our need to recognize pattern. One creates individuality while the other subverts it. Simple symmetry more easily favors the figure (object), tessellation the ground (field). We have a natural tendency to filter out the figure from the ground, the signal from the noise. In such images the repetition of figures turns them into ground. The individual made plural no longer retains its unique identity as it is subsumed into the larger collective. We might well ask, "Does this repetition desensitize the viewer to the particular qualities of the original, as it does in the work of Andy Warhol?"

The complexity of a tessellated field is quite a bit different from the simplicity of a Ganzfield, a field where there is little or no information. Tessellated fields offer a wealth of information, perhaps even an overabundance. One offers sensory deprivation, the other sensory overload. One has nothing to focus on; the other has too many things to focus on simultaneously. In tessellated images we can focus on individual figures while attempting to screen out the surrounding field of figures they are embedded in, or we can focus on the overall substructure (the grid for instance) deflecting our attention away from the specific characteristics of the individual components. Curiously both encourage association. Submitted to a Ganzfield, we are prone to see variation where there is none. No matter how chaotic, against a background of nothingness, this still reads as order, an interesting reversal of standard ways of seeing. Any tendency toward optical illusion is strengthened. Association and projection is encouraged as information from our internal worlds frequently wells up. Subjectivity is forced to confront itself. The mind has a very hard time being still and accepting "emptiness" but it can learn to do so with practice. Similarly in tessellated fields, association can well up as new patterns not specific to the individual (the seed) but drawn from within the larger whole (the field) are found. One prompts "free" association, the other "guided" association. One draws forth the internal through relaxation, the other through overstimulation.

The identical duplication and repetition of the cell can be visually exhausting, as the back and forth perception of figure versus ground and the ambiguity created by shared contour is challenging. It is interesting to disrupt rigid formality with variation, to substitute a syncopated or irregular rhythm for a regular one. Changes in hue, saturation, brightness, proportion, or slight variations of information within certain cells can provide diversity. If you do not wish to emphasize the cell structure,

9. The unfolding continues.

10. The space at right is filled with repetitions of elements found within the cell.

variations must be managed so that the transitions between adjacent cell structures is fluid.

You can offset a tendency toward pure artifice by introducing elements that disrupt the formal repetition. Gaps and irregularities stand out more in these types of images. So do subtle changes, amid such sameness their nuances carry greater weight than they ordinarily would. In an interesting reversal of roles, they can become the signal rather than the noise.

To some, this aesthetic seems like Chinese water torture; to others, it is reminiscent of religious chanting. Comparisons might be drawn to the compositions of Philip Glass. Each demonstrates the power of repetition and subtle variation within it.

Tessellated images, particularly those found in Islamic figures, still the apex of their sophistication to my mind, are akin to fractals — both explore order at a level of greater complexity than that typically found in Euclidean geometry. The abstraction of order from nature is one of man's greatest and most enduring quests.

METHOD

1 Establish a grid. With the ruler displayed (View: Ruler) click and hold the Move tool on the ruler (top for horizontal lines, left for vertical lines) and drag a guideline to the top, bottom, left, and right of the primary cell. Repeat this at regular intervals until the grid is established.

2 Copy the information in the primary cell. Select it using the square Marquee tool and copy and paste it creating a new layer.

3 Using the Move tool reposition the new layer. It will snap to the guidelines for easy placement.

4 Repeat until the cells are filled.

5 Optionally, flip the new layer, either horizontally or vertically (Edit: Transform: Flip Horizontal or Flip Vertical). Flip vertically if you moved the new layer up or down; flip horizontally if you moved the layer left or right.

Check your alignment carefully.

Give each layer a useful name. You might title each layer based on its location in the grid — 1x1, 1x2, 2x1, for instance.

Increase the size of your canvas as needed (Image: Canvas Size).

To reposition the point at which two areas meet, add a layer mask to one side. Unlink it and move both the image and the mask into position to achieve a desired effect.

Clone seams as needed. For maximum flexibility clone from a base layer to a new layer that contains only the repairs.

EPILOGUE

In a Master Class, learning is a continuum. So, I would be delighted to receive your feedback on this book and the material in it. If there are things that you liked or disliked, things you felt were clear or could be clearer, things you agree or disagree with, I would enjoy hearing from you. Just as the feedback from my students helps me clarify processes and challenges me to expand them, I imagine your feedback will do the same. You can e-mail comments and inquiries to info@johnpaulcaponigro.com.

While I read all of my e-mail personally, due to a very busy schedule and an already high volume of inquiries, I may not be able to answer your questions myself. I have created a resource on my web page — www.johnpaulcaponigro.com. — to help address frequently asked questions. It will grow as the number of questions does.

My web page contains a great deal of information, including the kinds of equipment I currently use, service bureaus I work with or can recommend, answers to specific technical questions, a guide to other useful resources in print and on the internet, and chapters not included in this volume. In addition, you can find information on prints, posters, cards, exhibitions, seminars, workshops, magazine articles (past, present, and upcoming), upcoming publications, other web features, artist's statements, and a gallery of images. This information is updated regularly. I hope it can be an additional reference for you.

C O L O P H O N

This book was produced using Adobe Photoshop and QuarkXPress on Apple Macintosh computers (PowerMac with 212MB of RAM, G3/400 with 512MB of RAM, G3/350 Powerbook with 128MB of RAM, and G4/450 with 384MB of RAM) with Apple 17 inch, Radius Pressview 17SR and Sony Multiscan 100sf monitors. Removable media used included Zip 100 and 200 discs and Kodak CDR discs written on FWB 4x and Yamaha 6x CD writers. The fonts used are the Adobe multiple-master typefaces Aldus and Minion. Photographic images were made with Canon A2, Canon D2000 and Mamiya 645 cameras. Kodak Ektachrome film was scanned on a Howtek D4000 drum scanner. Initial proofing was done on Epson Stylus Photo 1270 printers with Epson Photo Ink and Canon BJC-8200 printers using Adobe PressReady. Final output was on a CREO Prinergy Work Flow CTP. The book was printed on 80-pound Orion Matte Text paper at Commercial Documentation Services in Medford, Oregon. John Paul Caponigro's exhibition prints are currently produced on Epson Stylus Photo 2000P and Epson Stylus Pro 9500 printers with Epson Archival Ink.